Pilgrim River

A Spiritual Memoir

KENNETH GARCIA

Pilgrim River
A Spiritual Memoir

First published
by Angelico Press 2018
© Kenneth Garcia 2018

For information, address:
Angelico Press
169 Monitor St.
Brooklyn, NY 11222
angelicopress.com

ISBN 978 1 62138 338 3 pb
ISBN 978 1 62138 339 0 cloth
ISBN 978 1 62138 340 6 ebook

Cover design: Michael Schrauzer

CONTENTS

Preface

LET'S SAY you are raised a *not*—a not anything: neither religious believer nor unbeliever, Christian nor atheist, Jew nor gentile; not even a thoughtful agnostic. Further, let's say you are suspended somewhere on the spectrum between extreme introversion and mild autism, but you don't yet know it. Your outward life as a diffident young man appears to reveal an inner hollowness, even though obscure energies percolate deep inside.

Then, in your early twenties, while hiking the outback and wilderness of Nevada, something holy reveals itself through the austere beauty of the deserts and mountains. Sacred reality overflows wordlessly and sweeps you away. Your mind and soul swell, yet there are no precise words to describe the power and glory of the revelations. Metaphors have to suffice: volcano; earthquake; unquenchable flame. Spiritual fire burns uncontrollably and you cannot extinguish it, nor do you want to. It is bliss. It is euphoria. Spirit swirls around and in and fills you and transforms your life. The visions contain the germ of a calling to a deep spiritual life, though the call is nebulous. The fire burns throughout a summer and well into autumn. Then winter. You exalt God's holiness—that is what you call this force: the Holy, the Sacred, God—and you want to communicate your visions to others but don't know how. There are no adequate words and you lack a religious tradition through which to articulate the raw experience of this God. So you withdraw from the world and, alone and isolated, slowly sink into darkness—down, down into a fevered madness from which you drift in and out, shorn now of your virgin sanity.

Even so, the fire doesn't die out—it remains a living ember throbbing with insistence. It nags and cajoles, though your mind is now but a burnt out forest of dreams and visions. Yet you stubbornly follow its call, like a pilgrim river struggling through the desert seeking the sea. Many years into your journey you begin to wonder, *am I merely one of the many who are called, but not among the few chosen?* After all, you spent decades of your adult life trying to respond to a summons from an elusive God who doesn't always give clear directions; who, knowing your many shortcomings is sometimes stingy with the grace that would enable you to fulfill it, once you did finally discern what this God wants. Would you consider it your own fault for not being up to the task, or conclude, in the end, that you were deluded all those decades? Would you curse God and all his empty promises, as if he were some junior Satan in disguise, luring you into an abyss? Or would you stay the course, hoping the voice from the wilderness is holy and real, and will lead you to the sea?

Tell me, what would you do?

Whatever your response, and however your life turns out, you'd want to tell your story, in hopes someone might benefit, and that your children and grandchildren might understand why you are the way you are, what dreams you once dreamed (and sometimes still do), and what visions motivated, even enthralled you throughout life.

Notes to the Reader

I have written most of these memoirs without the aid of the writing journals I kept for decades. One day—I don't remember the occasion, but it had to do with religious fervor—I threw out dozens of journals in which I had recorded my observations and experiences beginning at age nineteen. I wanted to break from my chaotic past and make a new start. A new spiritual life. Only a few journals escaped the purge. As a consequence of that abrupt—and thankfully, short-lived—zealotry, I was unable to compare my memories with observations I'd made at the time events occurred, or details of landscape. When possible, I've revisited places described herein, but in more than one case, circumstances—such as drug cartel violence in Southwestern Mexico—prevented it. Those who participated in some of the events described might remember them differently, or interpret them differently—in chapter fifteen, dramatically so. I have tried to check facts and events with other sources when possible. I have scoured the fields of memory, and this is an account of what I found.

I have changed some proper names in this book with privacy—and, in two cases, aesthetics—in mind. Quotation marks around dialogue indicate that that's how I remember *the gist* of a conversation (I follow the lead of Mary McCarthy in *Memories of a Catholic Girlhood* here).

I am grateful to those who have read and critiqued all or portions of this book, especially three superb editors and writing coaches: Lisa Ohlen Harris, Michael N. McGregor, and Lindsey Crittenden. The book could not have come together without their insights and advice. Thanks also to Celia Wren for valuable feedback on a very early draft of the manuscript.

This book is made possible in part by generous support from the Institute for Scholarship in the Liberal Arts, College of Arts and Letters, at the University of Notre Dame. I am deeply indebted to various directors of the Institute who have encouraged and supported my research and writing over the years, especially Tom Merluzzi, Christopher Fox, Agustin Fuentes, and Alison Rice. I have received generous support from the Indiana Arts Commission for assistance with this book, for which I am grateful. The Virginia Center for the Creative Arts, set in the beautiful Blue Ridge Mountains, provided me with five weeks of free time to write the final version of this book. Special thanks go to John Riess, editor at Angelico Press, for his confidence in my work.

Some chapters in this memoir were published in whole or part as stand-alone pieces in the following literary reviews: the *Gettysburg Review*, *Hunger Mountain*, *Notre Dame Magazine*, *Saint Katherine Review*, and *Southwest Review*. I am grateful to their editors and reviewers for their confidence in my work.

Prologue
In the Land of
Disappearing Rivers

Ocean once lived here, years ago, in the lap of high mountains. It filled valleys to the brim, and life teemed in its deep waters. Then it drained away through a weak point breached, leaving a vast desert of slow growth and silence. A pilgrim river winds its way through the desert now, struggling, sometimes, just to be a river. It meanders slowly, searching for Ocean, then evaporates or disappears into the ground.

Now and then a welling up, or a cloudburst floods the basin, satisfying river, then subsides. The high water marks are visible up among old bristlecone pine trees that grow on dry hillsides, gathering wisdom. The ancient trees remember Abraham's long journey and a promise. They wait patiently. The river makes a long bend, then continues on its way, watering the land as it can.

I grew up wild and uncultivated in the deserts and hills of Nevada's Great Basin Desert, a world of wide-open spaces, vast horizons, and cattle ranches; of gold mines, gambling casinos, and whorehouses. I wandered through them all without moral or spiritual compass. What I remember most about my early years is a vast, semi-arid land of limitless horizons, intermittent mountain ranges, broad, sagebrush-covered valleys, and little water; of uninhabited landscapes as far as the eye can see, and the seeming barren emptiness of it all; of long, lonely roads between towns; and an inner loneliness commensurate with the landscape.

The Great Basin, my homeland, comprises some 206,000 square miles, of which 190,000 are desert. The region is bounded by the Sierra Nevada Mountains on the west and the Wasatch Mountains of Utah on the east. Its rivers and streams have no outlet to the ocean—they flow into one of many salten lakes, where the water stagnates, evaporates, or sinks into the earth, leaving behind alkali flats hostile to life. The mountains and highlands once encircled a small ocean teeming with life. Fifteen thousand years ago, a breach in an alluvial dam—created by deposits from receding glaciers— caused the sea to drain away through a massive flood with a volume three times the flow of the Amazon at its mouth. The basin is now dry, silent, and empty, a no-man's land of deserts, middles of nowhere, and solitary mountain ranges.

The basin is geologically active. The movement of tectonic plates has stretched the earth's crust, creating hot holes, warm ponds, geysers, volcanic seepage, and fissures in the earth through which steam rises. The surface appears calm—serene even—but not far under its crust seething, turbulent energies seek to rise through its attenuated skin.

I live outside the desert now, and happily so, but it abides in me, as if a living, breathing thing. In *Wolf Willow,* Wallace Stegner writes of how one's early environment is permanently etched in the deep recesses of the mind, influencing one's thought throughout life. Expose a child to a particular environment in his formative years, and he will always perceive things through the lens of that environment. Stegner likened the environment's sway to the manner in which a duckling becomes attached to the first object it sees. Whether that object is an alarm clock, a stuffed animal, or a cat, the duckling's mind is "imprinted" with it, and it will always follow that object as if it were its mother. The desert holds such an influence over my perceptions, even four decades after I left it: it gave me birth, raised me, and haunts me still.

Anyone who has driven across Nevada and western Utah has experienced the seeming desolation of the region. I say "seeming" because if you spend time there, away from the throughways, you may discover a subtle but powerful beauty. That beauty instilled in me a deep and irresistible nature mysticism and, later, the kind of "desert spirituality" found among contemplative monks in the ancient Christian tradition: a love of solitude and of wide-open spaces, far from the maddening bustle of cities. I began my religious journey as a young adult, following a hunting accident that laid me up for several months. After this experience, I spent a summer in solitude in the mountains and deserts of Nevada. From this solitude came a rich influx of spiritual energy that transformed every dimension of my life. I knew that I was called by a force both mysterious and holy—but to what? Someone else might have sensed a summons to the priesthood or the ministry and consulted a parish priest or a congregation's minister for guidance. The next step might be seminary, then ministry. But what if you start out without any religious tradition at all, not even a humanistic moral tradition? What paths will your imagination open for you, if any?

The sense of being called by the divine has never left me; it has importuned me throughout life. I have struggled to discern just what it demanded: I wandered through the forests of contemplation and the dry deserts and dark nights of insanity and despair; I followed the path through marriage and family life with their joys and trials, and found refuge in the serene groves of academia; and I returned again and again to the awesome beauty of the natural world for inspiration. My trail has twisted and turned through this bent and grieving world that, in spite of pain and sorrow, remains a house of radiant colors, suffused with divine luminescence. I have carried out this journey in conversation with the traditions of a number of religions, especially the one I joined and studied later in life: Roman Catholicism. And even though I have spent decades trying to acculturate myself to this tradition, I have remained on the margins of its theological controversies. The Catholic Church—with its seemingly intractable flaws and its resistance to reform and change, yet, simultaneously, with its rich spiritual and theological tradition and its openness to grace, which it strives to mediate to a world in need of it—became a home, a sort of base camp from which I have launched explorations and that I have returned to for rest and sustenance. A home full of flawed people with whom you nevertheless have an unbreakable bond because you are joined in a sacramental family, even when you dislike one another. The Church, like most of us, is a wayward pilgrim in search of holiness and salvation.

Pilgrim River is not the story of a holy man, but a first-person account of a deeply flawed man who persistently seeks the Holy because he is summoned by it. It is not a guidebook by a religious guru claiming "higher" and secret knowledge; nor is it a self-help book leading the reader through sure stages of spiritual development. Neither is it a pious book that will confirm the cherished beliefs of conventional believers. Rather, it is one man's attempt to come to terms with the overpowering experience of God as he experienced it in the deserts and mountains of Nevada and Utah, through his sojourns in the country of marriage and in the republic of letters, and through a meandering and life-long quest to find the calling announced inchoately in the thunder and the whirlwind by a wild and elusive God.

1

Cattle, Casinos, and Cathouses

C ALL IT original sin if you like; blame it on the normal way-
wardness of adolescent boys; attribute it to the rough edges
etched in youth growing up in harsh, wild places. Call it all
those things; you won't be wrong. My friends and I roamed freely in
open country vast enough to absorb the wounds we inflicted. Our
hometown was Elko, Nevada, a one-stoplight town in the northeastern part of the state, near the middle of nowhere. We swam in
raw sewage dumped into the Humboldt River, even as we breathed
in fresh air and spread our wings over the hills and mountains in a
land of wide-open spaces, vast horizons, cattle ranches, gold mines,
and gambling casinos. We got in fistfights, attended frequent beer
parties, and trolled for girls who were easy lays. At the same time,
we had steady girlfriends. And, when drunk enough, we sought out
ladies at the local whorehouses.

Almost every town in Nevada, no matter how small, has at least
one whorehouse. On the outskirts of most towns you can find a bar
or trailer house with a name like the *Kit Kat Ranch* or *Moonlite
Bunny Ranch*. Small town whorehouses might employ only two
prostitutes, but they do not want for customers. In the larger
whorehouses, a dozen or more girls might ply their trade. My
hometown had three such establishments: *Betty's D&D Club*, *Sue's
Bar*, and *The Lucky Strike*. Each employed from six to ten whores.
Not yet aware of more sophisticated words like *brothel*, we used the
local term, *cathouse*. "Cattle, casinos, and cathouses," one of my
neighbors said, "that's what keeps this town running."

Knowing about such places fueled an adolescent boy's imagination. Older boys told stories to the younger ones, and we learned that gaining carnal knowledge in a cathouse helped earn a badge into the society of Western manhood. It conferred bragging rights. One night in early fall of 1966—my junior year in high school—my friends and I decided it was time to find out what this brand of manhood meant. But not before a chaotic and dissolute weekend— the weekend I first became aware that I was different from most of my friends and, indeed, most of the rural boys I knew. I had just turned sixteen.

My friends were a carousing, brawling lot. John and Larry Arangüena, first cousins and the sons of sheep ranchers, worked with their dads on a ranch south of Elko. Larry lived on the ranch year around, while John lived in town during the school year. Stocky, muscular boys accustomed to hard ranch labor, John and Larry lifted, docked, and sheared sheep; carried and installed fence posts and dug out the holes for them; operated and repaired heavy machinery; and mended decaying barns and sheds. They carried loaded rifles on racks in the cab of their pickups and shot coyotes at any opportunity. They hunted deer in the high mountains, carrying their quarry over their shoulders for miles. Larry regularly competed in the summer games at the annual Basque Festival in Elko, particularly the log-chopping and weight-carrying contests. The latter required entrants to carry two eighty-pound weights, one in each hand, as far as they could, in Larry's case almost 800 feet before his wrists gave out. He came in second place almost every year—his father always carried the weights a few paces past Larry's mark, then dropped them. Year after year, this father-son rivalry marked one of the highlights of the festival games.

Hank Brunner and Tom Nisley were tall and athletic, basketball players and all-state wide receivers on the football team. They loved the bump and grind of jockeying for a rebound, throwing elbows, and fighting for the ball. They relished jumping into the scrum of football players after a fumble, where the refs usually missed the gouging, elbowing, and kicking. Hank, Tom, and the Arangüena boys liked to drink beer and carouse as much they liked to brawl.

I was a diffident boy, average in sports and occasionally, but not often, thoughtful. I suppose I was assertive, at least in a pretentious way, hoping others would think I had the pluck and daring of my friends. In reality, I was too much the introvert and lacked the dynamism that enabled me to stride confidently in the world, though I tagged along with my friends—all alpha males—for the carousing. The five of us rented an apartment in town, unbeknownst to our parents, for weekend parties, splitting the $90 a month rent evenly.

One Friday afternoon in early October we skipped school and ended up at the Deep Creek Ranch, fifteen miles east of town. The cattle ranch encompassed nine thousand acres of undulating hills covered with wild grasses, sage, and juniper groves. Gullies cut through the landscape, and the towering peaks of the Ruby Mountains, still covered with snow from the previous year, lay just to the south. The father of our classmate Jimmy Callahan owned the ranch, but we had not invited Jimmy because we considered him an arrogant prick. We did not have permission to be on the land, so we found a secluded spot in a gully along a spring-fed creek about five miles from the main ranch house where no one would notice us. We spent the afternoon drinking beer, hunting ground hogs and rabbits, and plinking tin cans with our .22s. As we had done many times on past hunting trips, we killed, skinned, and gutted two cottontails, then roasted them over a sagebrush fire.

While we ate, a large jackrabbit appeared in an open space amidst the brush, about eighty feet away. He lingered a while, nibbled the grass, then raised his head to survey the surroundings. I slowly reached for my rifle, took aim, and shot. The rabbit leapt in the air, then flailed wildly for a few seconds after it hit the ground. I walked over to have a closer look, to see where I'd hit it. Right behind the shoulder. A perfect shot.

I knelt to inspect it. A slight breeze ruffled the hairs of its gray-black fur, then caught the flap of its long pointed ears, causing the tips to quiver. The rabbit lay inert and lifeless, its eyes still wide open. The eyes looked like doe eyes: big, shiny, and black. I saw the blue sky reflected in them, and could even make out my own form, distorted by the convex lens. The eyes had a penetrating, questioning look that unsettled me. I stood, then looked out over the landscape in all directions. The valley extended both north and south as far as the eye could see. The Ruby Mountains loomed: their shadows had begun to creep toward us as the evening drew on. I looked back down at the jackrabbit, then out again across the vast landscape. I remembered what a schoolmate—Cleve Fletcher—told me several weeks earlier, right before the opening of deer hunting season. Every year his father bought a hunting license, stalked deer in the mountains, then photographed them. That struck me as so odd—people here *hunt*; they don't take pictures.

"Why does he bother to buy a license?" I asked. "He doesn't need to pay just to photograph them."

"Because for every photographer that buys a license, there's one less hunter out killing deer," he said.

I was not an avid hunter, but I hunted with my father or friends on occasion. I had no objections to hunting. It provided food and recreation. I had learned to skin and gut cottontail, and de-feather and eviscerate a duck. So why was I unsettled looking into the rabbit's eyes? No one ate jackrabbit; many of them carried tularemia, a disease causing stomach ulcers and fever in humans, so it wasn't as if we planned to roast it. *So, why had I killed it? Why the hell am I doing this? Does it have any meaning?* These modest questions arose, I suppose, from the dissoluteness—the aimlessness—of what we were doing, the lack of meaningful focus and purpose. I did not conceive it in those words, exactly, or any words really, but as an amorphous intuition that years later I construed to mean something like *do these actions have any meaning in the scheme of things, if there is such a scheme?*

The questions flashed instantaneously, making me pause a few moments, then just as quickly passed away. I returned to the encampment.

As evening drew into nightfall, we unloaded our rifles and gathered our gear, preparing to leave, when two sheep wandered over a hillock just to the south.

"Sheep?" Tom asked. "On a cattle ranch?" Sheep and cattle don't mix on the same land. If sheep stay in one area, they eat the grass down to the roots so that it cannot grow back. You have to keep them on the move. In fact, cattle ranchers in the nineteenth century warred with sheep ranchers to keep them off their ranges.

"Ol' man Callahan probably breeds them for lamb meat," said

John. "Tastes better than beef." John's father raised sheep, but kept cows on the ranch for meat when they tired of mutton and lamb. "See, there's a lamb right there." He pointed to a nearby rise.

John and Larry looked at each other, eyes glazed from too much beer.

"Let's get it," said Larry. They stumbled up the hill, gesturing with arms and hands outstretched, whistling and calling, "Here, sheep. Come here, little lamb. Come on. Right here. Come here, little sheep." The rest of us laughed in amusement.

"Get 'em, cowboys! Round 'em up. Whoop!"

The two sheep bolted, but the lamb remained. And not only remained; it walked right up to John and Larry with their outstretched hands. Larry grabbed it, threw it over his shoulder, and carried it down the hill to our campsite.

"Come on," he said. "Let's get out of here! We're going to have a lamb roast."

John and Larry shoved the lamb into the back seat of Hank's car and held it down on the floor with their feet. Hank jumped in the driver's seat.

"We'll meet you at the apartment," John shouted to Tom and me. "Stop and get some more beer on your way back in." The lamb bleated plaintively as they sped off.

Forty minutes later, Tom and I arrived at the apartment. John and Larry had snuck the lamb in under the cover of dark. They knelt over the bathtub, dressing the lamb with their hunting knives. The fleece lay at one end of the tub. They were now gutting it. They worked efficiently—they'd grown up doing this kind of work.

Larry asked me to turn on the shower to rinse away the blood. As I turned on the faucet I surveyed the gruesome scene: blood, organs, head, fleece. It both engrossed and repelled me. I felt queasy. *Why?* I had never experienced squeamishness about skinning and gutting a rabbit or removing the innards of a trout. I was accustomed to casual Western violence. Was it less repelling in the open country than in a bathtub? I went into the living room and sat on the sofa. I leaned my head back against the cushion and closed my eyes. My mind swam in a sea of beer; images floated by: the jackrabbit's questioning eyes, the lamb's frightened bleating, the blood and guts in the tub. And there was this, too: we could have been shot for stealing the lamb. John and Larry, the sons of sheep ranchers, knew the rules—you don't steal other people's livestock, not even when you're drunk.

The dressing completed and the meat stored in the fridge, John and Larry jumped in the shower and washed up.

The next day we announced a lamb roast and bring-your-own-beer. Friends from school and neighbors from the apartment building joined us. John and Larry brought charcoal and a large roasting spit from their dad's garage. About thirty people showed up, both the invited and uninvited—including Jimmy Callahan, who dated John and Larry's second cousin. He had tagged along with her.

"Oh, shit!" said John. "Don't tell anyone where we got this."

"Fresh lamb?" said Jimmy looking at the spit. "Where the hell'd you get that?"

"From my dad's ranch," said John. "God damn coyotes killed it before the old man could shoot 'em. Third time this month. He brought it back to town, so enjoy!"

It rang true. Coyotes regularly marauded the ranches.

"I wonder if that's what happened to Becky's nursing lamb," said Jimmy. "It went missing yesterday. Just wandered off. Dad sent the ranch hands out to look for it this morning, but they haven't found it. My sister's been crying all day. God damn coyotes."

"Yeah. Damn coyotes," said John.

John and Larry exchanged glances. No wonder the lamb had walked right up to them; it was used to being nursed from a bottle at the end of someone's outstretched arm.

After the meat was nearly gone and the beer dwindled, people drifted away to other activities. We cleaned up the spit, refrigerated the left-over meat, and went for more beer.

We rarely had trouble getting booze. We could easily find a drunk at one of the downtown saloons who would buy us a case of beer for a fifty-cent tip. A small Shoshone Indian colony lay just outside town, and on any night of the week a number of the Indians hung out at one of several downtown saloons, sitting drunk on the sidewalk or lying in the gutter. The Shoshones lived about two miles out of town in government-built wood shacks without indoor plumbing, electricity, or heating, except a wood stove. The majority of the adults were alcoholics. Whiskey had contributed to their ancestors' ruin in the nineteenth century and they were still hooked on it. They lived in squalor, generation after generation caught in cycles of poverty and alcoholism. They received monthly checks from the government; much of it they spent on booze. Few townspeople gave a thought to their plight.

Elko's downtown covered a four by four-block area. Only the bars, casinos, and—on the other side of the railroad tracks—the cathouses, remained open. We went to the Pioneer Hotel Saloon, which the Indians frequented nightly. There, on the creosote-stained logs along the railroad tracks behind the saloon, amidst empties of white port and bottles of beer, sat some drunken Indians. Port wine and cheap beer got them through the night, helped them sleep better in gutters stained dark with layers and years of dried Indian vomit. They slept there because they could not make the two-mile walk back to their shanties at the edge of town. They could not even make it one block, and those wives who didn't join them in the gutters no longer waited at home for their staggering return.

We approached one of them with our money, but quickly backed away when we saw commotion and heard angry shouting. A fight had broken out nearby. The Sorensen brothers, Mick and Lenny, and their pals Danny Woodson and Butch Erikson, were kicking someone laying on the sidewalk. The man tried to fend off the kicks with his arms, and then went limp. A crowd gathered. We got the hell out of there.

At a safe distance, I looked back and saw the man on the sidewalk. It was Pacheco Little Tree's father. Pacheco, shy Pacheco, who sat quietly in the back of our classroom, seldom offering a word, but who always snickered at our jokes. At school he shared with us the deer jerky and pine nuts he brought from the reservation. He played on our baseball and basketball teams. He was a good outside shooter and a crafty defender. Then one day he just quit coming to school, without notice. No one knew why. Now, a short distance away, his father lay on the ground, unconscious.

"Hey, guys," I said, "that's Pacheco's dad they're beating up."

We all knew his father, Sampson Little Tree. We liked him. Grown-ups referred to him as a "character" with affection, humor, and pity, a kind of Rip Van Winkle whose frequent drunkenness was his long sleep. Sampson Little Tree had a cheery disposition despite his alcohol addiction and poverty. He always wanted to chat when he met people on the sidewalk. He came drunk to his son's baseball games, but he always showed up. He sat on the top bench at the edge of the bleachers, away from the other parents. When Pacheco hit a home run he stood with his right fist raised high, pumped the air, and said, "That's my son!" He sometimes bought us beer. Now, he lay on the ground, bleeding.

"Those bastards!" said Hank. We knew we had to go back. We ran as one into the midst of the fray. Hank rammed his shoulder into Lenny Sorensen, knocking him to the ground.

"Leave him alone!" Hank shouted. "You get the hell out of here!"

Lenny's brother Mick was defiant. "We're not afraid of you. We'll kick your asses, too!"

Action swirled. Tom confronted Mick, but the Woodson boy came at him from the side, throwing a fist. Tom pivoted quickly, blocked the swing, and punched him squarely in the jaw. Woodson's knees buckled and he staggered backwards a few paces. Mick drew a pocketknife but Larry tackled him before he opened it, got him face down on the ground, and wrenched his right arm tight behind his back. The knife lay nearby. John kicked it away. Butch faced off with me, fists raised, in a boxer's stance. *Why's he coming at me?* I wondered, but then realized that was the safe choice. John would have done to him what Larry did to Mick. I had been in previous fistfights but was not known as a tough fighter, despite my self-image as one. Fortunately, Butch had no more fighting skills than I did. We danced around each other trying to land punches, without much success. We had been there barely more than a minute when we heard a police siren in the distance. Everyone in the melee perked up.

"We gotta get out of here," said Hank. The police would smell liquor on our breath. They knew our parents; would tell them we were involved in a brawl at the saloon.

The Sorensen gang ran to their car. "We'll get you motherfuckers!" one of them yelled as they drove away. "You better watch your back."

A group of Indians surrounded Pacheco's father, trying to wake him. They lifted his head and back into a sitting position. A saloonkeeper brought a pitcher of water to pour on his face. There was nothing more we could do. We took off.

We had to get beer elsewhere.

Deer hunting season had arrived in Northern Nevada, and hunters came to Elko from the surrounding counties and states. Elko County is the third largest county in America, larger than some states in the northeastern U.S. Deer congregated during rutting season in the numerous mountain ranges, drawing out-of-town deer hunters to Elko. As we drove away from the fight, Hank noticed the many out-of-state pickup trucks—hunters' pickups—parked near the casinos. Many had tarps tied down over the truck beds. The hunters went to the mountains provisioned with camping gear and coolers full of food and drink. After a few days or a week of hunting and camping in the wild, they came to town to gamble or visit the whorehouses. They parked their trucks in the casino parking lots.

"I bet we can get some free beer from these pickups," Hank said. We patrolled the parking lots, looking for a truck with an empty parking space nearby. We found one. Hank pulled into the vacant space, jumped out of the car, and slashed the cord of the tarp with his pocketknife. He lifted a cooler and put it in the trunk of his car. We drove away quickly. The cooler was full of beer, sodas, and half a ham. We feasted on and drank the spoils of our theft.

Pleased with our cleverness and bravado over the previous two days and high on the excitement of the fight, we were feeling the adrenaline, even at 1:00 a.m.

Hank asked, "Have any of you been to a cathouse yet?"

"No," we answered, aware of the expectation conveyed by the word "yet."

"Let's see if we can get in."

"I don't have a fake ID," I said.

"Me neither," said the others.

"C'mon," said Hank. "Let's give it a try."

"Not me," said John. "You can catch venereal disease in those places." John's mother was a nurse at the Elko Clinic and likely had warned him about contracting syphilis or gonorrhea. I wondered if his hesitation came also from his Catholic beliefs. His extended family—aunts, uncles, second and third cousins—were descendants of Basques from northern Spain and they were serious Catholics. John didn't talk much about religion, but I suspected Catholicism had something to do with his unwillingness to visit the whorehouse. He didn't mind brawling and drinking and thieving, but I guess he drew a line at whoring. Religion was a foreign country to me. I had been inside a church twice: once as a child when my mother took my brothers and me to a Presbyterian Church on an Easter Sunday, and once to the Catholic Church for a funeral. That was the extent of my acquaintance with things churchy.

Unlike John, the rest of us had no religious compunction. We dropped John off at his house and drove to the cathouse.

Giddy and drunk, we knocked on the front door of *Betty's D&D* (we never knew what the *D&D* stood for). A large black woman—the *Madame* as she was called—opened the door and welcomed us heartily. To our surprise she did not ask for IDs. We recognized the Madame right away: Bella, formerly the cook and housekeeper at the rectory of the local Catholic church. News of her new job had created quite a stir in the parish. The priest even went to *Betty's* to persuade her to give up her evil new way of life. Bella, for her part, tried to persuade him to come in for some rest and relaxation. The priest's exhortations failed: Bella remained at Betty's for a number of years. No one knew for sure whether or not Bella had been persuasive.

Bella was well known to the boys of Elko. Big Bella, black and sensuous, the ritual guide. That first night, she led us through poorly lit corridors to the choosing room, which was also the barroom. A chime rang down a hallway. Ladies filed out of their bedrooms and lined up, side by side, showing their barely clad wares. *Wow. Whores.* Six of them: young ones with glowing skin still taut over firm flesh; a middle-aged woman with hair bleached blond, hiding wrinkles beneath layers of make-up; and a tall black one in a striking white negligee. Bikinis, short negligees, and high heels were the dress code.

Three men sat at the bar, treating other ladies to drinks. One of the men was a sheepherder visiting town after several months in the mountains. We knew him. He used to herd sheep for Larry's dad before going to work for another rancher. He winked at Larry and shook his head affirmatively. Near him sat a trucker, taking a break from a cross-country haul along Highway 40. Next to him was the local real estate agent, recently divorced. The men smiled at us, perhaps wondering if the courage from beer would see us through. Hank chose his girl right away—the tall black one. She led him to a room in the back. The rest of us, reticent in unfamiliar circumstances, sat at the bar to order drinks (I ordered a Vodka Collins, the only hard drink I knew the name of). I wondered who these young women were—definitely not locals. If they were, we'd have known whose sisters or daughters they were. *Where did they come from? Did they get mail from their mothers? Was it addressed "in c/o Betty's D&D," or just the street address? Did their dads know where they worked?*

As these questions swirled in my mind, one of the ladies sat on the barstool next to me, placed her hand on my thigh, gave it a squeeze, and asked, "Hey, sweetie, would you like to buy a girl a drink?"

She was a pretty, black-haired girl with gleaming white skin, probably in her early twenties. She wore a short, silky black slip. Other ladies did the same with my hesitant comrades. What could we do? We bought them drinks.

The black-haired girl said, "You're sure a young one. What's your name, honey?"

Hesitant to tell her my real name, I said, "Jimmy. Jimmy Callahan. Yours?"

"I'm Samantha."

"Samantha. Really?" I had never met anyone named Samantha

and wondered if everyone used fake names here. "Where you from?"

"Massachusetts."

"Massachusetts? Wow, that's a long way. What are you doing way out here?"

She put her arm on my shoulder and whispered in my ear, "Earning my way through college."

"Really? Where do you go to college?"

"Smith."

"Smith College? Where's that?"

"Northampton, Massachusetts."

Puzzled, I asked, "So how come you're not at school? It's fall. Aren't there classes?"

"I'm taking a semester off. I go back in January." She began to stroke my thigh again.

"How did you find out about this place way out in the boondocks?" I asked.

"A classmate of mine used to work here. They like East Coast college girls out here."

After a poignant pause she added, mischievously, "And so will you, Jimmy Callahan."

I smiled giddily, burning now with desire, but my curiosity right then was still stronger than my lust. Not knowing protocol, I followed the curiosity.

"So how did your classmate find out about this place? Does she have family here or something?" *Who in Massachusetts would even know this little town existed, let alone that it had whorehouses where you could get a job?*

My curiosity wasn't scoring any points. Other customers were arriving. She inhaled deeply, trying to be patient, then softly sighed. She gently took my right hand between hers, set my palm on her thigh, and helped me caress it. It was warm, smooth, and soft.

"Let's talk more about it in my room," she said, and gave me a tug.

That was all the coaxing I needed. Samantha the Smith girl took my hand and led me down a long hallway to the inner room. On the way, a curious thing happened. I was struck by the strangeness of a window with open curtains at the end of the corridor, in which I glimpsed, through my own pale reflection, dim lights in the distance. I was discomforted and puzzled. *What's with those dim lights in the darkness?* It was as if I were on the outside looking at myself on the inside. *Is that apparition in the window really ME?* I wondered during my twenty minutes in the room, and then wondered it some more in the weeks ahead.

The questions that flickered through my mind that weekend—about what the hell I was doing and why—came not in the form of some epiphany, but as inklings—flashes of intuition that something was awry, that I was not quite at home in this world, certainly not in the way my friends were. And what, exactly, did I mean by "this world?" Certainly not a sense of something profane in contrast to something sacred, concepts with which I was not yet familiar. What then? Killing? Human sordidness that debased sexuality by buying it? The comings and goings and doings and aspirations of the people I knew? A little of all of these things? Maybe. Yet, I admired some of those doings: the skills and practical know-how of my friends; their daring confidence; the quick realization that something had to be done to rescue Sampson Little Tree, and their unhesitant jumping into the fray. We grew up as so many youth did in that time and place: fighting and drinking and hunting and whoring. We played sports, had girlfriends, lived mostly in the present. My friends went on to do well in life: one a civil engineer, another a corporate vice president; one a sheep rancher, the other a state government official. That weekend was nothing out of the ordinary. I envied my friends' ease with the world and loved their camaraderie, even as I gradually grew aware, over the years, that I was ill fit for the world, that I belonged somewhere on its margins.

2

The Hollow Places
of the World

The ores of divine providence are everywhere infused, and everywhere to be found.

—St. Augustine, *De Doctrina Christiana*

T HE MARGINS of the world surrounded me—at least in the
physical sense—for hundreds of miles in every direction.
They were full of emptiness and full of hidden treasure. During my last two years of high school and first two of college, I spent
summers searching for gold in the remote mountains and hills of
Nevada and Utah, assisting geologists from Newmont Exploration
Company. We hiked rocky hillsides covered with gnarled brush and
pungent with the smell of juniper and sage. We scoured long-aban-
doned mining towns and uninhabited landscapes searching for hidden traces of ore. We crisscrossed rugged terrain far removed from
towns and highways, accessible only by dirt road or no road at all.
When the land became too steep or rugged for a four-wheel drive
pickup, we hiked in with pack mules. The mules hauled our tents,
sleeping bags, shovels, metal placer pans, canned and freeze-dried
food, water jugs, and rifles. I scooped soil into small canvas bags,
labeled them by location and soil type (gritty, loamy, clay-like), and
loaded the bags onto the mules. The geologists carried compasses,
maps, and binoculars to orient us in the vast open spaces. It was big
country, country to get lost in, scorched in, or find oneself in.

I graduated from high school in 1968 and spent that summer working with an assistant geologist, Fred Buechel: a gruff, overweight man in his mid-forties. He was a crank, a heavy drinker, and socially inept. Most of the summer employees disliked his sarcasm and cynicism, but I liked the way he used geological terms as cussword intensifiers, which I suspected he picked up from reading Mark Twain's accounts of Mississippi riverboat pilots. Given his profession, it suited him well. He called prominent landforms by anatomical names (tits, pricks, thumbs, elbows), and sexualized references to digging and drilling into the earth. His language had color. He had once been married to a Russian woman he found through an advertisement in the back of some magazine. After receiving her citizenship papers, she divorced him. After that, he despised women. His sole contact with them now was an occasional visit to a whorehouse. When he went to town for "business," we knew which one.

Geologists from Newmont were certain gold lay hidden in the hills and mountains of northeastern Nevada, even though prospectors had discovered and removed most of the principal veins of gold and silver ore in the nineteenth and early twentieth centuries. Mining boom towns with populations ranging between a few hundred and 10,000 sprouted throughout Nevada—towns that were home to opera houses, churches, hotels, newspapers, hardware stores, grocers, schools and, of course, saloons and whorehouses. Once the ore gave out, the populations dwindled, turning the once-bustling towns into ghost towns. Only a few decaying buildings and mine tailings—the waste ore dug from the mountainside—remained.

Although miners had extracted the principal veins of ore by the early twentieth century, plenty of gold remained hidden in microscopic flecks diffused over a broad area. Newmont hired me and other young workers to help look for it. And we found lots without ever seeing it. Only special assaying can detect it. Twenty-five miles west of Elko, a vein of gold runs northwestward by southeastward along about a sixty-mile length, dipping deep underground at places, rising near the surface in others. The gold flecks are dispersed widely, so it is not really accurate to call it a vein; rather, geologists refer to it as a "trend," the "Carlin Trend" to be precise, named after the small town nearby. The trend does not run in a straight line; it twists and turns as it dives and rises. Around 1960 geologists from Newmont had discovered where the trend rises near enough to the surface to extract, and one of the country's most profitable gold mines—the Carlin Gold Mine—sprang to life.

Buechel and I worked at Bootstrap, a site fifteen miles north of the Carlin Gold Mine. Bootstrap had been home to a small mining operation in the early twentieth century. Prospectors had followed and extracted a vein of gold running horizontally through a large hill that stood alone in a great, broad valley. The tunnel, carved through solid rock, remained. Newmont bought the mineral rights and began assessing its gold content.

I did mostly grunt work and heavy lifting, but the pleasure of trekking the backcountry made the hard work worthwhile. We worked in shifts around the clock throughout most of the summer. I volunteered for the graveyard shift, from 8:00 p.m. to 5:00 a.m., to avoid the scorching daytime sun with no recourse to shade. At night the temperature in the high desert dipped to around 50 degrees Fahrenheit—jacket-wearing temperature—contrasted to the mid and upper 90s during the day. Bootstrap was about an hour and a half drive from Elko, so Newmont provided a small trailer for us to live in during the week. The trailer, without air conditioning, was insufferable during the day, however, so the night crew slept on cots in the old mining tunnel, where it was cool, dark, and silent. A heavy wooden door at the opening sealed the tunnel enough to keep critters out. The interior of the tunnel presented us with both a temptation to explore and a fear of the unknown. The fear kept us near the opening; none of us ventured into the darkness.

During much of the summer, I worked on a drill rig that bored deep into the earth. The rigs used 20-foot steel poles, about five inches in diameter, with a hollow center. A steel drill bit was attached to the lower tip of the pole, a bit designed for scouring rock and turning it to dirt. As the drill bore into the ground, an air compressor forced air through the hollow tubes of the poles, blowing the loosened dirt up the shaft to the surface, where I collected it in a tub. I took samples of the soil at five-foot intervals, placed a portion of the dirt in a canvas bag, labeled the bag with a number and, on a separate note pad, noted the depth, color, and consistency of the soil. Once the pole drilled down twenty feet, we attached another to it and continued boring. Each drill rig carried thirty or forty of these poles, so we could drill down 500 to 600 feet if necessary. When the lead bit hit a very hard layer of rock, it wore down, forcing us to raise all the poles out of the ground, one at a time, and replace the steel bit with a diamond one. Normally we drilled down several hundred feet before moving on to another site fifty yards or so away.

Based on the assay results, geologists created a composite map of the mineral content underground. I marveled at human ingenuity, at the ability to investigate nature, to test, explore, and discover what is beyond the range of our five senses.

On a few occasions, some of the other workers and I hunted rattlesnakes in our free time—one of the drill rig operators said we could sell their venom for cash: medical researchers used it to produce anti-venom. The snakes denned in the cavities of rock outcroppings about ten miles north of Bootstrap. We took poles made of cut tree branches, about six feet long. The tips, sharpened with our pocketknives, formed a Y-shaped fork that looked like your index and middle fingers when you spread them. On our initial hunt we came across the first rattler on the road to the outcropping. It crossed the road in front of us. We jumped out of the pickup and grabbed our poles. The snake, sensing danger, slithered up the embankment on the side of the road and coiled itself into a small cavity near the top. We poked at it with the tips of our poles, arms stretched—a good-sized rattler can bite through a pair of leather boots, so we kept our distance. The poking made it angry and its rattler buzzed frenetically, but it soon slithered off to escape the annoyance. As it crawled, one of my comrades forked it right behind the head, the pointed tips stuck in the ground. The head was immobilized and couldn't strike. The rest of its body writhed, trying to get free, but couldn't. My comrade grabbed the squirming body with his left hand to hold it still. With his right hand he firmly grabbed the neck just behind the head as I held the Y-prong tight. I removed the pronged stick so he could lift the snake. I then placed a small glass jar up to the snake's open mouth, its fangs on the inside of the jar and its lower mouth on the outside. The pressure against the fangs forced the snake to secrete its venom into the jar.

We milked five more snakes that day, then let them go. Their venom wouldn't be replenished for some time, so they weren't dangerous. Before driving back to Bootstrap, one of the other guys suggested we take a rattler back for Buechel. We knew just what he had in mind. We caught and milked one more snake, then killed and took it back to the tunnel. While Buechel was in town "on business" that evening we coiled the snake up inside his sleeping bag, then waited up for his return.

As he got into the bag, he recoiled in panic. "Holy crap! There's a fucking snake in there!"

When he heard us snickering he cursed up some graphic geology words that grew in number of syllables as he went.

"Goddamn sons of bitches! I'm going to fire your Paleozoic asses! Fucking carboniferous potheads!"

In our spare hours, when we weren't hunting snakes, we played cards and drank beer. Buechel shot at wildlife, mostly lone coyotes and jackrabbits. His rugged temperament seemed just right for these places—places for men in dusty boots who broke rock with handpicks and penetrated the earth with drill rigs and bulldozers. Men who passed the tracks of cougar and deer, and kicked away the shed skin of snakes and bleached antlers, without wonder, seeking no messages, wishing only for a gun. They extracted the gleaming substance of earth, stripped away its mystery, without reverence. I was comfortable among them.

Yet, I found solace in the vast, silent spaces, too.

The more time I spent in the wide-open country, the more I noticed an austere beauty that awakened an inner recess of my psyche I had not known was there. Like a man gazing into a long, dark mining tunnel—a place at once forbidding but also mysterious—I felt lured to explore its depths. Something subtle drew me, though I barely recognized it at first. A sense of the land's awesomeness, even sacredness, filtered gradually into my mind. I had no words to describe it at the time, and even if I had my co-workers, especially Buechel, would have thought me "touched." Treasure of a different kind, I slowly discovered, can be found in out-of-the-way and unexpected places, even this seemingly desolate region of it.

I began to sense a primordial power that permeated the world. Could I call it *Spirit?* And that power is a stealthy hunter. It does not gather in packs to surround you, like coyotes. It does not remain downwind lest you detect its presence. It rides the wind and filters through the grasses, suffusing the quiet, hollow places of the world.

We shut down the drill rig for an hour during lunch, which for the night shift came around midnight. I took solitary walks over the hilltop while the other workers took naps in the pickup trucks. I lay on the ground gazing at the stars and listening to the night sounds: the howling of distant coyotes, the scurrying of small animals in the dark, the flutter of owl wings swooping down. I carried a flashlight and a rifle, but on many nights I didn't need the flashlight; the moon illumined the way. The distant hills and valleys gleamed like quicksilver. Something living yet invisible seemed to suffuse the land. Something mysterious, like when you lean over to hear an infant's soft breath, to detect whether it's still breathing. When you realize it is—what wonder!

One morning, in the tunnel before we fell asleep, Buechel asked, "Where the hell do you go during your lunch breaks? You got a coyote sweetheart out there or something?"

I laughed. "I just wander around. Have you ever really observed the country out there in the moonlight? You can see so far. And it's so quiet. Eerie, but beautiful."

"Beautiful! This desolate place? There's nothing out there but dust, sagebrush, and coyotes."

"Yeah, but not just those," I protested. "There's beauty, too."

"Yeah, well what's that stuff covering your boots and pant legs every day? And what are those thorns in your socks, *beauty incarnate?*"

I knew just what he meant. The land got so dry it turned powdery. With every step we made, the ground belched a miniature dust cloud that settled on our boots and pant legs. The little burrs from cheatgrass seeds clung to our cotton socks and irritated the skin. We had to stop occasionally to pluck them out.

"But seriously," I said, "there's something mind-boggling out there, something mysterious, you know?"

"Oh, Jesus!" he said, "All I see is a bunch of dirt and weeds. Mysterious! You get some sleep so we can go out tomorrow and find more gold. Then you should go invest in Newmont and be rich as hell. They've found a mother lode, for sure. That's why they've brought in more workers to work the drill rigs around the clock."

"We kind of are already, aren't we?" I said before he finished speaking.

"Kind of what?" he asked.

"Rich. You know, with all that—I don't know." I paused to find the words. "With all that spiritual beauty out there."

Beauty. Spirit. Nature. All kind of mingled and interwoven in ways that were inexplicable to me, as hidden as those flecks of gold, unless you knew how to look for them.

"You're full of it," he said as he turned over on his cot. "The earth's just a lump of inorganic stuff with an itty bitty covering of organic stuff, that's all." I intuited otherwise, but didn't have the language with which to express my emerging awareness.

I brought my bicycle to work, and began riding in the evenings before my shift began—wandering aimlessly along dirt roads and cow paths. One weekend I didn't return to Elko with the others.

"You're staying here all weekend?" asked one of the other workers. "Alone?"

"Yeah."

He looked at me, puzzled. "What about Jan? Aren't you seeing her this weekend?" Jan was a red-headed girl with a bubbly personality whom I had dated since high school. We usually went out together on weekends. "What's she going to think?"

"If you see her, just tell her I'm working through the weekend."

"Just tell her he's a weirdo!" interrupted Buechel, "that he's got a breccia brain—you take a handful of jagged little rocks and squeeze them together with cement-like mud, and you get a brain like his that doesn't think too keen. If he wants to stay here and commune with dirt, let him."

The next day I biked on a gravel road leading northward. After half an hour I reached the top of a rise where I caught sight of a vehicle about ten miles away, heading in my direction—not really the *vehicle,* but a cloud of dust billowing upward from a moving point on the road. The dust formed an elongated cloud held aloft by air currents before gradually spreading out and floating back to the ground. I didn't want to eat that dust, so I left the road and biked over the untrodden countryside: across creases in the land, through tall sagebrush and Russian thistle that scratched my legs and ankles. I stopped at the edge of a narrow ravine and climbed down it, wondering if I could discern something of its history. Had it formed from the waters of ancient streams, or had the earth cracked and split like wood drying too fast? I rode from one rise to another, horizon to horizon, crisscrossing the valley in a general northward direction, just to see how far the unbounded space could go before I reached something human—a fence, a ranch house, a windmill, anything. *Such an immense land.* An inner void, pregnant with something I didn't know, opened as I gazed on the ever-receding horizon. A void at once frightening and comforting. I couldn't explain it.

I came to a large rock outcropping surrounded by brush. One side of the outcropping had a large overhang about six feet up, creating a shady spot—a good place to crawl into and have lunch. I wriggled through the brush on all fours until I got under the ledge, and sat with my back against the rock. The rock felt cool. It was utterly quiet except for a breeze whispering through the brush. A few bird feathers and bones of small animals were scattered here and there. *A hawk must use this place for lunch, too. Good choice.* I wondered if any other human had sat here. Probably not. As I ate, I slipped into a reverie and imagined this recessed nook as a kind of sacred space, and thought something like this: *around the hollow, sacred places revolves the busy world that, uneasy with a presence unseen, refuses to know its own quiet center.* I sat still in the nook, listening. The wind whirled about, raw and pure; it filtered through the brush, gently, rhythmically. The place was lonely. Severe. Comfortable.

During my walks and bike rides I began collecting the sheddings and remains of animals: deer antlers, snake skins, golden eagle and hawk feathers, and dry animal bones bleached by the sun. I hung them from the timber just inside the doorway of the tunnel. I hung the jar of snake venom, too—we'd never bothered to find out where we could sell it. Buechel pretended to scorn my decorations, but I knew he liked them because on one occasion he brought me a badger skull.

"Here's something for your freak art show," he said, and tossed me the skull. A few days later he brought a coyote tail he'd cut from one of his kills. I hung it with the rest.

One day several of us were assigned a double shift—all night and the next day. We gouged soil samples from the wall of a ten-foot-deep trench dug out by a Caterpillar. After a few hours in the mid-July sun we needed a break. I sat in the last sliver of shade against one wall of the trench. A hard, pointed rock, barely above the surface and hidden by a layer of dirt, jammed into my tailbone. Unwilling to give up the only shady spot around, I began to dig at the rock. It was firmly lodged. Digging further, I discovered a horn-shaped object extruding from a large boulder below, of a different material than the rock, yet encrusted to it. *Could it be the petrified horn of some ancient animal?* It was too thick to be a deer or antelope antler—more like a bull's horn. Yet if buried ten feet underground it must have been deposited there millennia ago, long before cattle came to this part of the world. Perhaps a bison horn? No, it had spiral-like wrinkles around it. It didn't look like any horn I'd seen. I chipped off the extrusion from the rock with a hand pick and stuck it in my rucksack. In the evening I showed it to Buechel.

"Any idea what this is?" I asked.

He turned it over a couple of times, spat on it, then wiped off the wet dirt with his shirt-tail. He examined it with a magnifying glass. His facial hair showed several days of growth. He wiped sweat from his forehead with his handkerchief.

"Coral" he said. "*Coral rugosa* to be exact."

"Coral? Here? I thought coral grew on the ocean floor, in the tropics."

"It does. Hundreds of millions of years ago this place was under a tropical ocean."

"No way! You're pulling my leg."

"No, I'm not," he said. "The slow movement of tectonic plates shifted the continent way up here. That's a piece of coral, alright, probably from the Devonian Period."

"When was that?"

"About 400 million years ago, give or take a few years."

Buechel was a crank, but he sure knew his geological history.

"So was this thing alive at the same time as the dinosaurs?"

"Earlier," he said. "About 150 million years earlier." He paused a while. "If you go over to the Toquima Mountain Range, you'll see plant fossils that are 600 million years old. And I'll tell you something else. Someday many valleys in the Great Basin will be filled with ocean water again. This entire basin is stretching and expanding, just like the Atlantic basin did after North America separated from North Africa. Eventually the stretching will open a breach to the Pacific Ocean—maybe in Southern California, maybe in Northern California—but when it does, this land will be an ocean again and a big chunk of California will be an island. The scrawny rivers and streams running through the area will have an outlet to the ocean instead of emptying into alkalai flats. That's inevitable. Probably not before we get the gold out of this hill, though." Buechel, it seemed, knew something about the geological future, too, and I wondered, *How can someone who knows the deep history of this land not see beauty in it?*

I held the coral up to have a close look. "So this thing lived 400 million years ago?"

"Yeah. Maybe only 398 million."

"Ah, so it's not very old, then."

"Nah. Not much older than your mama," he said.

"Your mama, maybe," I said as I tied a string around a wrinkle of the coral and hung it along with the coyote tail, deer antlers, and other items. I pondered my decorations.

"Could any of these animals hanging here have descended from this coral?" I asked. "You know, maybe the coral evolved into an animal and one of these things is its descendent."

"Probably not, but you might be, with that fucking Precambrian fossil brain of yours."

It was the night of the full red moon of August. We had finished our work at Bootstrap several weeks earlier. We knew it was time to move on when the big yellow earth-movers started arriving. Mining engineers, geologists, and surveyors wandered the hillside, surveying, calculating, pointing things out to one another on maps and drawings. Newmont would soon blast the hill with dynamite and shovel loads of earth into the giant trucks that would haul the ore to the Carlin Gold Mine for crushing and heap-leaching. In a typical heap-leach operation, miners remove tons of ore from hillsides or open pits, crush it into dirt, and pile it onto clay or plastic liners. They then spray large quantities of cyanide solution over the ore. As the cyanide percolates through the layers of crushed rock, it draws microscopic flecks of gold and extracts up to ninety-seven percent of it from the rest of the ore. This "pregnant solution" concentrates at the bottom of a drainage system, where the miners distill and process it further. We completed our work without seeing a speck of gold. Buechel had predicted it right; the increased activity and earth-movers confirmed it.

Newmont sent Buechel and me to the Prospect Mountains in central Nevada, just south of Eureka—a nineteenth-century boomtown now turned into a lethargic community of around 350 inhabitants. As we drove through town we noticed a handful of old-timers sitting on benches in front of decaying buildings.

"What do you think these old guys do all day long?" I asked.

"Probably reminisce about the old days and hope a new deposit of gold gets discovered so the town can spring back to life, vibrant with saloons and whorehouses."

Buechel and I explored the region surrounding Prospect Peak, the highest mountain in the range at 10,400 feet, and the site of significant mining operations in the nineteenth century. Extensive tailings fanned out from the mouth of several tunnels. Tons of dirt had been removed, so the tunnels went in deep, forming honeycombs inside the mountain. We planned to spend two weeks there.

I collected soil samples at 100-foot intervals while Buechel analyzed rock outcroppings and applied drops of chemicals to the dirt I dug up. He broke chips of rock off with his hand pick, then smelled and licked them, tasting for hints of certain minerals. We worked our way gradually over a nine square mile area, with frequent stops, side trips around ravines, and slow climbs up the mountainside. Because of Buechel's weight, he had to take it slow. We pitched a tent alongside a spring, gathered firewood in the evenings, and cooked our meals. We hunted cottontail or grouse for dinner.

The alpine terrain, well above the sagebrush zone, boasted rich grasses, berries, Pinyon pine, wildflowers, and springs—good country for sheep grazing. We chanced upon a flock almost daily. A Basque sheepherder made a point of visiting us regularly, glad for human contact. He spent nights alone in a metal-covered wagon stationed near the bottom of the canyon. During the day he rode up the mountain on horseback to check the flocks and share wine with us from a leather *bota*. He spoke little English, so we conversed in pidgin and by gesture.

One morning Buechel and I discovered two dead sheep lying in the brush. We walked over to have a closer look. As we approached we saw others. Three. Four. Five. Then many others, twenty-three in all. Dead sheep strewn everywhere.

"What the hell happened here?" I asked.

"Dunno," said Buechel. "Maybe they ate some poisonous plants clustered in the area."

Later that day, we met the sheepherder and pointed out the site to him. On the following day rangers from the Fish and Wildlife

Service came to inspect the scene. They determined a lone mountain lion had killed them, not for food, but for sport. None of the sheep—not one—had been eaten.

Buechel and I did not sleep in the tent that night or out in the open, knowing a killer was on the loose. We slept in one of the mining tunnels on the side of Prospect Peak. Its shabby wooden door closed well enough. We kept loaded rifles close at hand.

The night witch set loose by the full moon forbade me sleep. I lay for a long time on the cot, pondering the great expanse of geological time and our miniscule span of life within it. Though just a microscopic fleck within its enormity, I felt a strange kinship toward the natural world. I wanted to walk about, but dared not because of the cougar. I decided instead to explore the tunnel. I put on my boots, grabbed a flashlight and rifle, and walked into the darkness.

I shone light on the walls and felt the layers of earth, one upon another. *Such ancient rocks.* If a primeval coral fossil ten or twelve feet below the surface was 400 million years old, how old was this rock deep inside the mountain? A billion? More? It boggled the mind.

The tunnel went straight into the mountain for at least a hundred yards, then branched off in three directions. I took the branch on the right, the wider one. After another hundred feet or so, the tunnel descended steadily, deeper into the darkness. More branches. Then cross branches. Again I took the larger one, reasoning it would be the main branch. I should be able to find my way back by following the larger tunnel consistently. After a time, the air became tight. It grew warmer. Another branch veered to the left.

My mind drifted. I thought about the prospectors who'd discovered gold in this mountain back in the nineteenth century, way out in the middle of nowhere. What obsession lured them into such a search? Why did they willingly spend so much of their lives as near hermits, traipsing the rugged countryside and living weeks or months on end in inhospitable places for a slim hope of striking it rich. I had met prospectors who filed mining claims in remote areas and spent their free time trekking the outback, digging trenches, gathering soil samples, and sending them to the assay office. Some of them contacted geologists at Newmont with the assay results if they looked promising. The seduction of future wealth was certainly a factor, but the likelihood of that was so slim that there had to be some other motivation, some indefinable enticement that lured and kept them at it, year after year. Perhaps the pursuit itself drove them, the hope of unearthing and beholding that gleaming, intoxicating substance.

I began following a rise. Walking became labored, breathing more difficult, though I was used to climbing hills. I stopped frequently to catch my breath. *Altitude sickness?* I felt a momentary disorientation. *What if I got lost in this maze of passageways?* Would Buechel think to look for me here? He was accustomed to my nighttime walks; he would assume I had gone outside, would look for me in the morning and wonder if the mountain lion had dragged me off to its lair.

What would happen if I died in here? Would they find me? If not, I imagined two endings. One was this: if Newmont found gold, they would tear down this mountain and my remains would end up in a heap-leach pile, dissolved by cyanide. The second was less dispiriting. The earth's movement would close the tunnel and fuse my bones with Devonian or Ordovician rock. Some geologist would discover them ten million years from now and place them on exhibit as an example of a primitive hominoid form. Viewers would speculate on what thoughts I might have had, and what dreams and promises I never fulfilled. Would they be able to deduce from DNA that I *had* thoughts and dreams? Could scientists, by then, *recreate* my memories—such as the wonder and mystery of riding a bike toward a seemingly endless horizon?

I continued along the passageway. If I got lost I could shout for help from Buechel—if he could hear me, anyway. I imagined him banging on a placer pan repetitively, and I would follow the sound back. That image led to a curious question, given the circumstances. *Would I even want to shout for help from Buechel? Would death be any worse than the smirk on his face when I found my way back?* I could hear his words, "Hey, Tonto, did you find some creature back there with an Archaean brain like yours?" Yet, I knew he would worry.

Soon I noticed a musty, acrid smell. And foul, like the odor of death. It grew stronger. Soon I entered a widened chamber, a small cavern of sorts. I shone light all around. There were bat droppings agglomerated on one side wall. They spread onto the floor, rank and hot, the outer layer still moist. *Ugh!* I started to turn back, but then noticed there were no bats. They must be outside, hunting insects. *There had to be an opening somewhere nearby. How else could they get out?* I continued past the chamber. Soon a hint of outside air mingled with the musty, stale air of the tunnel. As the outside air became stronger I perceived a soft light up ahead. It came from an opening above, right where the tunnel came to an abrupt end.

A wooden ladder, old and decrepit, rose to the opening. Miners must have used this opening as an escape route. One of the ladder's rungs was missing, another creaky. I pressed against it, shook it, pulled on the rungs within reach, stood on the bottom one. It was usable. I carefully ascended.

Outside, the full moon glowed fiery orange above the eastern horizon. I walked to the top of Prospect Peak to get the best view, and peered over what seemed the edge of the world. To the north a few dim lights from Eureka shone in the distance. In all directions the sky extended limitlessly and the earth seemed to stretch out with it. The great valley below waited expectantly, like a womb. There was a mountain range thirty miles beyond, and another, ninety miles, stretching like millennia over the vast empty spaces. Far to the southeast, a peak rose above the intervening mountain range: probably Wheeler Peak—just under 14,000 feet—the tallest mountain in Nevada and the home of ancient bristlecone pine trees, thousands of years old. The moon's light bathed the earth in a soft amber sheen like the luster of the ocean just after sunset, or before sunrise. *Yes, something mysterious but real hovers over these boundless spaces. Seeps in and fills them. It doesn't become exhausted, doesn't run out; it just keeps on going, farther and deeper. The great valleys are like lungs through which it breathes.* Something expansive filled me, and I intuited this, too: we no longer expect to hear, out of those silent spaces, a word that will bless.

3

The Hunter
and the Hunted

The wind arises from a place unknown, blowing where it will. Spirit breathes into the hollow and lowly places. The ocean churns and heaves, sending waves of heat to the surface where the air is warmed and sent scurrying across the face of the earth. No one has seen the wind, yet it encircles and buffets us; it wears down high hills and jagged mountain peaks; it rustles the dry leaves and blades of grass, raising the hidden undersides of things into view.

In the hills and valleys of northern Nevada a dry and solitary wind blows like a spirit unseen, and the voice it carries is seldom heard unless spoken in the thunder and the whirlwind, or discovered in the margins of the world and the quiet, hollow places seldom inhabited.

MY EYES were covered, wrapped with cotton gauze to discourage them from roving and possibly dislodging the pellet, causing a hemorrhage in the brain. The doctors did not yet know the exact location of the pellet—a single BB from a shotgun blast. I was propped up in the hospital bed, barraged by unfamiliar voices and sounds: nurses, doctors, orderlies, visitors. Hospital aides pushed dinner carts; nurses took pulses and temperatures and checked blood pressures; visitors came and went. Calls to doctors came over a loudspeaker in the hallway. The bustle and pother vibrated through my skin. An elderly couple, the Bonhams, friends of my mother and former neighbors, stopped by to visit and check on me. Mr. Bonham placed an envelope in my hand. "Here's a little something for you," he said, "for Christmas. There's five dollars inside. Maybe you can get yourself a sweater." I thanked him but did not know where to put the envelope. I could not see. I set it on my abdomen and kept it in place with my fingertips resting near the edge.

Another patient occupied the bed across the room. He screamed incessantly and cursed the nurses. They were not, he complained, relieving his pain and discomfort. I experienced no physical pain right then; the morphine had taken care of that. But the rush hour-like hubbub, and the combination of sightlessness, opiates, chaotic activity, babble from a television, and the grating screams disturbed and disoriented me. The walls pressed in, then expanded to a distant point where I imagined myself seated in a far corner. Human shapes, distorted and constantly shifting, reeled across a movie screen surrounding me, 360 degrees. The other patient's shrieks pierced through loud speakers behind, above, and to the side. I lost my composure. I, too, yelled; told him to shut-the-hell-up, then threw off my blankets and tried to get out of bed.

That would not do. The doctors didn't want me agitated. They injected a sedative and moved me to another room.

Earlier that day, my friends and I had gone chukar hunting in Kittridge Canyon, ten miles north of Elko. Chukar, a small partridge-like bird imported from India, thrives in the brush-covered hills of the West. John and Joel, both avid hunters, had returned home from college for the holidays, as had I, now halfway through my sophomore year. We were twenty-years-old.

Six inches of snow had fallen the night before, covering the countryside. We drove in John's four-wheel-drive pickup. Sunlight glared off the unbroken whiteness. Only the occasional track of a rabbit, bird, or coyote broke the snow's surface. The open country spread out before us, serene and beautiful. Although chukar are plentiful in the western United States, we had no luck that day. We climbed the hills here, without success; then drove further, and climbed the hills there. Still no luck. As dusk approached we decided to call it quits.

Though we hadn't had success, we felt no disappointment: our cooler was well stocked with beer, the snow-covered country lovely, and the companionship of friends good.

John made a bootleg turn. As we headed back toward town, a flock of chukar flew in front of us and up the hill. John stopped and turned off the engine. We jumped out with our shotguns and fanned across the hillside, trying to flush the birds. John and Joel stood about sixty or seventy feet above me and about fifty feet apart from each other. Suddenly, a flock flew up near Joel. We began shooting. The birds made a wide turn and flew in my direction, about ten feet over my head. John and Joel continued shooting. *Whoa!* I thought as I ducked, *this is dangerous.* We were tired, half-drunk, and getting careless. I do not know why I didn't shout out that they had almost shot me, but I did not. Instead, I decided to return to the pickup and wait outside of shooting range. As it happened, Joel had hit one of the birds and it fell to the ground near me.

"Hey, will you pick that up for me?" he called.

I turned back for the bird. As I was doing so, another flock flew into the air. More shots rang out and that is when it happened.

Things invisible sometimes alter our lives in unexpected ways. On that crisp winter day, a pellet from the shotgun sped through the clear, dry air, unnoticed and unimpeded, creasing the air with unseen waves, then cracked through bone, penetrated the left eye and lodged in the muscle behind it, pulsing there, hot. The force of it knocked me to the ground.

"Hey!" I shouted. "You shot me!"

Joel yelled back, "I *did*?" He and John rushed down the hill.

"Are you okay? Where did you get hit?" They helped me to my feet.

Shocked and disoriented, I had difficulty balancing myself. John and Joel steadied me. My coat and pants were covered with snow from falling to the ground. My head throbbed with pain. I covered the right eye, then opened the left. Darkness. "In the left eye," I said. "I can't see out of it."

John drove me to the Elko clinic where his mother worked as a nurse. Elko had no eye specialist at the time, so the doctors sent me on the next flight to Salt Lake City, the nearest city with a specialist.

Harsh, fluorescent lights glared off the white walls of the hospital examining room. Doctors and nurses hovered over me. They coaxed my face up against an apparatus designed to help find the location of the pellet. It had to be in there somewhere; there was no exit wound. They eased a thin metal rod horizontally against my cornea and urged me, again and again, to resist flinching my eyelids when they did so. They had to take a picture using radiography, someone said. The eye must not move. It took eight or ten tries. Who can resist flinching with a cold, foreign object touching the cornea?

Once they determined the location of the pellet, a doctor inserted a long thin needle into the eye, probing the pellet's channel. Based on the trajectory, he determined it had ricocheted off the nose bone and nested in the muscles behind the eye. I asked if I would be able to see out of it again.

"I don't know," he said. "I can't see into your eye because blood is clouding the eyeball. We won't know what damage the pellet has done until the blood clears up and we can see into it."

"How long will that take?"

"It could be months."

"Can you take the BB out?" I asked.

"It's better to just leave it," he said. "I don't want to disturb anything else in there and cause internal hemorrhaging. The best thing to do is let the eye stabilize. Eventually, the eye will clear and we can see what's up. In the meantime, the body will form a protective layer around the pellet and keep it in place."

They laid me in the hospital bed, propped me up, and wrapped both eyes with white gauze.

I spent seven days in the hospital under close observation, my eyes bandaged the entire time. My girlfriend, Jan, flew in from Reno to see me. She spent two nights sleeping on the reclining chair in the room. My mother and brother Brian came from Elko. Joel and John called to see how I was doing. After a week, the doctor sent me home with a rigged-up pair of glasses that covered my good eye entirely except for a small peephole through which I could see straight ahead only. This reduced the eye's natural tendency to wander. They ordered me to not exert myself for several months. I had to take a leave of absence from the University of Utah for the remainder of the academic year. I had completed only a year and a half of coursework, and assumed I'd be going back in the fall.

The months passed slowly.

I had time to reflect. What was my life about, anyway? Where was it going, if anywhere? I thought about my time at college, how unprepared I'd been. I had gone to the University of Nevada my freshman year, where I'd lasted only a semester. I spent evenings and nights in the bars and gambling casinos. I would arrive home at 3:00 or 4:00 in the morning, set my alarm for 8:00 to make a 9:00 o'clock class, then sleep through the alarm. I missed more classes than I attended, and never studied. I flunked out after my first term.

After that failure I went to the University of Utah in fall, 1969, after working at a grocery store during the spring and then Newmont during the summer. At Utah, I began to take studies more seriously.

One night in early May 1970, my roommates and I received a call from a mutual friend from Elko, Sonny Jones. He invited us to help organize a demonstration against the killing of four students at Kent State University by the Ohio National Guard during a campus protest of the American invasion of Cambodia. We made signs and passed them out the next morning to fellow protestors. We gathered in front of the Marriott Library, then marched *en masse* from building to building, chanting:

Four dead at Kent State
War Continues to Escalate
Students Strike Now!

We marched through classroom buildings, disrupting classes in progress, and urging the students to join us. As the day progressed, the column of marching protestors grew steadily. Students at universities all across the nation were doing the same. It was a heady time. The Students for a Democratic Society (SDS) organized an open mic forum outside the student union, where anyone could express their concerns. The line leading to the mic was long, disorganized, and the protest quickly became about much more than Vietnam and the invasion of Cambodia. Adherents of multiple left-wing causes got into the act: anti-capitalists, minority rights advocates, feminists, advocates for the legalization of marijuana, anarchists. Professional protestors travelled from campus to campus, agitating for this cause and that. A shaggy-bearded Caucasian man, claiming to be from UC Berkeley, spoke on behalf of Native American rights and passed his hat around for donations. A tall Native American man pushed his way to the podium, took the mic, and challenged the bearded man's right to speak on behalf of Indian people.

"Who the hell gave you the right to speak for us, White Man? You're not from Indian Country. Who authorized you to collect money for us, and what are you going to do with that money?" He stood face to face with the bearded guy in a confrontational pose. We thought a fight might break out.

"Heh," said the Berkeley guy, addressing the crowd. "This guy's challenging *me*? I was a wrestler at Berkeley, and a damn good one!" He paused a moment, then improvised. "Hey! We'll have a second collection. Somebody pass around another hat for this guy. Who's got a hat?"

The rally became a hodge-podge of grievance airing without focus. A few incidents of violence erupted. During the first night of the protests, someone threw Molotov cocktails through the window of the ROTC building, starting a small fire. Fifty-three protestors, including Sonny Jones, took over the main administration building for half a day. The police carried them out one by one.

On the third day of protests, the student body voted on whether or not to close the university. The nays were over eight thousand, the yeas around five thousand—a resounding defeat for the protestors, but five thousand seemed a lot to me in as conservative a state as Utah. By the time the vote was held, I was already beginning to doubt the value of a strike. What purpose would it serve? Was this protest movement really a principled cause, or just a way to enhance the egos of some of the lead instigators? Prior to the take-over of the administration building, Sonny and I had been walking across campus to have a look at the ROTC building. One of the SDS leaders passed us, going the other way. Sonny greeted him, "How's the revolution going, comrade?"

"Just fuck off, man! Don't bother me!"

Sonny and I exchanged glances. *What the hell was that about?* We later learned that the leaders of the SDS had argued over strategies for campus action—violent or non-violent—and Comrade Fuck-off's pro-violence strategy had been voted down.

After witnessing some of the internal struggles among the various student leaders, I realized that the pursuit of power and self-glorification was a stronger motivator for some leaders than principle. Over the course of the four-day protest, I gradually backed away from the center of activism; first, to being more of a detached participant-observer, and eventually, just an interested observer.

The events, fortunately, led me to take an interest in political philosophy. I started reading Marx, Locke, Jefferson, and Hobbes. I sat in a shady spot on the lawn near the library during the afternoons, underlining passages from Locke's *Treatises of Government* or Marx's *Das Kapital*, and writing comments in the margins. An intellectual spark flamed, then spread to other subjects.

I began going to the Marriott Library early in the morning—well before classes started—to study, fascinated even by dry textbooks on evolutionary biology that my high school biology course had only a brief unit on. The theory of evolution opened my eyes to the slow, intricate development of life forms on earth—the role of genetic mutation in adaptation to changing environments, the role of geological and climactic changes, and the nature of population dynamics. I had learned a bit of geology while working for Newmont and had an appreciation of the great expanse of geological time and changes in the earth. Evolutionary biology, coupled with geological history, was mind-boggling. And astronomy mind-*blowing*. Yes, Astronomy 101. The universe began almost fifteen billion years ago through a cosmic event known as the Big Bang. It began with all the matter in the universe compacted into a super-dense grain (seed?) only microns (one millionth of a meter) in circumference! Some ancient and unknown energy set it loose and let it expand wildly, furiously, uncontrollably. Over time it formed into galaxies, supernova, planets, elements, space. Not all astrophysicists, however, accepted this theory of the universe's beginning, first proposed in the 1920s. Even Einstein rejected it at first because there was no empirical evidence to back it up. But evidence accumulated over succeeding decades until it became the dominant paradigm in astronomy. Even then, I learned, some scientists dismissed it. Fred Hoyle, for example, the famous British astronomer, proposed the Steady State Theory in its stead. The universe, said Hoyle, has always existed and has no beginning and no end. Hoyle, in fact, coined the term "Big Bang" as a pejorative because he disliked the theistic implications of the theory: if the cosmos began at a certain time, that would suggest a *Creator*. Why, I wondered, is that implication unsettling? I was neither a theist nor or an atheist, but theism did not offend whatever certainties I might have then had.

Order and intelligibility reigned in the universe, even amidst constant change and upheaval. My mind slowly awakened. I began to envision a future of study in academia, a place where I could pursue knowledge wherever it might lead. I could become a philosopher, an astrophysicist, a molecular biologist. *How awesome science is! No: how wondrous is the universe discovered by science!* And our minds have the ability to know and understand it and love it.

The following winter, before that vision of a life in academia led anywhere, the hunting accident occurred.

In June, 1971, six months after the accident, the blood had cleared enough for the ophthalmologist to see into my eye. He discovered what he'd feared: the pellet had severed the retina from the optic nerve. The eye could receive no blood, no nourishment, and would slowly shrivel. They would have to remove it to prevent other complications, such as "sympathetic opthalmia," a phenomenon in which the good eye, "sympathizing" with the lost one, grows weak itself, eventually going blind also. Even the ancient Greeks knew of the condition. In the early nineteenth century Louis Braille, the inventor of the Braille writing system for the blind, lost his sight precisely in this way. He had punctured one eye accidentally, and his good eye eventually lost its vigor and vision, too.

The Hunter and the Hunted

The surgeon removed my damaged eye and replaced it with a prosthesis, a glass eye that closely resembles the intricate features of a real eye, even the tiny blood vessels.

Following the operation, the hot July days dragged. I slept in a bed in the basement of my mother's home, where the air stayed cool. The eye socket healed slowly. I had to refrain from activity a while longer, and had to continue looking at the world through that damned little peephole. It constricted my vision, allowing me to see only a portion of things. I couldn't even enjoy watching the Fourth of July fireworks. I lost depth perception and, for a while, clarity. But, thank God, I was alive and still had vision in the other eye, though I had to reconfigure my perception to find my way in an altered world.

The heat of August bore down. I read in short but frequent spurts. I took leisurely walks. I pondered life. I began for the first time to write reflections on the books I was reading—Dostoevsky's *The Brothers Karamazov* and *The Possessed*, Steinbeck's *The Grapes of Wrath*, and Hemingway's *A Farewell to Arms*. I wrote unsubtle commentaries about the large egos of the student protest leaders at the University of Utah, and wondered: if they had their way, would they resemble the radical nihilists in *The Possessed*, who seemed to want only to destroy, or would they instead construct a new and wholesome political order? *Would they be Comrade Fuck-offs, or principled, visionary leaders?* The former, I concluded.

I speculated on the nature and lure of *horizons*: physical horizons that I'd experienced biking near Bootstrap and hiking to the top of Prospect Peak; and philosophical horizons that I'd picked up from Heidegger in an intro to philosophy class. One horizon leading to another, seemingly without limit—each drawing you forward to the next in hopes you'll arrive at a final one. A mysterious lure behind visible things keeps the human mind searching for something ultimate. I suppose I was expressing a kind of spiritual yearning, though I'd had no religious upbringing. In fact, my father had a strong animus against religion and wouldn't let my siblings and me go to church, even when a friend invited us. My mother's religious sensibility was tepid.

Mostly, though, I wrote down fragments of my childhood and family life.

My parents didn't have a happy or successful marriage, not by a long shot. Their union was loveless and violent. A cold silence hung thick between them and they avoided talking to each other, even being in the same room. My father was an angry and moody man who exuded a brooding darkness that made us want to steer clear of him. At times, my parents got into bitter and heated arguments. My siblings and I were awakened countless times in the middle of the night by angry shouting. We arose from bed to find our father beating our mother. I impulsively forced my way between them, trying to push my father away, and as a result received some of the blows. During many of these quarrels, my father threw my mother out of the house, late at night, and locked the door so she couldn't get back in. Sometimes she walked in her night robe to the Schlagers' house down the street and stayed the remainder of the night with them. On other nights, she slept in a small camping trailer parked in our backyard. Sometimes she feared for our safety and pounded on the front door, shouting for my father to let her in. On more than a few occasions, this woke up the neighbors who, irate, called on the phone to complain. My father, aware that the household strife was now public, would then let her in. Knowing that the entire neighborhood knew of the discord in our household embarrassed us all. Equally humiliating was the fact that the Schlagers were the parents of my classmate, Joe. Though Joe was not in any way judgmental—he never said anything about it—I resented his knowing my family was a mess.

Even after my parents separated, the violence continued. One day I came home from school to find my father at the house berating my mother. He was red-faced and agitated. The construction company he worked for had just been sold to a new owner and his job had been eliminated. He was without work and upset. He blamed my mother.

She protested, "It's not my fault you lost your job! I can't help it if they sold the company!"

But his ire and urge to strike out had to be satiated and my mother was the one he went to. Soon after I arrived, my father started hitting. At that very moment my oldest brother, Barry, home on break from college, entered the front door. He intervened immediately. He grabbed my father in a headlock and hurled him across the living room. My father fell onto the sofa, stunned. He turned and sat upright. He stared at Barry, speechless for a few seconds, both enraged and bewildered. His hands clutched the sofa cushion; his arms tensed, ready to push himself up and go after my brother. Barry clenched his fists, ready for him to get up. My father weighed the situation, but hesitated. His son was bigger and stronger than he was. He knew it. We all knew it. Finally, he said contemptuously, "That's the way! Go ahead and throw your father around! This is what I get for supporting you all these years!"

"You better leave Mom alone," Barry said.

Five more seconds passed. Eyes still wide open and in shock, my father finally stood up and walked out of the house, shaking his head in dismay, as one who has been unjustly wronged. To my knowledge, he never again came to the house to beat my mother. He moved to Reno shortly after that, and took a job as a bookkeeper in a hardware store, where he still worked at the time of the hunting accident.

I suppose writing about my family life—objectifying it—was a form of therapy. I had never looked at our family life from the outside; I had merely lived it—not knowing what normal family life might be like—and repressed it, wanting to believe all was well. But I knew with certainty that I didn't want to be like my father. When he died years later, I refused to even go to his funeral.

I sat under the elm trees in our front yard to escape the August heat, journal in lap. A light breeze brought a bit of relief. My friend Warren Hardie and his father drove into their driveway across the street. They saw me and strode over to greet me. Mr. Hardie, a mining engineer in charge of Newmont's western U.S. operations, wore his geologist uniform: light brown khakis and Red Wing leather boots. Warren wore blue jeans and a sage-green khaki shirt. Warren was studying to be a mining engineer at the University of Nevada, following in his dad's footsteps. Their arms and faces were tanned from the summer sun. They had just returned from examining a mining claim southeast of the Carlin Gold Mine. They were strong, confident, and practical men, comfortable in their own and the world's skin. They asked how I was doing.

"Doing alright, except for having to look through this little hole. I can only see half of you."

"Which half?" asked Warren in jest.

"The ugly half, but only half of that, so move around some so I can see the all of it. The doctor says I have to take it easy for at least another month, so I'm not supposed to turn my head much."

Warren chuckled. "So, will you be able to go back to college next month?" he asked.

"Probably not," I said.

"I'm sorry to hear that," said Mr. Hardie. "Do you have other plans?"

I wanted to sound pragmatic and decisive, as if I knew where my life was going, but I wasn't, and didn't. So I made light.

"I don't know. Maybe I'll wander into a cloudburst and disappear into oblivion."

Warren and his dad laughed; they got the cloudburst reference right away. Both had been present when it happened.

During the previous summer, Warren and I had worked with his dad and another geologist in the Oquirrh Mountains of Utah, west of Salt Lake City. We searched for gold in Mercur Canyon. The Oquirrhs rise nine- to ten-thousand feet above sea level and are rich in precious metals. Just thirty miles to the north of Mercur was the Kennecott mine, the largest copper mine in North America that also extracted large amounts of gold and silver. Newmont purchased the mineral rights to the land in Mercur Canyon and began exploring the area. Bulldozers carved out roads that crisscrossed the mountainsides, allowing pickup trucks and drill rigs to travel up and down the mountain. We collected underground and surface soil samples across a broad swath of the mountainside.

The Hunter and the Hunted

One day in July Warren and I collected samples on the north face of Eagle Hill. It was sunny and warm, around 80 degrees in mid-afternoon. We stopped to take a fifteen-minute break, and sat on a rock outcropping to enjoy the view, eat snacks, and drink from our canteens. The sky was clear blue, the canyon opened up below us, and the mountains stretched to the north. To the east we saw the towering, snow-covered peaks of the Wasatch Mountains, twenty miles distant. It was utterly peaceful and quiet. No one sitting there would expect to encounter danger, certainly not violence. At this altitude, we did not even expect to encounter a rattlesnake. What could possibly disturb such serenity? We soon found out.

Looking down toward the dry creek bed on the canyon floor, we noticed what appeared to be grayish-white smoke moving rapidly from the west.

"Look," I said to Warren, "what's that smoke?"

"I don't know. Did something blow up at the storage site? I didn't hear an explosion." Newmont stored diesel fuel in fifty-five gallon barrels near the mouth of the canyon for the drill rigs and bulldozers (the nearest diesel station was over thirty miles away). *Had the barrels exploded? Was there a fire?* But that could not be the cause: smoke from burning diesel would be black; this was grayish-white. Soon, a flash of lightning and a clap of thunder simultaneously burst forth overhead. We looked up and saw storm clouds speeding over the mountaintop, just above us. That was cloud, not smoke, rushing up the canyon floor.

The sky suddenly darkened and the air turned cold. The clouds opened with fury. Rain poured in sheets, then in buckets as the cloud burst open. Spellbound, I stood to take it in, wanting to remain in the midst of it, unsheltered, to experience the full, raw power of nature. Transfixed, I shouted for joy. "Wow! Look at this!"

Fortunately, Warren had good sense.

"Come on," he shouted, "let's get the hell out of here! This is dangerous!"

Coming to my senses, I turned and followed him up the mountainside—straight into the storm—to where our pickup truck was parked, about three hundred feet above. It was a steep climb. Warren, taller than I, had a longer stride and reached the truck about thirty seconds before I did. The truck was parked in a recently cut road, so the downhill bank was formed of loose dirt, which had become oozing mud. I tried to scramble up it, but with every step I took, I slid back down. Water rushed along the road itself, cutting ruts in it. Warren saw my plight. He opened the truck door wide so that it hung near the edge of the road. He grabbed the door handle with one hand, reached down to me with the other, and pulled me up through the muddy bank. We jumped into the relative safety of the vehicle—a vehicle with rubber tires was the safest place right then. The lightning flashed around us; we sensed electricity flowing through the truck—like the quivering of a small buzzer—and into the ground.

Warren drove the truck down the now slippery road, hands gripping the steering wheel, struggling to keep us from sliding over the bank. He tried to hug the side of the road opposite the drop-off, but at times the truck slid sideways, following the flow of mud. He accelerated a bit, turned the steering wheel clockwise then counterclockwise, hit the brake, accelerated again, trying to pull us out of the slide. We were fishtailing on a mud floe. Our hearts pounded. It was a long way to the bottom of the canyon.

By the time we got to the canyon floor, the storm had passed. The gravel road through the canyon had been washed away by a flash flood that rushed through just minutes before. The soil on the mountainside could not absorb the torrent. The water surged into a raging stream on the canyon floor, cutting deep gullies through the roadbed. There was no longer a passage out of the canyon to the west, our usual route in and out. We had to find another way out, to the east. The time that had elapsed since we first noticed the cloud rushing up the canyon was about twenty minutes.

After the storm, the sun shone brightly again, glistening through rain droplets that clung to the low brush. Birds sang. Serenity reigned. Except for the wide and deep gullies cut in the roadbed, it was as if nothing happened.

Had it not been for Warren's presence of mind and quick action, I might have died on the mountainside, enraptured in the glory of nature's power. The incident displayed our respective approaches to life: Warren was analytical, problem-solving, and decisive; I dreamy and quixotic, receptive to what the environment offered, ready to accept and participate in its power and life, even to merge with it. I had become aware of some deep and abiding reality that dwells in the natural world, at the heart of things, and this abiding reality was the source of its awe-inspiring beauty and power.

Warren recognized the danger of that power, and got us out safely. I lacked his good sense.

As we chatted beneath the elm trees in my front yard, remembering the cloudburst, I wanted Warren and his father to think that I, too, was sensible and pragmatic, that I had a life plan mapped out. But I didn't. "I don't have any definite plans," I answered. "Maybe I'll travel some," but I had no idea where I might travel.

4

Land of My Ancestors

I NEVER dreamed of having so much money. As a result of the hunting accident, I came into over $19,000 from the insurance company, after medical expenses. That was almost double what my parents had paid for their house, and more than my father's $12,000-a-year salary. What does a twenty-year-old from a modest middle-class family do with a cache of money like that? The insurance agent advised me to use it for college; my brother Barry, to invest it in the stock market. Sound advice, but I was too unwise to take it. Instead, I bought a new four-wheel-drive Ford pickup truck with a shell camper for $5,400 and prepared to move permanently to the wilderness of British Columbia, where I would live off the land. Already, some of my older college roommates, along with campus activist Sonny Jones and his wife, had emigrated to Canada and formed a commune with other dissidents. I had narrowly avoided the draft in the lottery system instituted in 1969, so my objection to serving in Vietnam had no bearing on my desire to go to Canada. Nor did I have an interest in joining a commune. I wanted to go it alone, like Henry David Thoreau, or at least the idealized Thoreau based on the book *Walden.* I had become increasingly aware of my need for solitude. The thought of becoming a hermit appealed to my imagination far more than joining a socialist commune. Canada—I imagined—had the space where I could do that and, at that time, leaving the U.S. to live in Canada held a certain romantic appeal.

I was young and idealistic enough to think that living in the wilderness would be easy. I planned to build myself a log cabin in the Rocky Mountains, hunt and fish for my meat, and eat berries, wild asparagus, dandelions, and watercress. I would become a solitary mountain man. I had learned some wilderness survival skills as a Boy Scout. I bought books on living in the wilderness: Bradford Angier's *How to Stay Alive in the Woods* and Larry Olsen's *Outdoor Survival Skills*. I outfitted myself with gear: a 30.06 rifle for hunting, a deer hunting knife, and a pole for fishing; a tent, goose down sleeping bag, and backpack; sturdy warm boots and clothes; an axe, hatchet, and Swiss army knife; a Coleman camp stove with camp pots and pans; a compass and binoculars; flint and steel with which to start a fire; two hundred feet of sturdy rope; and topographical maps of British Columbia, similar to those I had learned to read while working for Newmont Exploration. I was ready to go—almost.

Winter had just arrived—not the best season to get settled in the Canadian Rockies. So, instead of heading north, I drove south to Mexico in late December of 1971. I would settle in Canada once spring arrived.

I was twenty-one.

Although my great-grandfather hailed from Mexico, I knew nothing about the country, not even the language. My father came from a family of leather workers and silversmiths from Sonora, Mexico, some of the best craftsmen in the western United States in the first half of the twentieth century. My great-grandfather, Guadalupe Santiago Garcia (or G.S. Garcia as he was known), immigrated from Sonora to San Luis Obispo, California, in 1868. There he became an apprentice in the silver-smithing and leather-working trade. In 1896 he moved to Elko and set up his own shop, where he made saddles, bridles, harnesses, bits, and spurs for horsemen. G.S. Garcia quickly became renowned throughout the western U.S. for the quality of his craftsmanship. Horsemen and cowboys wanted articles manufactured in his shop, and they saved to purchase them. G.S.'s reputation spread; presidents, actors, and famous cowboys such as Will Rogers rode on Garcia saddles. His crowning achievement was an intricately engraved saddle that won a gold medal at the 1904 St. Louis World's Fair, and another gold medal at the 1905

Lewis and Clark Exposition in Portland, Oregon. The saddle was decorated with silver and diamonds, with gold medallions engraved with the face of President Teddy Roosevelt and two early governors of Nevada. The "Garcia Beauty," as the saddle came to be known in the press, was a legend in our family and, indeed, among the ranchers of Nevada. It is now in the permanent collection at the Nevada State Museum in Carson City, the state capitol. Because of the success G.S. Garcia achieved, combined with the fact that he was the first of the ancestors to achieve some fame in America, he held a legendary place in Garcia family lore.

But G.S. Garcia was the only ancestor we learned anything about. My paternal grandfather, whom I never met, was buried in the Elko cemetery, but I had not known that, was never taken to visit his grave, and never knew my father to visit it, either. What was my grandfather like? What was my father's childhood like? What did he do for fun? Who were his friends? Did they still live in Elko, have kids my age? My friends all knew their aunts and uncles, their cousins, their grandparents, and were proud of their heritage, whether Basque, Irish, or Italian. I grew up unaware of my ancestry—apart from the skeletal outline of G.S. Garcia's success. My family had forgotten its heritage.

I did not know the ancestral link I had to many of my peers—those whose grandfathers and great-grandfathers had worked in G.S. Garcia's shop: the clans of Jayo, Cruz, Flores, and Capriola, whose progeny I went to school with but with whom I had no bond of history or affection. The ties between our families were lost.

Lost, too, was the cultural and religious past of my ancestors. My family did not go to church. None of my siblings or I had been baptized or catechized. We had no beliefs, or even unbeliefs. I grew up without a communal, historical, and religious narrative to encompass and orient my life. Stories of ancestors give broad context to a life, but for my family the stories had evaporated and memories became ghosts.

As a result, I considered Mexico not a place to find my roots, but a good place to spend the winter before going to Canada. I borrowed an introductory Spanish language book and a bilingual dictionary from Warren Hardie, who had recently moved to Tucson, and drove down the west coast of the Mexican mainland. I slept in the back of my pickup along the beaches of the Sea of Cortez. I travelled from site to site throughout January 1972, spending a few nights in each.

The coastal city of Guaymas, about 250 miles south of the U.S. border, was known for its tourist beach, the Miramar, with several elegant hotels and a beachfront that overlooked the sea. Too touristy. I found a dirt road that traversed the hills west of Guaymas and followed it to a small, isolated cove occupied by only a few daytime fishermen. Steep, rocky cliffs surrounded the cove and made it inaccessible but for this one dirt road. Coarse rock rather than sand formed the beach, so it was unattractive to beach-bathers and tourists. An occasional local fisherman came to the cove during the day, but otherwise I had the place to myself. I camped for a week, swam in the ocean, fished for my dinner, read, wrote in my journal, and enjoyed the vistas. The sunsets from the cove were like none I had seen before. When the giant red orb of the sun dropped below the sea its rays created layers of crimson, orange, and yellow above the horizon. About two miles out from shore stood Roca Gringas, a massive rock jutting above the sea, imposing and solitary. The rock was home to thousands of sea birds: pelicans, gulls, and murrelets. After sunset the birds flew to and fro from the island in elongated lines, dipping and soaring through the layers of colored evening sky. The sea's silver sheen reflected the sunset.

There I beheld and felt for the first time the power of the ocean. I swam freely in its waters—albeit in a protected cove—and felt the attraction of its deep mystery, abiding peace, and power. The sea spoke in a deep, rhythmic language unknown to me. At night its waves soothed and beckoned. At sunrise and sunset its waters gleamed a liquid silver, polished and buoyant. A space opened inside my chest, resonating with the waves. Some primal portion of my brain aroused from slumber.

By happy chance, in early February I discovered a small town where I would spend almost five months, and to which I would return again and again in later years: Álamos, Sonora, tucked in the Sierra Madre Occidental, about fifty miles inland. The town has long been referred to as "the colonial gem of the Sierra Madre," an apt designation. It also bears the designation "la ciudad de los portales" because of the tall, arched portals that cover the walkways at the front of many buildings and homes facing the cobble-stoned streets. Most of the homes are built around a central, rectangular garden courtyard.

I did not go to Álamos to admire the architecture, though. I went for a shower. After living on the beach several weeks without running water, a hot shower was a major draw, and Álamos had a guest ranch for gringos. At the guest ranch, I met a number of retired American snowbirds, enjoying the pleasant winter climate in Álamos. They lived in silver Airstreams or truck campers.

After showering, I ambled about the town, which in 1972 had around 5,000 inhabitants, was densely packed, and easy to walk. I immediately fell in love with the town and its people. I made friends with some of the young men of the town—Chui, Ramón (El Guero), and Guillermo (Billy)—and fit effortlessly into their society, a new experience for me. In Nevada I had been a bit player in my friends' escapades, never quite in my element. Chui showed me around town and introduced me to his friends. We made occasional weekend trips to the beach in the small fishing village of Huatabampito on the coast, and enjoyed the mariachi bands that frequently performed in the town square or at fiestas on nearby ranches. At one fiesta, the four of us sat drinking beer. Chui put his hand on my shoulder and said, "You're a cool gringo, you know? You have a Mexican soul. Most Americans keep their distance from the local people. They treat us like servants."

El Guero seconded him. "That's right, man. We like you."

I liked the idea of having a Mexican soul, and intuitively knew what he meant: I belonged here; I felt at *home*.

One weekend in February, Chui, Billy, El Guero, and I attended an exotic and lively religious festival in the nearby town of La Aduana. Chui told me the legend behind the festival. In the early seventeenth century, the Virgin Mary had appeared atop a cactus and showed the local Indians the location of a mother lode of silver ore.

In honor of Our Lady, a stone church was built in 1630 on the site where she appeared. It remains standing today. The Catholic Church established an annual religious festival to celebrate and honor the Virgin's apparition. Thousands of pilgrims, most of them *campesinos* from farms and villages in the surrounding region, make an annual pilgrimage to La Aduana. Some pilgrims walk as far as thirty miles.

The festival itself mixes solemn religious events with celebratory singing and dancing. Mariachi bands and dancers in brilliantly colored-costumes (all colors of the rainbow) perform; vendors sell religious articles (rosaries, crucifixes, figurines of the Madonna, pictures of the Sacred Heart of Jesus); food pavilions line the road and fill the town. The pilgrims, vendors, and parked cars clog the road, making it impassible except by foot.

I parked the pickup several miles away from La Aduana and we walked the rest of the way. The sleepy village of around one hundred people had swollen to around 30,000 by the time we arrived. As we wove our way through this teeming mass of humanity, I noticed a number of people crawling on their knees along the dirt road. I asked Chui why they did this.

"They crawl for many kilometers," he said, "to suffer as Christ suffered. It's crazy, no?"

It certainly did seem strange. I had never before experienced such folk religious energy: a bizarre combination of medieval Christian piety and native customs and beliefs; of joyousness and self-inflicted pain; of sacred rites and commercial crassness. All of it fascinating.

And there were the young ladies, too. Later that February a group of singers and musicians—the *Estudiantina*—from the University of Hermosillo, came to town. They sang traditional folk songs of love and romance, of sorrow and joy, and swayed from side to side as they sang in unison, accompanied by guitars, mandolins, and lutes.

That February night they performed on the steps of the *palacio*, the town hall. The townspeople stood in the street and the plaza, entranced by the music on a cool but pleasant winter night. After the performance many of the assembled moved to a nearby building for a dance. Chui introduced me to a young lady named Fabiola, who had asked him about me. She wore a dark blue dress and black pumps, her hair curled up at the shoulders. I do not remember what dance we danced together first, only that we held one another's gaze as we did so. After the dance, I reached to hold her hand, as a young man might commonly do in America, but she quickly pulled it away, took my mid-arm in her hands, and walked me over to meet her mother, who was seated nearby.

As the winter chill gave way to spring in the Sierra and birds began migrating northward, I visited Fabiola occasionally at her home, sitting in the parlor, conversing with her and her mother. Sometimes we went to dances or weddings together, but not just together. Having a *novia* in traditional Mexican society was quite different from having a steady girlfriend in the United States. In the U.S., this often conferred lots of privileges on a young man: holding hands, kissing, heavy petting, and sex in the back seat of the car. Not in Mexico. You visited her at her home with her mother present; you accompanied her to a wedding party or a dance with her mother present, seated at the same table with you; you walked around the town's central plaza with her on a Sunday evening after Mass, under the watchful eye of her mother. There was no hand holding. No sneaking off to a corner for a kiss. No back seat liaisons. Her mother's eyes were always on Fabiola and me, glancing back and forth between us, scrutinizing us as we conversed in the parlor or sat at a table at a wedding party. Even when Fabiola and I walked side by side on the opposite side of the plaza from her mother, I felt those eyes near, making me, in their watchfulness, an honest man. I did not have a well-formed conscience, but those eyes did the same work.

The central plaza—a small park the size of one square block—forms the heart of social life in most Mexican towns. Townspeople gather to catch up on one another's stories; young men and women exchange the first glances of romance; the community learns of its comings and goings, its challenges and promises, its births and deaths. A Catholic church usually faces one side of the plaza, so after Sunday evening Mass the plaza comes alive. Vendors appear with carts to sell *carne asada* and *nieves* or to hawk potions made of *manteca de coyote* (coyote lard) and *veneno de abeja* (bee venom) that—according to the vendor—cures colds, the grippe, headaches, cramps, congestion, and constipation. Children run and play; grown-ups converse; young men and women make the *paseo*, or *la vuelta*. The young women file out of church and walk around the perimeter of the plaza in groups. Young men in clean white shirts, their hair slicked back neatly, circle the plaza in the opposite direction, hoping to casually catch the eye of one and strike up a conversation. If all goes well, they circle the plaza for a time together— under the watchful eye of the girl's mother, of course, and, often, the father's, too. This custom of the *paseo* is, I believe, nearly universal in Spanish-speaking countries. Thomas Merton described a similar scene in *The Seven Storey Mountain*, where he visited Cuba before entering a Trappist monastery.

In March, about two months after arriving in Álamos, I met an expatriate American named Hal D., who lived on the outskirts of town with his wife and children. Hal opened his home to me. He and his wife, María Antonieta Rábago, set up a cot for me in a small storage room attached to the back of their house, a step up from sleeping in the bed of my pickup truck. I ate and lived there as if I were a member of the family.

Hal was a tall, husky man with blond hair, probably in his mid-fifties when I met him. He had been a farmer in Illinois in his younger days and knew animal husbandry well. He kept chickens, pigs, goats, and a donkey. An automobile accident had rendered him lame. He hobbled when he walked such that both elbows jerked upward in unison as he did so. He drank and smoked heavily. He was eccentric, a drunk, and mentally deranged much of the time. He, María, and the children lived on a pension that arrived by check from the U.S. each month.

María was a full-blooded Yaqui Indian with pitch-black hair, dark brown skin, and a sharp tongue. She had once been a prostitute in a nearby brothel, which is where Hal had met her. She had three young children, a son and two daughters, by different fathers. Hal brought her into his home as a housekeeper, to rescue the children from growing up in a whorehouse. Maria wanted to be more than a housekeeper, though, and did not want to appear like some cheap, live-in mistress. She persistently pressured Hal to marry her, and he finally did. They seldom seemed to share a bed, though: Hal slept in one room, while María shared another with her two daughters.

It was an odd household: a mad, expatriate, alcoholic farmer; a former prostitute; young children fathered by three different men, all unknown; and an assortment of chickens, goats, dogs, pigs, and a donkey. I felt perfectly at home. I was comfortable around drunks and whores. In Elko, I had frequented the places they frequent, drank at their tables, and walked with them down poorly lit corridors to their chambers. Hal and María had sat at similar tables and walked down other dusky hallways. But they had good hearts. They cared for María's young children and made sure they went to school and studied. Later, they would send them to university. Some of the most impoverished people of town came to Hal and María's house on occasion for a meal or a handout. Hal and María always fed them a hot meal and gave them clothing or blankets. They turned no one away. Their easy welcome of strangers and outcasts was a kind of grace, despite their derangements. In retrospect, it was the kind of household that Jesus might have visited and asked for a meal and a night's lodging. Hal and María would have welcomed him without hesitation. Jesus would have then healed them and made them whole. As it was, they dwelt in their curious, demented marriage, and I drifted freely and comfortably in and out of their house, rested and fed. They never charged me a peso.

Several mornings a week, Hal and I went to market for provisions. I enjoyed talking him during the mornings before he hit the bottle. I had the Ford pickup truck, but we went to market in a small wagon hitched to a donkey. The wagon rumbled and creaked over the cobblestone streets. On some of our wagon trips into town, we stopped at a poor family's home and gave them a large can of powdered milk and other canned goods.

The Alameda, the town's central open-air market, boasted half a dozen fruit and vegetable stands, a tortillería, two clothing stores, a newspaper and magazine stand, a canned goods store, and a butcher's shop. Hal introduced me as *escritor* (writer) to the proprietor of each store we stopped in. The owner of the canned goods store, Señor Benavidez said *"Ah, periodista? Like Clark Kent?"* At that time, I wore glasses with thick black frames and hardened lenses to protect my good eye. I chuckled at his humor.

"No, no," I answered. "Like Carlos Fuentes," returning the jest. He had not heard of Fuentes, however, and continued to refer to me as Señor Clark Kent.

Life in Álamos was simple, with an air of innocence. But innocence is fragile. Late one night, I lay in the cot, listening to the comforting cacophony outside: donkeys braying, dogs barking, a rooster crowing, an owl hooting.

Incongruous with the nighttime noise came a light knock on the door. I sat up.

"Who is it?"

In a quiet whisper, a voice said, "María."

María? *Something must be wrong.* I turned on the light and opened the door.

"What's the matter?" I asked.

"*Nada.*" She raised a cigarette to her mouth, inhaled, then blew it out to the side, all the while looking into my eyes. Her right arm hung diagonally across her body when she wasn't puffing on the cigarette, her left hand grasped her upper right arm. She came in and closed the door.

"Is something wrong?" I asked, clueless.

"No," she said with a wry smile.

She looked at me some more, sizing me up. She turned the light switch off and continued smoking. The cigarette glowed orange intermittently. When she took the last drag, she opened the door half way, threw the butt out, then closed the door again. I could hear the rustling of clothes in the dark as she lifted her shirt over her head.

"What are you doing? Why are you here?" I asked.

"You know why."

"What about Hal?" I asked, no longer clueless.

"He's asleep."

"He might wake up."

"No. He's drunk. He never wakes up before morning."

She continued removing her clothes. Almost no light entered from the outside, and no resistance welled up inside me.

Not that night or other nights.

On the following morning, I joined Hal and the family for breakfast. Our conversation centered on the oranges that were ripe for picking at Mr. Haywood's ranch nearby. Mr. Haywood, another American and the owner of Haywood Hardwood Floors, allowed us to gather the windfall from his orchard. He owned several acres of citrus trees: orange, lemon, and grapefruit. We decided to go for the windfall later in the morning, after returning from market. Breakfast completed, Hal consolidated the scraps from the plates to feed to the pigs, then said, "Should we hitch up the wagon?"

"Sure," I said, "I'll bring the donkey around."

We hitched the wagon and rode into town, sitting side by side on the wagon bench, feet resting on the buckboard, chatting affably as we rolled past small adobe houses, greeting townsfolk as we passed them. *Campesinos*, coming in from the countryside, their donkeys laden with baskets of produce or sticks for firewood, converged with us as we neared the central market. The mid-morning sunlight reflected off the windows on the west side of the street. Through the old and warped windows of a small adobe house—a shack really—I noticed my distorted reflection as we passed by; I sensed movement from behind the windowpanes. *Eyes are watching me*, I sensed, and wondered what they knew.

By June, the Sonoran heat was stifling. Animals hunkered in the shade and people stayed within the cool of their adobe houses. The town languished. I planned to return to the United States with the intention of coming back to Alamos the following November. I had, by then, lost interest in Canada.

Mexico had a profound effect on me. It introduced me to a different culture and way of life; it took me out of the stream through which my previous life had flowed into a stagnant lake with little depth. It was the first place where I had felt at home with others, truly myself. I lived there for various periods of time—ranging from one to six months—over the next eight years. Had I been able to work in Mexico and make a living, I might have stayed for the rest of my life.

Something else came of the trip. A few days before I left Mexico, I went to the bar at the Hotel Los Portales for a cold drink. There I ran into an American snowbird who had not yet returned to the U.S. for the summer. I knew him from the guest ranch where I'd stayed for a while. We had drinks together in the shade of the veranda. As we made small talk, a group of townspeople filed out of church following the weekday evening Mass. The man asked if I went to church regularly. "I assume you're Catholic"—a logical assumption given my surname.

"No, actually I'm not," I said. "I've never gone to church." I had not even entered the colonial church across the street, even out of curiosity.

"So, you don't believe in God?" he asked.

I paused.

Did I? I had no religious upbringing. My parents didn't go to church. My father was hostile to religion. He wouldn't allow my siblings and me to attend church, even if we had wanted to. My mother had taken us to a Presbyterian church once or twice, on Easter Sunday, but I was baffled by the unfamiliar service. At age thirteen I came to the sudden conclusion that God does not exist. I was sitting at a desk in my room doing homework. But then I remembered a scene in Nicholas Ray's *King of Kings* when, after Christ dies, dark storm clouds gather and lightning flashes on the mountain. At the same moment, the curtain in the Temple rips in two from top to bottom, the earth shakes, and rocks split apart. Moreover, I had earlier seen Cecile B. DeMille's *The Ten Commandments* and had been awed by Moses's parting of the Red Sea. *There must be a God to make those things happen*, I thought, and returned to my homework. That fifteen-second rumination was the extent of my theological thinking, and I thought about it no more. But my lone forays in the outback of Nevada had awakened a nascent sense of spiritual awe and given me a strong appreciation for the beauty and mystery of the natural world.

"I don't know," I said. "I don't go to church, though."

"I don't either," he said, "I think religion is right here in the heart." He patted the left side of his chest with his palm a couple of times. "It's how you treat other people. You don't need formal religion for that."

I didn't have much to say one way or the other, but, days later, as I drove back to Elko along long stretches of lonesome highway through Sonora, Arizona, and Nevada, I had time to reflect on my life: a chaotic adolescence; the experience of spiritual wonder in the backcountry of Nevada; the intuition of not quite belonging in the world and my preference for solitude. I had a strong sense that God *was*, though didn't know exactly what God *might be*. I lifted my right hand above the steering wheel and wrapped my middle around the index finger and wrapped them tightly. "God and I are like this," I thought, "intertwined somehow. There's some kind of fellowship." An odd and pretentious thought, perhaps, for someone un-churched, but the memory of it remains.

5

The House
of Radiant Colors

To lose oneself in the unfathomable, to plunge into the inexhaust-
ible, to find peace in the incorruptible, to be absorbed in the definite immensity, to offer oneself to the fire . . . and to give one's
deepest self to that whose depth has no end.
> —Teilhard de Chardin, *The Divine Milieu*

A FTER six months in Alamos, I returned to Elko and rented
an apartment on Cedar Street, just up the hill from the
Safeway grocery store. I paid $145 a month for rent, and
another $60 for food. The owner had converted the basement of his
house to a one-bedroom apartment furnished with only a refrigera-
tor and a sofa. The couch cushions sagged. A fitted, brown couch-
cover hid the worn-out spots, but the covering no longer aligned
with the contours of the sofa; it had been pulled this way and
stretched in that, so much so that the cover had its own frayed
spots. A dark red shag carpet covered the floor throughout. I borrowed a mattress from my mother's basement. I bought a floor
lamp, a metal desk with sliding drawers, and an office swivel chair at
Lundgren's Office Supply store. I found a two-burner electric
counter-top stove at the hardware store, and a folding card table at
which to eat. These furnishings sufficed.

About $11,000 remained from the insurance money, so I had the
luxury of leisure. Life felt open-ended, full of promise. Being free for
the time being of financial worry, I lived at the margins of society and
continued to do so for several years. I had no job and no boss to tell

me what to do, no professor to tell me what I must study. I did not belong to the student-academic class, belonged to no organization or church, had no family ties with any force, no commitments. Groups and organizations to which we belong—churches, workplaces, and social classes; labor unions, kinship networks, and friends—form us in multiple ways, both consciously and unconsciously. They let us know what is expected of us to get on in life and be accepted. Through word and gesture they inform us about acceptable and unacceptable forms of behavior: explicitly and implicitly they reveal to us what beliefs make us fit well into the group and what interests and activities we must participate in to belong.

I did not belong, and interacted with the few friends I had infrequently.

I spent summer nights reading, and slept during the day. I read widely and eclectically, from Russian novels and scientific inquiries into the possibility of extraterrestrial intelligence to accounts of the quest of medieval alchemists to transform base metals into gold—to find the philosopher's stone and discover the elixir of life. I wanted to explore all areas of knowledge—my mind felt both willing and absorbent. I drove to Salt Lake City several times a year to buy books. I built bookcases and filled them: works by Emerson, Thoreau, and Whitman; Spinoza, Hegel, and Plato; Toynbee's history of the rise and fall of civilizations (condensed version); Tolstoy's *War and Peace* and *Anna Karenina;* Dostoevsky's *The Brothers Karamazov* and *Crime and Punishment;* Virgil's *Aeneid* and Dante's *Divine Comedy;* Augustine's *Confessions.* I bought a copy of the *Encyclopedia Britannica* and the *Harvard Classics.* I read wantonly, without plan. Who needed college?

Cedar Street was five blocks from the northern edge of town. Going north, I crossed Maple, Elm, then Sage, Walnut, and Willow streets. After Willow, open country, hundreds of miles of it, sagebrush-and-juniper-covered hills forever. The open spaces drew me and I wandered in, glad to again drink in the beauty and mystery of the natural world. After reading all night, I hiked into the hills surrounding town and watched the sunrise.

A strong new force entered my life. The distant wilderness lured me even further into solitude. The voice from the thunder and the whirlwind became more assertive. Sparks of the divine began to flash regularly and insistently. They beckoned. I backpacked alone a week or more at a time, hiking deep into the Ruby Mountains, and into the Jarbidge Mountain wilderness along the Nevada-Idaho border, about ninety miles north of Elko. The raw power of a wildness-beyond-horizons called.

The Jarbidge mountain range extends about thirty miles long and twenty miles wide, with eight peaks over 10,000 feet in altitude, all attached by interconnecting saddles that form a seven-mile crest. The range lies so far from a paved road that few people even know about it, let alone visit it. The town of Jarbidge, population 107 in 1972, was the largest in fifty miles. Local hunters go to the mountains during the fall hunting season because of the abundance of deer and elk. Cougar and black bear also make the Jarbidge their home.

John, one friend I did interact with, had often invited me during our youth to join him on trips to his father's sheep camps in the Jarbidge. His father maintained two cabins for his sheepherders: one on the western flank along Seventy-Six Creek, and another on the eastern just above Sun Creek. By day, the herders kept the sheep moving from one area of the range to another, while by night they slept in the cabins. John and his father regularly took a truckload of provisions to the sheepherders: flour, sugar, coffee, tobacco, canned goods, red wine, toilet paper, and bullets for shooting coyotes and cougar. They took me along during the summers of middle and high school. We'd fish in the creeks and beaver ponds and explore the countryside. I spent many three-day weekends at these sheep camps and knew the area.

I went alone to the Jarbidge on my first extended backpacking trip several weeks after returning from Mexico. I parked my pickup near the sheepherder cabin above Sun Creek. My goal was to travel along the mountain crest to Seventy-Six Creek, dipping down into the valleys along the way to camp, then make my way to the town of Jarbidge before returning to Sun Creek. I carried the backpacking gear intended for my now forgotten Canadian Rockies adventure and a .357 magnum pistol in case I encountered cougar or bear. I brought my writing journal and a few books.

Spring wildflowers bloomed throughout the lower basins in late

June: purple fireweed, found throughout the Intermountain West, and arrowleaf balsamroot, a yellow flower with long pointed petals and wide green sepals that look like stretched-out maple leaves. I hiked between fir, limber pine, and white bark pine trees in the higher elevations, setting up camp in the shade of aspen groves lower in the basins, along streams or beaver ponds. I filled my canteen in the creeks.

The first night I pitched tent alongside a beaver pond full of rainbow trout, visible in the clear mountain water. Hundreds of hungry trout, easy to catch. I pinched off a piece of worm and slid it onto the hook of my fishing line, then cast it into the pond. A trout struck immediately. It had been several years since I had felt the tactile sensation of a trout nibbling the bait on a hook—a slight pull at first, followed by a gentle wiggling of the fishing rod; then the thrashing surge as the hook grabs and the trout flails and communicates its struggle through vibrations in the line, up into the bent rod, into my palms, through nerve circuits and into the brain. *Reel it in slowly; give it leeway now and then so the line doesn't break; so the hook doesn't tear through its mouth, freeing it and, thereby dissolving too soon the wash of adrenalin in me.* The feel of that brief surge of struggling, writhing muscle, the art of reeling it in slowly—I knew well—is what makes fishermen arise at 3:00 a.m. and go out into the dark. I reeled in the trout, cleaned it, then cooked it over a fire. In the morning, I caught another for breakfast. I could have lived for months off that one pond.

The next afternoon I stripped down to my shorts and waded in. The afternoon sun had warmed the shallow pond—just off the snow pack above—to a tolerable temperature. I knelt, knees planted in the mud at the bottom. The surface of the water came to just above my waist. I placed my hands in the pond and let my skin cool to near water temperature. Fish swam lazily about. A twelve-inch trout moved near, then right in front of me. I gently wrapped my hands around it, without it feeling me until I had a good grip, one hand behind the other. The trout then felt the pressure and wriggled to free itself. Its body became a sleek, wriggling muscle in my hands; the throb of it felt good against my palms, without fishing pole or line as intermediaries.

The House of Radiant Colors

After five or six seconds, the trout relaxed and went still, then thrashed more. I lifted it from the water. Its gills opened and closed as it tried to breathe—it was drowning in air. A pinkish red band lined each of its flanks; black spots adorned its back and fins; its tail flapped like a butterfly wing. I laid it on the shore. It flailed wildly, in spurts. Between spurts I grabbed it tight in my left hand, then strung fish line through its gill and mouth, and hung it from the bare twig of an aspen tree.

After hanging the trout, I returned to the pond and dove in, immersing myself in the cold water. I swam to the far side of the pond and back, then rose to feel the warmth of pure sunlight and to breathe deeply the fresh mountain air.

I stayed two or three days at each campsite, explored the surroundings, then moved on. I zig-zagged methodically up the slopes to reach the mountain crest, which I followed two or three miles before dipping down into another valley. Along the crest the view was clear in all directions until everything merged with the horizon. I hiked slowly—the oxygen at that altitude was thin and the footing precarious. Loose, broken rocks lay piled one on top of another, randomly, so there was real danger of rockslides. Deep snow covered some sections of the crest, so I walked gingerly to avoid falling. I had not told anyone where I was going (an affront to my Boy Scout training). I descended into a valley in late afternoon and set up camp along a stream or beaver pond.

On clear nights, I lay in my sleeping bag, entranced by the stars. The nighttime sky in the sparsely populated western U.S. is like no other. There's no light pollution and no moisture in the dry desert air to absorb and block the starlight. The vast expanse of stars appeared to be within reach. The Milky Way floated across the sky like a stream. Something deep opened within me, allowing what I thought of as some ancient and mysterious force to seep into the crevices of my mind. I spoke, to whatever that force might be: *how wondrous you are.*

About a week into the Jarbidge trip I camped in an aspen grove beside a pond along Saint Mary's Creek. In the evenings I read and wrote in my journal. I had recently discovered the work of Pierre Teilhard de Chardin and brought along two of his books, *The Phe-*

nomenon of Man and *Hymn of the Universe*. Teilhard had articulated a vision of an evolving cosmos guided by Spirit. Spirit, he said, is both the origin and the goal of the evolutionary process. I read *The Phenomenon* one evening and throughout the night, by firelight and flashlight. As dawn slowly transformed night into day, I looked up from the book and over the countryside. I envisioned the end of one world and the beginning of a new one ablaze with the Spirit of God. Tremors shook my world. Subconscious volcanoes, long slumbering, erupted. It was the beginning of an extended religious awakening that would overwhelm me with the radiant colors of a world alive with Spirit.

The natural world, says Teilhard, is as much spiritual as material, and evolution exhibits a *telos*—a directionality—and an *eros* impelled by love, writ broad and deep. Teilhard's thought gave form to my experiences in a powerful way. In *Hymn of the Universe* he writes:

> I bless you, matter, and you I acclaim; not as the pontiffs of science or the moralizing preachers depict you—debased, disfigured—a mass of brute forces and base appetites—but as you reveal yourself . . . in your totality and your true nature. I acclaim you as the divine milieu, charged with creative power, as the ocean stirred by the Spirit, as the clay molded and infused with life by the incarnate Word.

I did not know the meaning of the "incarnate Word," but I understood clearly that nature is a bearer of Spirit. The German philosopher Schelling says that nature is visible spirit, and spirit is invisible nature. And I experienced this directly—I, one speck of humankind—sitting amidst an aspen grove along Saint Mary's Creek near a beaver pond, trying to grasp the incredible beauty of this unfurling cosmos.

The sun peered over the edge of the eastern mountain. Dew from the meadows began evaporating into mist that floated delicately several feet above the ground. Vapor rose from the pond. Trout were rising, ready to feed. A rainbow trout jumped out of the water to catch an insect. Sunlight caught the colors along its flank and glistened through the drops of water as they fell back to the pond, creating multiple tiny prisms. More trout jumped; water droplets fanned out and spread like mini-fireworks; radiant colors glistened, again and again.

Felled trees, denuded of bark and bleached gray by the sun, lay scattered around me. One end of each had been tapered to a blunt point by a gnawing beaver. The chewed shavings—chips of pine and aspen—decomposed slowly into soil. I set the Teilhard book down and scraped the surface of the ground—dug several inches down with my fingernails, then scooped the dark, cool dirt into the palm of my hand. I squeezed it tight into a clod, then broke it up with my thumb and let it sift slowly through my fingers. Again and again. *This stuff is alive!* It quivers with energy, breaks down, recombines with new elements, gets taken up into larger wholes, part of a cosmic process that organizes the scattered elements of the universe into ever-more complex unities, with each new level of complexity rising to a higher state of sentience and love, until evolution reaches humankind, with its enormously complex brain and a degree of self-consciousness never before attained, at least on earth: a world where Spirit becomes incarnate in the form of matter, then matter evolves toward Spirit, impelled by an inner dynamism. Why, I wondered, had my college course in evolution focused only on the material mechanisms of evolution—natural selection, genetic mutation, and population dynamics—but not also its directionality, its movement toward Spirit?

On returning from the Jarbidge, I entered a sort of monastery of one, secluding myself in my basement apartment. I read, wrote, and studied, became both teacher and student. I sallied forth into the world only when I needed food or other supplies or to hike the sage-covered hills. I ceased almost all contact with former friends and family. I fasted, sometimes for days at a time, drinking only water, a concept I borrowed from Hinduism. I rarely ate meat, relying on lentils, legumes, eggs, and milk for protein. I ceased going to bars and casinos and whorehouses.

I had entered an entirely new world and eagerly explored its contours, its wonders and intricacies, the hidden underside of things seldom noticed. Now I wanted to learn all things religious. I added to my book collection the *Upanishads*, the *Bhagavad Gita*, the *Tao te Ching*, the *Koran*, the *Analects* of Confucius, and the Bible, which I began to read for the first time. I used Huston Smith's *The Religions of Man* as an introduction to these traditions. Alongside Augustine's *Confessions*, I added Bonaventure's *Journey of the Mind into God*, Basil of Caesarea's *Hexamaeron*, Clement of Alexandria's *Stromateis*, Henri de Lubac's *The Discovery of God*, and Idries Shah's stories of Sufi mystics.

During subsequent hikes and backpacking trips—throughout the summer of 1972 and into the fall—something for which I had no name nudged its way stealthily, but steadily, into my consciousness. A fleeting movement, noiseless, passed through the grasses and brush as I walked the hills; a stalking presence, out of sight, would brood in the shadows of the junipers; a wind-like breathing murmured in the tall grasses and the sage, evoking an unknown voice inside my soul. Divine presence stalked me. Its breath was warm and earthy, yet fresh. It was both lightning and a calm deep lake; it was earthquake and water from a mountain spring; it was volcano and a woman's nourishing breast; it was galaxies exploding and a soaring on wings. It was cloudburst and she-bear—yet was none of these things. It was giver and taker and transformer of life.

I frequently hiked up Graystone Hill on the outskirts of town, not far from my apartment. The sage and juniper were faded and dull, the semi-arid land dusty and parched, all color bleached by the sun. I had spent many days in these hills as a child. My brothers, friends, and I roamed the town and countryside freely, without care or prohibitions on what we could do and where we could go. Our parents knew we would return home when we got hungry or tired. We caught lizards (blue bellies and white bellies) and horned toads and brought them home in rusty buckets. Sometimes we took pellet guns or bows and arrows to shoot birds, rabbits, or ground hogs—anything that moved. We chased and captured tumbleweeds rolling across the land, or freed them from captivity to barbed wire fences. We pulled them from the fences and tossed them to the other side, giving them another chance to roll and bound across the country-side in the wind. They bounded with determination, and it seemed they might reach Utah or even Colorado before the first snowfall, spreading their seeds across hundreds of miles while crossing unin-habited land marked only by the occasional dirt road or windmill— or alas, another barbed-wire fence.

In the summer, hot air currents formed swirling dust devils that frequently scurried across the land. The wind funneled down to earth like a mini-tornado, picking up dust and tumbleweeds into a swirling vortex. We ran into the thick of the whirlwind with eyes closed, and tried to stand firm without getting blown to the ground. We emerged, and laughed to see one another's crusty masks formed of dust and sweat.

After the three-week excursion into the Jarbidge, these familiar hills surrounding town seemed different. I saw them differently. County road crews had cut into the eastern side of Graystone Hill for gravel, exposing drab brown, gray, and rust-red pebbles—ordi-nary, unremarkable rocks that I had passed numerous times with-out notice. Yet one morning something gleamed just under the surface. I fingered through the dirt and pulled out a handful of small, smooth rocks, and held them in my palms. I wiped the dirt off on my pant legs. The colors were luminescent; I knew at once they reflected a divine light. The pebbles exuded a kind of energy, and that same energy flowed through everything in creation and through all time—*traces of God encoded in physicality,* I thought. Drab, lifeless dust and bitter sage became sweet fruit. This uncanny experience turned the dreariest of landscapes into a house of radi-ant colors and swung open the doors to a many-roomed mansion inside me I had seen previously only through a peephole. I looked up from the rocks and out over the land, now transformed and luminous in the morning light. *How,* I wrote in my journal, *does one reckon with the infinite wilderness that is God?*

I used the word *conversion* in my journal to describe my experi-ences. But conversion *to what?* No religious tradition had informed my transformation. I didn't join a church. To what, then, did I convert? To a sense of the all-encompassing presence of—what exactly? God in the cosmos? I felt as if I had come upon an ancient book— the book of nature—that smelled of earth, sage, and sky, that I now had to learn to read as I journeyed toward a home I didn't know, but knew was mine. A spiritual resplendence flooded my mind, altering my horizons entirely, leaving me with a totally new frame of reference and a new territory to explore. The mind that had slept listlessly for almost twenty years—awakening only on occasion to the twilight—was now aglow.

It has taken a lifetime for the implications of this conversion to take hold, for as I realized later, the conversion marked only the beginning of a lifetime quest.

God, I discovered, dwells in the natural world and also in our inner- most being. Spirit *wants* to emerge in us; indeed, it hunts us through the forests of our preoccupations and stalks us through the mazes of self-made obstacles that keep us from our deepest and tru- est selves. That, anyway, is how I experienced it. If I'd have voiced that idea to anyone I knew, they'd have thought I'd gone Looney Tunes. But, when I retreated into solitude and lived on the margins of society for a time, the Spirit broke through, capturing me. Some- times it came peacefully and gently, sometimes it erupted like a vol- cano. When it surfaced, psychosomatic effects followed: nerve cells, long dormant or unconnected, linked and produced an effect as if light were infusing my mind—a state of illumination, a word reli- gious seekers frequently use. St. Augustine, addressing God directly in *The Confessions*, writes of this experience:

> Urged to reflect upon myself, I entered under your guidance the innermost places of my being; but only because you had become my helper was I able to do so. I entered, then, and with the vision of my spirit, such as it was, I saw the incommutable light far above my spiritual ken and transcending my mind: not this common light which every carnal eye can see, nor any light of the same order; but greater, as though this common light were shining much more powerfully, far more brightly, and so extensively as to

fill the universe. The light I saw was not the common light at all, but something different, utterly different, from all those things. Nor was it higher than my mind in the sense that oil floats on water or the sky is above the earth; it was exalted because this very light made me, and I was below it because by it I was made. Anyone who knows truth knows this light.

God had illuminated my mind with Spirit. At the same time, there were passages in *The Confessions* I couldn't agree with, such as, "In my unloveliness I plunged into the lovely things which you created. You were with me, but I was not with you. Created things kept me from you." *No, no,* I thought, the natural world does not take us away from God and from our deepest selves: it evokes both. The Spirit of God lives deeply both within us and within the structure of the cosmos—is its ancient and always-guiding energy. The sacred permeates the world. I knew this with certainty.

The Upanishads say that the individual soul (Atman) of all things is one with the universal, or cosmic, soul (Brahman). That idea resonated deeply with me at the time. I suppose a form of pantheism was forming in my mind; perhaps even some kind of nature worship. I remembered the cloudburst in the Oquirrh Mountains of Utah, of my desire to merge with the elemental power of nature, to be absorbed into and consumed by it. Yet, neither pantheism nor nature worship quite described my experience, though at the time I did drift toward pantheism. I sensed the powerful presence of God's Spirit in nature, and Teilhard's writing gave me the evolutionary framework for understanding it. And, although Teilhard's writings frequently referred to Christian concepts—Alpha and Omega, the Logos, the Incarnation, Christ-centered universe, the Pleroma— those concepts did not mean anything to me since I had no Christian frame of reference in which to place his work. The Christian connection seemed to me peripheral to his evolutionary thought, which I understood without knowing its Christian context.

I understood that God utterly transcends the universe, even while inhabiting it intimately. I later learned that the more apt word for this is *panentheism:* the divine both transcends and pervades the universe. *How could that be?* It seemed contradictory, but through my readings, I discovered that numerous Christian and Jewish mystics, and even theologians, throughout the centuries had experienced the sacred through nature. I began jotting down examples in my journal:

> From the Psalms: "The heavens show forth the glory of God and the firmament declares his handiwork" (Psalm 19:2).

> St. Paul: "The invisible things of God are clearly seen since the creation of the world, being understood by the things that are made" (Romans 1:20). Paul was a tent maker. Maybe he camped out in the wilderness on his journeys.

> St. Basil of Caesarea: the natural world is "the school where the mind normally exercises itself" and is "the training ground where [it] learn[s] to know God; since by the sight of visible and sensible things the mind is led, as by a hand, to the contemplation of invisible things." Basil saw intelligent design everywhere in the universe and had great appreciation for the intricate details of the smallest things in the world, such as a blade of grass or the function of the various parts of an insect. Basil the proto-botanist, or entomologist?

> St. Bonaventure: God shines forth in all created things and, therefore, they bear witness to him. Bonaventure's classic book is *The Journey of the Mind into God*—not to or toward, but *into*, right into the heart and mind of God.

> Teilhard de Chardin: "God is not remote from us. He is at the point of my pen, my pick, my paintbrush, my needle—and my heart and my thoughts." *Even this disposable Bic medium point pen that conveys my thoughts?*

> Gerard Manley Hopkins: "God plays in ten thousand faces; lovely in limbs and lovely in eyes not his."

> Henri de Lubac: "every living being is a theophany. Everywhere we find traces, imprints, vestiges, enigmas; and the rays of the divinity pierce through everywhere." God appears to us through the world, "to solicit our attention." Hunts us, and when he finds us, merely

solicits attention. We can ignore, and most people seem to, but what a lost opportunity!

I kept a list of these examples in a manila folder, and it grew thick over time.

We need only be attentive to discern God's presence everywhere. So, rather than being a hindrance, as it was for Augustine, contemplation of the divine traces in Creation enabled Spirit to rise from my dark interior into consciousness. Living in solitude at the margins of the world, on the periphery of society, made this possible.

6

Mask

I N NOVEMBER of 1972, I returned to Mexico as planned, to spend
a second winter in Álamos. I still had $9,500 left from my insur-
ance settlement, so I flew into Ciudád Obregón and from there
planned to take a bus to Álamos. After passing through customs, I
stopped in the restroom before going to the bus stop. I glanced into
a mirror above the washbasin, and what I saw astonished me. I
stared for a long time, startled by my image. I turned my head to the
left, then the right, to inspect my nose, cheeks, and eyes. I saw my
face, but did not at first recognize it. I saw the same face I'd always
seen, yet I appeared somehow different. I beheld *my real self*, in
some uncanny sense, in a way I had not before seen. I looked, for
the first time, as if a mask had been torn away.

I stayed with Hal and María for a week until I could find a room
or apartment to rent. On about the fourth night in Álamos, María
came to my room, as she had many times in the past. I refused her
advances. She persisted, as did I in my refusal. She reached her arms
around my neck and tried to kiss me. I took her wrists and pulled
them down. "No. It's wrong," I said.

When she realized I was not going to give in, she blurted out
angrily, "*Hipócrita!* You didn't think it was wrong last year."

"I know, but that was a sin," I said.

"Sin? *Mierda!*" she huffed and slammed the door behind her.
"*Pendejo cabrón!*" she said, loud enough for me to hear.

As she walked away, I wondered why I used the word *sin*. It had
not been part of my vocabulary in the past. Where had I picked it
up? I knew what it meant, of course, but why did I apply it to my
relationship with María? Yes, she was legally married to Hal, but
they didn't live as man and wife, nor share the same bed except per-

haps on occasion. He needed a cook and housekeeper, she someone to support her and her children. Both María and I had sexual desires that needed satisfaction. Throughout adolescence I had sought that satisfaction, and it was no big deal, a normal thing for a young buck. So what was the problem now? I had read bits and pieces of the Bible, where the word *sin* means "missing the mark," or *hamartia* in Greek. The word *sin* appears regularly in the letters of St. Paul to describe the many ways humans give offense to God. We're off-kilter. The last of the Ten Commandments proscribes coveting another man's wife. Hinduism and Buddhism teach that adultery and the inordinate gratification of sensual desires directs attention away from spiritual progress. But, I wondered, must sensual satisfaction and spiritual progress oppose one another? Are they mutually exclusive? The physical world, I knew, is no illusion; it is a bearer of Spirit, is sacramental. So, then, what of the physicality of sex? How can it be a sin? It's part of our nature. *Is there is a difference,* I wondered, *between sacred and profane sex?* How did I come to that intuition? Is there a moral law within us that asserts itself under the right circumstances, even when our culture tells us the opposite—and American culture loudly broadcasts the opposite?

I also worried what might happen if we were found out—not for my own sake, but for the children's. Would Hal throw María and the children out of the house? I doubted that he would, but—*what if?* That would be on my conscience, which, though not well-formed, had at least awakened from slumber. I lacked the theological language or moral framework for adjudicating my questions, but I knew with certainty that my relationship with María had been sinful. I had to quit it.

As glad as I was to be back in Álamos, something in me had changed. The enchantment of a new and different culture receded into the distance. A mysterious new magic possessed me, and it dislodged every other interest. I was not the same. I returned to Elko after only a month, and greeted the New Year, 1973, from my apartment monastery, surrounded by my books, by the austere Nevada hills, and in view of vast horizons that I eagerly explored.

7

Falling

A YEAR LATER, the new magic began to wane. Solitude gradually devolved into loneliness. Nothing in my background or
mental frame of reference had prepared me to handle the
after-effects of the eruption of the divine, which psychologically
overwhelmed and led me to exclude all other interests. At the same
time, I had no outlet through which to express my discovery, except
through the cryptic writings in my journals. How does one talk
about the ineffable, especially if you don't have a religious symbol
system in which to articulate it?

God's grace, said the German theologian Karl Rahner, "wells up
from the depths of man's heart in a thousand secret ways, penetrating into all spheres of his life. It makes him restless; makes him
doubt whether existence is really finite and restricted to this present
world, fills him with a sense of the immeasurability of that claim
which can only be fulfilled by the infinity of God."

Grace had seized me, alright, yet I didn't know how to translate
my newly given insights into a language understandable to others,
or how to share them with a community of others. Perhaps I now
needed to move away from the margins of society into the communal. But *what community of others did I even have? What kind did I
need?*

I had no outlet for this new spiritual energy, and energy caged
turns dark and destructive, as I soon discovered through a long trial
in the desert.

8

The Valley of Shadows

MYSTICAL euphoria can be a kind of addiction: once you experience the high, you can't go without it. A year and a half after the summer of conversion in the Jarbidge wilderness and the hills surrounding Elko, the intensity and frequency of the euphoria decreased. It was like going through a slow withdrawal, against my will, and it didn't go well. And I had no one to shepherd me through the agony. I had no community of fellow seekers, no mentors, and didn't know how to seek help.

The inability to communicate with others was nothing new for me. With the exception of my time in Mexico, I had always been a diffident and private man—an introverted loner. I'd had friends and dated girls in high school, to be sure, but my friendships were not close or personal. I hung in the background, tagging along with the guys hoping to be "cool," but I wasn't personally close to any of them. I didn't have conversations with other boys about the things boys wonder about, those things that disclose something of one's vulnerability to the unknowns of life.

How do you ask a girl out on a date? What if she says no?
Have you ever gone all the way with a girl? What's it like? How, exactly, do you do it?
Do your parents help you with homework? Do they ever fight or argue?
Why is your family so close? Hardly anyone one at my house even talks to each other.

I'd wondered these things, but didn't know to ask, didn't know it was normal to talk about such things—things that reveal oneself in the questions themselves, and elicit personal experiences from others in a way that forms a bond of friendship.

My parents were not warm and affectionate people, not toward each other and not toward their children (at least some of us). They had a broken relationship that ended in a permanent separation. I remember most their fighting and their emotional distance from each other and from their children (I suspect my mother was closer emotionally to my sisters). I have no memory of my parents ever entertaining guests or ever being invited to the homes or parties of others. I don't remember my father having friends. I can see him brooding in the living room, watching TV, eating dinner off a TV tray, not joining the family in the dining room. I had no models for how to interact socially. I don't know what influence that played in my psychological state of mind; my brothers and sisters seemed able to socialize well. I was the diffident one.

Even so, I'd dated throughout high school: Diana, Judy, Debbie, Nancy, Jan, and another Debbie. I went steady with two of them, and they wore my class ring.

In spite of these romances, I began to notice a disconcerting reality about myself. I became aware, as others already knew, that I was inept at socializing—out of place and uncomfortable in groups of people. The space between myself and others mirrored the vast spaces between mountain ranges in the Great Basin: wide valleys yawned between.

I first became keenly aware of this social ineptitude during my sophomore year of high school. A classmate, George Winters, and I went with our dates to a movie, and afterward to George's house, where two other couples joined us for a pizza party. We sat around the kitchen table, chatting, laughing, and telling stories. Judy Chandler was my date. We had dated before and enjoyed one another's company; we talked, joked and, on occasion, kissed. Amidst this larger group, however, where the conversation was not intimate and one-on-one, but veered this way then swerved in that, gliding across the surfaces of things rather than deep down, I felt as if I were in a different culture whose language I didn't know. Conversation, chit-chat, banter, joking, and laughter. A normal social occasion. Yet, I felt ill at ease. I drifted into the living room and sat alone on the sofa, listening to the conversation wafting about the kitchen and spreading into the ether. I felt bewildered by its alien character. Ten minutes later, George walked into the room.

"There you are," he said. "We thought you'd gotten lost. Come back in and join us."

"I'm doing fine in here," I replied.

He looked at me, perplexed, then shrugged and returned to the kitchen. Faintly, from a distance, someone said, "Why is he so quiet? Did we say something wrong?"

"He's just a party pooper," someone else said, in a far-off voice from across a valley.

I was now barely tuned into the fading voices. I gazed around at the furniture in the room: the sofa that I sat on, the end table, and a reclining chair; a coffee table, a potted plant, and a television set, all resting on a recently-vacuumed carpet. The vacuum cleaner stood alone in a corner, incongruously. I was struck by the emptiness of the space between the pieces of furniture, and how dry and sterile that space seemed. I wondered: why is it so empty? Had the vacuum sucked it of life?

Perhaps I exaggerate the dissociation I felt sitting alone in that room, but sit alone I did, not knowing *how* to interact. And that carpet *was* well swept; the room was neat; it had no junk in it, no piles of books or magazines, no boys' baseball cleats, no footballs or baseball caps under the couch. I did not know how to *be* in that room, except alone.

At that time, I had no notion that the desire for being alone might be integral to a vocation of contemplative solitude. I did not even know there was such a thing as a vocation. But was it a calling? Or just an amalgam of religious fervor, empty landscapes, emotional distance from others, and a naturally extreme introversion and mild autism, all of it blending into some kind of psychological aberration? The conversion I experienced in the Jarbidge Mountains and subsequent forays into nature had intensified my natural tendency to solitude and avoidance of groups.

When my sister Karen married in late 1974, I skipped out on the family dinner party the evening before the wedding. The mere thought of socializing and trying to explain what I was doing with my life generated uncontrollable anxiety. At the reception hall following the wedding service I drifted to a back corner and stood alone, shrinking from conversation. At the first opportunity, I slipped out a side door and left, relieved to not have to talk to anyone.

I did grocery shopping early or late, when few customers were around, and looked for checkout registers with no one waiting in line—to prevent the possibility of casual conversation. I avoided cashiers who liked to chat. I rarely ventured out of my apartment, even to visit family, unless it was to the open country. My natural introversion had become extreme. *Did I have a mild form of autism?* I later wondered.

Shortly after Karen's wedding I returned to Álamos for a brief vacation. I stayed with Hal and María who, along with her younger sister, Julieta, did not know what to make of the changes in me. I did not interact with anyone in the household. I sat alone in my room, reading or musing, oblivious to anything going on around me.

"Qué pasó contigo?" Julieta asked one day, sarcastically. "Eres como un fantasma! Como algo que casi no existe."

Is that how people now see me? I wondered. *Ghost-like? As a specter that barely exists?*

I had not dated in a long time, and when I did, I hardly knew what to talk about. What in my new world was there to talk about when I didn't have the language with which to do so? An old girlfriend from high school (one of the Debbies) wrote me a letter from Hawaii, where she had spent a few years as a Mormon missionary. She was returning to Elko soon and asked if she could see me. Sure, I wrote back. We took a walk, and talked. Or maybe I just listened, but must have told her something about my experiences. Afterwards we went to her house and sat on the couch. I had no idea what to say. I merely sat and smiled at her, like a disembodied ghost. She seemed puzzled at the change in me. "You seem so sweet and nice," she said, incredulously. *Sweet and nice.* I had changed so much from the wild young man she once knew. Her words were not meant as a compliment. She might as well have said, "You don't have much personality. Nice, but boring."

Does religion *do* that to people? I wondered. Where do I turn for help? *How do I start to exist again?*

My brother Brian got married around the same time as Karen, and his friends threw a stag party that I was invited to. Brian is less than a year older than I am, so many of our friends overlapped. At the party, everyone made merry, as I had made merry during the years of adolescent carousing. But I was no longer at home with this group of young men—my friends and associates of twenty years. As the night wore on and drunkenness took hold, a movement arose to move the party to the gambling halls and (though unspoken, I knew) the whorehouses. Two pals, Dave Palmer and Jerry Spikes, asked if they could hitch a ride with me. I said I'd give them a lift, but wasn't joining them.

"You're not coming with us? How come?" they asked.

I believe I responded half in jest, and half not: "I don't want to soil my soul, like you princes of debauchery."

They stared at me, trying to grasp where I was coming from. "Are you serious?" asked Jerry.

"Yeah, kind of, I am."

"What are you, some kind of fucking saint?" asked Dave.

"Not yet, but trying to be," I said.

"Have you become a Jesus freak or something?"

"What's a Jesus freak?" I asked. I had been out of circulation a while and had not heard the term.

"Someone who thinks Jesus Christ is his personal lord and savior, and likes to let everyone know how holy he is and they aren't."

"No, I'm not that," I said, though I *was* becoming judgmental—not in a fundamentalist, Jesus-freak sort of way, but in a growing scorn of things worldly, of the world most people live in. The influence on me in that regard was more from readings in Hinduism and Buddhism than Christianity. I was no longer at home in the world. But where *was* I at home?

Though not a Jesus freak, I didn't know *what* I was. Did I belong in a category? The liminally lost? Phantoms of the sacred grove? Who do *they* hang out with? What would *they* do on the eve of a brother's wedding? Chant *Om* antiphonally?

In a small town like Elko, people who turned religiously serious tended to be evangelical or fundamentalist Christians. Catholics did not drift toward zealousness, and I wasn't that, anyway. The Mormons expressed their zeal by going on missions; the Seventh Day Adventists by going door to door. There were few, if any, non-Christian groups around. Acquaintances therefore placed me in the nearest category they knew: I must have become a Jesus freak. In truth, Christianity was barely on my radar screen at the time, only one of many religious paths to delve into.

Family and acquaintances began to wonder what happened to me. Some were just curious. *What exactly do you do all day?* What could I tell them? Read, write, sleep, go for walks. Repeat. Not having undergone anything like this themselves, they were baffled. I seemed a ghost of my former self.

Around that time—1974–75—I began reading William James's *The Varieties of Religious Experience,* a classic in religious psychology. James says that the person who leads a religious life, *exclusively pursued,* to the neglect of all else, tends to become eccentric. Those for whom religion is an "acute fever" rather than a dull habit often show "symptoms of nervous instability," with a "discordant inner life." They experience depression for a significant portion of their lives and have many behavioral characteristics "ordinarily classed as pathological."

Yes, pathological.

I had been intimate with that acute fever and, now, that discordant inner life and depression. I possessed a number of pathological traits that became increasingly pronounced: avoidance of close relations with others; "autistic thinking (i.e., thinking unduly directed towards oneself and the inner personal view of the situation, at the expense of information available from the external world); a shut-in, reclusive, withdrawn, introverted personality." These traits, described by Kenneth Leech in *Soul Friend,* had always hovered around me, but now surged to dominance. And, yes, religious experience was inextricably intertwined with those traits. I had been seized by what Rudolph Otto called the *numinous,* which transformed my life. *But what had it done to me?*

The Valley of Shadows

Years later, I learned that religious seekers in most traditions are escorted to the margins of society for a time by wise and experienced religious leaders who introduce novices into the mysteries of the sacred and to a deep knowledge of a religious tradition. The goal: spiritual transformation and illumination, a process that may take months or years. Following this marginal—or liminal—phase, they are ritually re-assimilated into society—either the one they left behind or a new one to which they will now belong and owe allegiance—prepared to be leaders within a given religious tradition.

I had no tradition, no mentors, no advisers. Separation from society and withdrawal into a liminal state, undertaken without guides and outside a structured, ritual process rooted in a living tradition, is fraught with danger. Labyrinthine passageways to a nether world split off from pathways to the mountaintop. How does one know which turn to take?

I had charged into the numinous realm enthusiastically, but had no one to guide me out. I got lost in my own psychic forest.

The mystical overflow that had suffused my mind and soul had no outlet. Like a pressure cooker with no relief valve, it began to melt and collapse inward on itself. The nether regions became infernal. I tied myself in a knot. I could not sleep, so tightly strained were my nerves. I became a hollowed-out man with a scorched psyche.

William James says that when someone is "converted" it means that "religious ideas, previously peripheral in his consciousness, now take a central place, and that religious aims form the habitual centre of his energy." New ideas and perspectives—let's call them visions of an expanded horizon—become "hot" and "alive" within his mind, and all other ideas and actions have "to crystallize around them." The experience seems to come directly from a divine source. I had become focused single-mindedly on that divine center, to the exclusion of all else.

After a period of euphoria, I lost my way, became a sick and divided soul, just like many of the eccentric characters described in James's *Varieties*. I saw myself in some of them. I withdrew into myself, into a private world with little contact with friends and family. And as I read James, I had to ask, *are my experiences just a manifestation of mental illness?*

The crises and mental disturbances of some religious seekers are, indeed, similar to those of the mentally unstable. In fact, some people believe religion *is* a mental disorder. Freud equated religion with neurosis grounded in frustrated sexual desires and the inability to face the adult world. Marx said religion is the "opium of the masses," giving them hope in the "next world" so they don't despair of, or fight against, the injustices in this one. No one can deny that such disorders characterize some religious believers. Religion can prevent maturation by keeping one in a state of "spiritual childhood," unable to face the adult world and accept its responsibilities. Or it can lead people to withdraw from the world in an unhealthy way.

Sometime in 1975 I ran out of insurance money. I had sold the Ford pickup for $4,000, but even that money was dwindling. I needed a job. I wrote a letter to Byron Hardie, then living in Tucson, to ask for work with Newmont. I told him I was willing to work anywhere in the world—perhaps, I thought, an adventure in some exotic place would bring me back to life. First, though, I faced the dilemma of how to address the letter. What was the etiquette of a formal letter? "Dear Mr. Hardie" would have been standard, but that didn't seem formal or dignified enough. I pondered this difficulty for several days, agonized over it. Finally, I remembered some letters written by the seventeenth-century philosopher Spinoza, in an appendix to a translation of his *Ethics*. I pulled the volume from a bookcase and found the letters. There I found my salutation:

Most Distinguished and Excellent Sir:

Mr. Hardie kindly contacted the local Newmont office—in spite of the inane salutation—and the head geologist put me to work. I worked a few weeks in the Independence Mountain Range about thirty miles west of the Jarbidge Mountains. I spent a month in Snowville, Utah, near the Idaho-Utah border, helping geologists explore an area mined in the early twentieth century. But the job didn't go well for me. I was in a bad state: wound up so tightly I couldn't sleep; and uninterested in things that were "common" and "worldly." I had difficulty carrying on conversations with other workers.

So I quit. Walked into the office, quit, then walked out. Later that day, the geologist in charge dropped by my apartment to see what was wrong, but all I could offer was a cliché: "I'm just dealing with personal problems right now." He tried to persuade me to come back to work, but I couldn't muster the energy or enthusiasm to go out into the world. A week or so later, Byron Hardie flew to Elko and took me to dinner. He was concerned. He asked if I had plans. I didn't—said I might go back to Mexico for a few months, that I needed to find out what I was meant to do in life.

"Listen," he said, "you don't find that out by going off somewhere and meditating in solitude. You find it out by trying out different jobs, interacting with people of all kinds. Eventually you'll find out what you're good at, where in the social fabric you belong. One of the greatest of gifts in life is to find the work that best suits you. But that can take some time."

He had such forthright, practical wisdom. No wonder his son Warren loved him so much, and why I admired him.

Psychological demons from the past beset me. Repressed memories of my father's violence ate away at me, and I had to exorcise them. I wrote him a long letter—six pages. I no longer remember its details, but it was a letter of repudiation for the hell he put the family through. I spent days writing and rewriting. Inexplicably, I also included my oldest brother Barry in the letter, criticizing him for something or other—I cannot now imagine why. Perhaps he had mocked me mercilessly when I was a kid, but so what? That's what older brothers do. Such was my state of mind. After days of torturous deliberation about what to say, how to say it, and whether or not to send the letter at all, I dropped it in the mailbox. I felt relief. One ghost exorcised.

But demons kept coming. Specters began to inhabit the dark rooms of my apartment, or so it sometimes seemed. On occasion, I sensed an eerie, malign presence in the apartment. I knew it was my imagination, but knowing that didn't make it disappear. It grew stronger. The only way to get it out of my mind was to confront it. I walked slowly into a back room where the furnace and water heater were, a space mostly vacant. As I approached the dark, a chill crept up my spine. Goosebumps raised the hair of my skin. I knew it would do no good to turn on the light—the phantasm would merely flee to the shadows, then return as soon as I turned the light off. So I stood for a time in the darkness—minutes perhaps—until I had conquered the fear and the eeriness. I spoke in a tremulous voice, "*G-go... awaay.*" The words knotted themselves tight and came out with difficulty, as when trying to dispatch a malign presence in a nightmare. I said it again more resolutely. "*Go away.*" The presence departed. This occurred on several occasions. Because I had no companions with whom to talk, interact, and from whom to receive regular reality checks, I lived in a phantom world of my own making. Indeed, I had become ghostly, neither enmeshed in this world nor able to cross over to the eternal. A void opened wide in my soul and darkness crept into it—darkness that eventually took the form of insanity.

For several months I drifted from job to job, unable to hold any down for long. Walks into the hills no longer felt like holy pilgrimages; instead, the world glared a harsh, searing light at me, parched and lifeless. *My God, My God, why have you forsaken me? Why did you call me only to leave me in desolation?* I thought I understood Christ's shriek of dereliction on the Cross.

I began to drink heavily, even tinkered with the idea of suicide. One day I was in the basement of my mother's house, looking for some books I'd stored away. I sat in an old cushioned rocker, and wondered what had happened to me, why the ecstatic visions of several years earlier had flickered and then died out.

I shouted in anger, "God, where are you!"

Silence.

I will force his hand. Amid the stored-away stuff in the basement were shotguns and .22 rifles that my brothers and I had used for hunting when we were young. I took a 12-gauge shotgun off its rack and slipped a shell into the chamber. *I will kill myself if you don't return!*

Silence.

"God, I hate you! Bastard!" I shouted, not realizing my mother had come home.

She opened the door to the basement. "Son, can I do something to help you?"

"No!" I shouted. "Leave me alone!"

"Please let me help."

"Just leave me alone!" Poor gentle woman, wanting to help; I, unwilling to be helped.

I was twenty-five years old. By then I no longer needed a wise spiritual guide; I needed a psychiatrist. I had enough sense to seek one out.

Elko had no psychiatrists, so I travelled 220 miles to Salt Lake City every other week. Dr. Roy Greene's office was in a converted mansion on North Temple Street. The wood walls in the consulting room exuded earth colors, warm and comfortable. Dr. Greene was a short, elderly man with white hair, thick-rimmed glasses, and penetrating eyes. He sat at a large oak desk opposite me. He asked background questions and took notes; I gave short, probably unhelpful answers, but he pried out enough information to get a sense of my mental state. He prescribed Valium (a tranquilizer) so I could sleep, and Elavil and Tofranil (anti-depressants). He asked me to record my dreams nightly and bring them to each therapy session. I did. He read them out loud, underlined certain passages, and tried to elicit from me some reaction to the vivid and troubling images.

In one dream, the lights in my house had gone out. I went to the basement to see what was wrong. There was old, useless stuff stored down there: worn-out dressers, decaying boards, boxes of junk. Wires hung from an electric generator that sat on paper bags. The wires dangled loosely, unconnected to the house wires. I searched for tools to fix the generator, but in every box and dresser drawer I found only gross, stagnant water.

In another dream I stood at the edge of a frozen lake. I wanted a drink but could not find water. I tried to chip some of the ice away, but it was too dense. I walked and walked around the lake, looking for something to drink, but found nothing but ice, everywhere. The psychic, spiritual energy that had flowed so abundantly several years before was now frozen, and there was no path to follow but one of endless, hellish frustration.

Unfortunately, I didn't understand the dream symbolism at all. I sat passively in the office, saying little. When Dr. Greene suggested a possible interpretation, I merely shook my head yes, compliantly and obtusely, a cipher. Years later, after I had read psychoanalysts like Carl Jung and Erik Erikson, I dug those dream journals out of my file cabinets—surprised I had even kept them—and re-read them. Their symbolism seemed crystal clear.

In addition to dream work, Dr. Greene encouraged me to exercise regularly and to take up painting or music to stimulate creativity. I took up water coloring.

In one composition, I tried to capture the serenity of the sunsets I'd experienced at the cove in Guaymas, Mexico. What emerged, instead, was a series of three paintings altogether different and more disturbing than what I had intended. With quick, clean brush strokes I colored streaks of orange, yellow, and red, mingled with faraway blue receding in the horizon. In the foreground were trees and above them I inserted a church steeple that pierced the evening sky. The colors bathed the steeple in eerie, calm light, reflecting the calm and beauty I sought—beauty I had once known walking the hills outside Elko at sunrise, watching the sunsets on the Mexican coast, and gazing at the Milky Way while camped out in the wilderness. Though the work was amateurish, I was moderately pleased until, in the upper right corner I began painting—without thinking—a hint of menacing black cloud. A streak of red sunset merged with the cloud and was transformed into a lightning bolt-like spear. It broke the calm. I stood back, looking at what I had done. Why did I ruin the picture with a menacing storm?

And, yet, it felt honest.

I took out fresh paper and began painting a new scene—same backdrop, new reality. Streaks of red from the sunset grew more vivid, strong, and threatening, developing into bolts of lightning that streaked to the ground. The faraway blue of the horizon turned to gray, and then black, ominous clouds in the distance. The trees and steeple were veiled in cloud; the hill surrounding town a seething volcano, glaring with orange rage.

I took out more blank paper. I painted a solid black background encircling a white egg. The egg had a crack in it. Blood-red lava in the form of a lightning bolt flowed through the crack and into the darkness. Something that had come to birth several years earlier had become a colorless, aborted shape, bleeding in the night.

I showed the watercolors to Dr. Greene. He looked them over carefully, in sequence, and shook his head knowingly. Then looked into my eyes. "You are hurting," he said. "I'll try to help you."

After reading William James, I knew I had to discuss my religious experiences with my psychiatrist: the experience of being *seized* by the sacred, how it had shaken up and transformed my life and mental horizon, making me lose interest in "ordinary" things; how it led me to lose touch with the few friends I did have. Understanding this experience, for me, far exceeded the value of interpreting dreams. I wanted to know what it all meant. I wrote a detailed summary of the experiences, page after page, revised and clarified, then typed them. He carefully read what I wrote, underlined some passages, then said, "I'm glad you're able to objectify this experience. It gives you distance from its immediacy. Some people never find their way out of mental states like this." Beyond that acknowledgement, he was not of a mind to explore it further. "I'm a psychiatrist. My job is to help you find mental and psychological balance, and able to function in society and interact with people satisfactorily. I'm not a spiritual guide. I'm afraid you'll have to go to someone else for that. Do you know a priest or minister who can help you?" I told him about my earlier visits to a Catholic priest and my short-lived church attendance.

A year earlier I had searched for some kind of religious community where I might find fellow seekers with whom I could articulate my experiences. I can't really say why I began going to Mass at the Catholic church—perhaps because it was only a few blocks from my apartment. Or maybe because I had noticed how close my friend John's extended family was, and how Catholicism seemed to be at the center of that cohesiveness. That familiar and social closeness— something I had not known in my family—had been apparent in the people of Álamos, too, and I associated it somehow with Catholicism.

At church I sat in the back pews. The ritual was new to me and baffling: kneeling, standing, bowing; the rote recitation of the same prayers week after week. I wondered why we had to spend so much time on our knees during the Eucharistic prayer. It seemed to go on interminably. I endured it patiently, though I did wait expectantly for the *Sanctus*: "Holy, Holy, Holy Lord, God of power and might. Heaven and earth are full of your glory! Hosanna in the highest!" That I understood. I resonated deeply with the belief that the earth is full of God's glory. I appreciated the exclamation marks, too, and approved the repetition of "holy" *three* times. Overall, though, the rituals lacked vitality.

I met weekly with the parish priest, Fr. Donovan, a short, nervous man with an air of impatience. He gave me two catechisms to read—Richard Wilhelm's *Christ among Us* and a Dutch catechism—both written following the Second Vatican Council (1961–1965). I read Thomas Merton's *The Seven Storey Mountain*, and some documents of the Second Vatican Council. Fr. Donovan and I met in the living room of the rectory to discuss the books. The room was spacious and clean, with a large picture window facing the yard (on first entering, I wondered if Bella used to clean this room before becoming a Madame at Betty's D&D). The meetings had little structure. I brought questions that had arisen from the readings, and he tried to answer them. What I really wanted to talk about, though, was how the Church's teaching related to my mystical experiences. I tried to talk about my unusual conversion in the hills and mountains, about Teilhard's vision of cosmic evolution. Where did my experience fit in, if at all? I needed a connection. But Fr. Donovan seemed uninterested in my experience. He probably had enough familiarity with Christian history to know the problematic nature of individual religious enthusiasms and the difficulty of aligning them with Tradition. Revelation had been given through Christ; what could my unformed mystical experiences in the mountains contribute to what had been handed down through many centuries? Maybe the priest wanted to discourage the acute fever in me—Catholics tend not to favor zeal.

I wouldn't let it go easily, though. I had underlined a passage from *Gaudium et Spes,* a document from the Second Vatican Council, brought it to a meeting, and read it aloud: "believers, no matter what their religion, have always recognized the voice and the revelation of God in the discourse of creatures." See, the *discourse of the created world, of nature. What about that?* I backed it up with my list of passages about finding God in nature. Fr. Donovan gave a cursory look at the list, but was not impressed. "God comes to us through the sacraments of the Church," he said, "especially the Eucharist. There's no salvation outside that. What you're referring to is a kind of *natural,* not *supernatural* revelation, which comes only through Scripture and the Church's sacraments." I remembered a section from Merton's *The Seven Storey Mountain* where he and his friends meet and befriend a Hindu man in New York City. Merton was moved by the Hindu's wisdom and spiritual depth—by his *holiness.* Yet, at that time (1940s) Merton felt obliged to assert that the Hindu displayed a merely *natural,* not a *supernatural* holiness. Merton wrote this at a time when Neo-Scholastic theology—which, among other things, posited a strict separation between nature and grace—reigned in Catholic intellectual life. I didn't understand the distinction. God's Spirit is God's Spirit, isn't it? *Does it matter what channel it comes through?* (Merton renounced his position years later.)

I had read in the church bulletin that a lay parish council had recently been established, and asked about it. Was it a group to which I might belong?

"Oh, those guys," the priest said, dismissing them with a wave of the hand. "I don't think you'll find anything of interest there."

The readings were helpful but our meetings were neither uplifting nor enlightening. Fr. Donovan seemed bitter about changes in the Catholic Church following the Second Vatican Council—changes I did not yet know the importance of. After several months, I stopped meeting with him and stopped attending church.

"Keep trying," Dr. Greene said. "Look for a wise priest or minister who will understand." He looked away a moment, in thought, clutched his hands in a finger lock, elbows on the desk, as if assessing whether or not to say what he was going to say. "You know, Hasidic Jews say no one under the age of 35 should read the Kabbalah. Do you know what Kabbalah is?" I did. "The Hasids say Kabbalah reveals a highly symbolic, esoteric world full of mystery that points to sacred realities. If one is not mature enough to handle those realities, they can go insane. I'm afraid I don't have the qualifications or training to help you in this realm, though."

Insane.

Pathological.

Sweet and nice.

A specter.

What kind of God would summon anyone with those traits—for any task?

After six months of psychotherapy Dr. Greene let on that he thought the loss of my eye probably had contributed to my mental condition. When a limb or other member of the body is lost, he said, the body "grieves," in a sense, and this has subconscious mental and emotional effects. I needed to bring this grief to consciousness, deal with it, and get it behind me. He hoped I'd acknowledge this, but it seemed too much of a stretch to me. I had never been troubled by the accident or the loss of my eye. And my religious experience was *real*, not merely an epiphenomenon of some physical trauma. I say "not merely," because the loss might have played some role—not in the conversion experience—but the psychological trauma later. My religious experiences, though linked to my mental illness, could not be reduced to it. I was altered. My consciousness was transformed. I was claimed by a presence and I could not reject or disavow its claim on me without destroying myself. Objectify it or not, I *couldn't* flee it; instead, *it* had abandoned *me. Why?*

William James, too, was unwilling to reduce religious experience to neurological or psychological disorder. If you go the route of reductionism, he said, then science, literature and every product of the human mind would have to be reduced to some organic, physical process. Beethoven's fifth symphony was perhaps traceable to a hyperactive spleen; Virgil's *Aeneid* to rheumatoid arthritis; Newton's law of gravity to cardiac excitation. James, a philosophical pragmatist, said beliefs should be judged not in accordance with whatever mental disturbance accompany them, but by their fruits. Do they lead to wholeness and enlightenment; to a life lived well?

His criteria for judging whether or not a religious belief or way of life is sound: "*Immediate luminousness,* in short *philosophical reasonableness* and *moral helpfulness* are the only available criteria." Does it lead one to wholeness or, conversely, to fragmentation and alienation? Using these criteria, I had strayed way off course. My religious experiences were real. They had taken me to the mountaintop. But I was now as far from whole as one could be, alienated from others, from myself, and from God. Christian Wiman says, "The way you ascertain the truth of spiritual experience [is that] it propels you back toward the world and other people, and not simply more deeply within yourself." I had felt that pull toward others, but did not know how to get there, or where exactly to go. Even a cloistered monk like Thomas Merton felt the need to write, to communicate his inner experience to others. He had many friends with whom he regularly corresponded. I had none.

Deep depression is a heaviness that pulls downward, incessantly, with a dense, dark gravity. I had to find a way out of that slow-burning state of limbo that I was trapped in. It would take years before I emerged.

Dr. Greene knew I had been out of college for a number of years and that I had not dated for quite some time. He encouraged me to return to college, where I could meet other people with similar intellectual interests, perhaps even a young woman. He encouraged me to seek the companionship of women, but I was now so socially inept that I didn't even know how to approach women. When I expressed reticence, he asked why.

"I'm too shy," I said. "Too quiet and boring. They won't like me."

"Oh, I think they will," he said with a confidence that surprised me. Perhaps he did not realize, I thought, how nice and sweet, even *spectral,* I had become in the eyes of many women—in the eyes of almost everyone. I was just so introverted, had so much difficulty conversing with others. Why would any woman be interested in me?

But Dr. Greene seemed certain they would. *Had some flesh returned to my ghostlike person?* Or was it just, as I wondered many years later, that the connections between extreme introversion and mild autism had not yet surfaced in the psychological literature? And he had misdiagnosed me, whatever his diagnosis was.

What struck me most, though, was his recommendation to return to college. The simplicity of the advice surprised me. *Well, of course,* I thought, *that's exactly what I should do. Why didn't I think of that?*

I reentered the University of Nevada in 1976, at the age of twenty-six. While there I met my first wife, Gloria Sanchez, who found me not spectral, but kind and caring. Through my first, brief sojourn in the country of marriage I would gradually emerge from the abyss and re-enter society—scarred, with a limp in one thigh from contending with the angel. I had not even won the wrestling match, as had Jacob, but I was still alive—psychically maimed, to be sure—but alive. Had I received a blessing, or a curse? Or both?

9

The Country of Marriage

I PLANNED to double-major in philosophy and history. I minored in Spanish in order to improve my language fluency, but was disappointed because Spanish courses were conducted primarily in English. I asked one of my Spanish professors if he knew of any native speakers I could meet with to converse in Spanish. He did, and introduced us.

Gloria Sanchez was from the town of Apatzingán, Michoacán, in the *tierra caliente* of southwest Mexico. She was the second of five children born to a peasant farmer who barely eked out a living for his family. Gloria had a number of half-brothers and -sisters scattered around, too, for though her father had few resources to support a family, he was not immune to the Mexican ideal of *machismo*. After secondary school, Gloria went to work in a local store and later came to the United States to search for a better life. She came on a tourist visa and soon found a job as a keypunch operator at a bank in Reno, Nevada.

Gloria was slender, with dark hair cropped short, and friendly, with a charming but not unseemly flirtatiousness. She had a good sense of humor, too. At first we met weekly at the University Library.

"Thank you for doing this," I said. "I really appreciate it."

"It's my pleasure," she said. "Dr. Romo says you are one of his best students."

"That's kind of him. Are you a student of his, too?"

"No. I'm not a university student. I know him through LULAC (League of United Latin American Citizens)," she said. "He volunteers his time helping Latinos with legal problems."

We agreed to read a book chapter out loud to one another in our respective languages. Each week I brought a book by a different Spanish or Mexican author: Mariano Azuela's *Los de Abajo*, Gustavo Adolfo Bécquer's *Los Ojos Verdes*, and Benito Pérez Galdós's *Doña Perfecta*, and the nineteenth-century Mexican poet Amado Nervo. I wanted to accustom my ear to different styles of writing. As Gloria read, I'd ask questions about the vocabulary or grammatical structure. In her turn, she brought novels by Danielle Steel. She loved romance novels.

On occasion, she invited me to gatherings of her friends, where everyone spoke Spanish and few knew English well. Some were in the U.S. on tourist visas, some had work permits. Others had crossed the border illegally. I enjoyed being around Gloria's circle of friends. Gatherings tended to become mini fiestas. People brought food, guitars, beer. We sang; we danced, spontaneously, as if it were connatural to us. Gloria loved to sing, and sang with gusto, especially after a couple of drinks. She enjoyed a good margarita, as did I. On occasion we had dinner at a local Mexican restaurant, *Mi Casa*, that served good food, excellent margaritas, and hired a strolling mariachi band on weekends. One margarita left Gloria mellow; two loosened her enough that she strolled from table to table, singing with the band. After a piece ended, she exclaimed, "¡la banda está borracha!" The band might have been drunk, but not as drunk as she was. Gloria's sister Hortencia and I had to help her navigate back to our table.

Getting into the United States and getting work was one thing; staying here was another. Tourist visas expire and if the records of "la migra" (Immigration and Naturalization Service) show you haven't returned to your home country, someone from the federal government contacts you to remind you it's time to leave. The reminder contains a threat of deportation, so immigrants search for means of staying. If they have specialized job skills, their employers can make the case that they possess a needed skill set. Gloria had completed only secondary school so could not make that case. Some women become pregnant and give birth in America so their child is automatically a citizen. The parents then get legal papers as guardians of the new citizen and, eventually, citizenship themselves. Others find that marriage to an American citizen is the easiest path to legal residency and citizenship. Immigration lawyers routinely inform their illegal alien clients of these options—without of course, advising them to marry or give birth for the sake of securing citizenship. They merely inform their clients that that is what some people do.

Gloria had married a man named George Stenson and had a two-year-old son, George, Jr. (Jorgito). Her first husband was, according to Gloria, a ne'er-do-well, a drunk, shiftless, unwilling to work, and frequently in trouble with the law. He had spent time in jail for several DUIs. From what she told me later, he had never been much of a husband or father, and they had divorced in less than two years.

Gloria's judgment about men had not improved after this mistake, and she soon married a man in the military who turned out to be an abuser. She knew she had bungled it again almost immediately after marrying her second husband, and they lived apart most of their short married life, she in Reno, he in Tucson. It was while she was married to this second man that I met her.

Jorgito took to me right away, and I to him. There is something about a child's simplicity, guileless affection, and natural trust that heals. It certainly had that effect on me, as did the camaraderie of Gloria's friends.

One weekend during a sing-around (we took turns choosing the song and singing the chorus solo), Gloria's first husband, just out of jail, showed up at the door, uninvited and unannounced. He had remarried and had his twelve-year-old stepson along with him. He walked in without hesitation and interrupted the singing as if it were his house. His eyes were bloodshot. No one introduced him, but I knew who he was. The room went silent.

"Where's my son?" he half-shouted, drunkenly jovial. Jorgito stood near Gloria's sister Hortencia. "There he is!" A bizarre scene ensued. Stenson got down on all fours in the living room, then starting aarfing and growling like a playful puppy. Jorgito was frightened. As his father crawled closer to him, he became terrified, and hid behind his aunt's chair. He didn't know this man. Stenson picked the boy up and held him in his arms. "Hey, buddy! Want to go for a little drive with your papa?" Gloria froze. Stenson was drunk. Jorgito cried and wriggled to get free. He looked around, pleadingly, and reached out to me. I had known Gloria only six months. We weren't romantically involved, but we had grown fond of one another. Moreover, I had developed a sort of fatherly attachment to Jorgito. I stood, walked over to the man, and firmly lifted Jorgito out of his arms and handed him to Gloria. The man reeked of liquor.

"We're having a friendly get-together here and are in the middle of singing," I said. "You're interrupting."

The man stood for a few moments, looked around, then said to his stepson, "Let's get out of this place."

That incident brought Gloria and I closer—more than just acquaintances.

More intimate.

We were both emotionally needy, desperate to find someone to rescue and comfort us. About a year after we met, we declared our love for one another and decided to marry. Before we did, Gloria asked, abashedly, "Does it not matter to you that I have belonged to two other men?"

"No," I said. She seemed both surprised and relieved. I was twenty-seven, she thirty.

I had earned enough college credits to be a year and a half shy of graduating, but I left school and we moved to Salt Lake City, where the economy was booming and jobs plentiful.

Running off with a married woman is no small moral failing. Is it something a man who has undergone spiritual enlightenment does, someone who had left behind the immorality of drinking, gambling, and whoring? Spiritual and intellectual conversion, I learned, are not necessarily the same as moral conversion. The latter, I would come to realize, requires formation into a moral tradition—whether religious or secular—and requires the hard work of tempering physical and emotional needs and urges, of resisting the tendency to place one's own emotional desires above all else. I was far from living a life of moral probity. My needs far outweighed any moral principles I had learned.

The Country of Marriage

Gloria had been raised a Catholic by her mother, but her father was anti-clerical to the marrow. As a boy, he had participated in the agrarian movement that rose up against the dictatorship of Porfirio Díaz during the Mexican Revolution of 1910–1917. He was barely old enough to carry a gun or use a machete, but, along with many other peasants, he fought the oppressive government and despised the Catholic Church's support of it. Gloria imbibed from her father some of the anti-clericalism that followed the Revolution. As a result, Catholicism was only an anemic component of her cultural background.

Gloria and I gave one another love and comfort, enabling each of us to begin the process of healing, emotionally and psychologically troubled as we both were. On occasion, we attended the Spanish Mass at Our Lady of Guadalupe Church in Salt Lake City. We frequently went to dinners and dances at the Guadalupe Center, a Mexican cultural center. The void within grew less dark. I legally adopted Jorgito and, at Gloria's suggestion, gave him my name: Kenny, Jr. (Kenito became his nickname). God saved us in some inexplicable way through one another.

The first year of my marriage to Gloria, I worked as a warehouseman and forklift operator for ACME Electric Company, a manufacturer of electrical transformers, located in the valley near the Great Salt Lake. I unloaded pallets of raw materials from delivery trucks, stored them on warehouse shelves, and took them when needed to the machinists on the manufacturing floor. It was not mind-numbing work, so I could dream of my next trip to the mountains. I spent my coffee and lunch breaks alone, reading or writing in my journals—at that time I was reading Gabriel García Marquez, Barry Lopez, Farley Mowat, Bernard Malamud, Saul Bellow, Chaim Potok, and Mark Twain. I took walks outside, listening for something clear in that nagging voice from within. The Wasatch Mountains rose in the east, the Great Salt Lake extended to the north, and to the west stretched a hundred miles of salt desert. Because I sat alone and seldom socialized with my co-workers, some of them considered me unsociable, others just odd. And why not? I wrote in my journal: I *am* odd. *Why did God make me so solitary and private?*

About a year into our marriage, Gloria thought she might be pregnant. The possibility distressed her and she made it known she did not want to have another child. *What would her family and people in her hometown say if she had children from two different fathers?* It would bring shame, more than her divorces. She made up her mind to have an abortion if pregnant. She visited a Planned Parenthood office to get information. I had not given the issue of abortion much thought—other than that I was vaguely against it. Gloria and I had not discussed having children when we ran away together: I neither strongly wanted nor rejected the idea of having children. The thought of it was just not on my mind at the time. Yet, I intuitively recoiled from the idea of an abortion. When she learned that she was not pregnant, she was greatly relieved, but the incident caused her worry about future possibilities. She asked me to get a vasectomy.

Whoa! I thought. *What if I want to have my own biological children someday?* Was I good enough to adopt and rear her son but not good enough to father one by her? I refused to be sterilized. Not that I was mature and financially responsible enough to bring up another child, but the incident became a sore spot for me, and put the relationship in a new light. *Was this not going to be a permanent thing?* I wondered. The initial gleam of marriage dimmed.

Restless energy beset me. I dropped in and out of both college and work. I quit my job at ACME Electric and began attending the University of Utah again. After two terms, I left and worked as a survey researcher in an alternative high school for dropouts, assessing students' post high school success and gathering data about former students' sense of the strengths and weaknesses of the school. That job lasted a year. I took a few more courses at the University between jobs. I then went to work as a mail and supply clerk for the Social Security Administration office.

I accumulated university credits in brief spurts, but struggled to put together a coherent degree program. My difficulty with university life was that I had intellectual interests in many areas and could not focus on one narrow academic field.

Through my spiritual awakening years earlier, I had experienced life whole, had seen the interrelationship of all things to one another and their groundedness in a sacred reality. To my frustration, one didn't—couldn't—study such interrelationships in the modern university, at least not in the public ones I attended. Knowledge in the modern university had become specialized and fragmented into isolated domains. Roaming freely from one domain to another in an attempt to see the whole of things was frowned upon. Things spiritual were *verboten*. So I drifted from one academic field to another, trying to piece together the whole of knowledge. I both loved and hated academic life, and did not fit well into its conventional structures.

Gloria disapproved of my ongoing aspiration to complete a university degree. She would have seen the sense of it if a degree would lead to a good job. But she couldn't understand what good a degree in the liberal arts would do. How would that pay the rent or put food on the table? One of her brothers had become a dentist; another was at law school. Those were studies that could *lead* somewhere. But the liberal arts? She didn't get it. Where does that take you? And since my university studies had followed such a desultory path, she wanted me to just quit it and get a regular job. Any job. Gloria had completed only secondary school. Her parents were illiterate. In her mind, work—any paying job—was preferable to a liberal arts education.

Although Gloria did not understand the value of the liberal arts, she enjoyed literature, even beyond her favored romance novels. In fact, to help me grow more accustomed to spoken Spanish (we did not have many Spanish-speaking acquaintances in Salt Lake) she read and recorded novels and poetry in Spanish onto a cassette tape player: Miguel de Unamuno's *Niebla*, Pio Baroja's *La Lucha por la Vida*, and Gabriel García Márquez's *Cien Años de Soledad*. In the evenings, she propped herself up in bed with pillows, tape recorder by her side, and read. Sometimes I'd hear her chuckling and poke my head in the doorway. She turned off the recorder. "Hi!" she'd say with a smile. "This book is so beautiful," she said of *Cien Años*.

"Some of the people in this book remind me of the *campesinos* in my town. They are so superstitious and funny and simple. I love these people. It makes me laugh."

I would listen to the tapes as I drove to and from work, to improve my command of the language. Gloria, though she favored romance novels, enjoyed this literature—laughed with it, argued with it, got saddened and enlightened by it—as much as I did. She had no antipathy to literature. It's just that, given her background of poverty, the specter of destitution always hovered just outside the door. She wanted me to work. Moreover, she could see that I wasn't getting anywhere, at least anywhere practical. She was right; I was disinterested in any practical end of higher learning. Instead, I sought to satisfy the gnawing intellectual and spiritual eros within that would not be still, even though the following of it had previously left me in wreckage.

Except for my life with Gloria and Kenito, I remained mostly solitary. Even within the family, I sought occasions of solitude. Intimations of the divine continued to haunt me. In quiet moments, I sensed its presence, as through a thin veil. The memory of euphoria experienced in the Jarbidge Mountains and the hills surrounding Elko during the summer of 1972, along with an undefined but insistent call, made my spirit restless. On occasion, I backpacked into the Uintah Mountains of northeastern Utah. The Uintahs are the highest mountain range in Utah, with some peaks rising to over 13,000 feet in altitude, and plenty of wilderness areas away from roads and campgrounds.

Gloria did not like going into the natural world; for her it was a place of danger and wildness. I invited her to join me on overnight camping trips, but she recoiled from the idea, and she didn't like it when I went.

"There are wild creatures out there," she'd say, "and no bathrooms."

"We'll go to a campground where there are bathrooms. And other people."

The Country of Marriage

On one occasion, Gloria reluctantly agreed to come along with me. We rented a campsite at Mirror Lake in the Uintahs. She enjoyed the scenery on the way, but as we ascended the winding road to Bald Mountain Pass, she grew anxious. The pass is 10,700 feet in elevation, and there are steep drop-offs to the valley below in some spots. Only a guardrail separated the road and the drop-off. Gloria pushed her feet tight against the passenger floorboard during most of the ascent to the pass, and her right hand clutched the door grasp.

"Look at those mountains across the valley!" I said. "They're so beautiful."

"No," she said, "It makes me dizzy." She would not look out over the guardrail.

We stopped at the pass and got out of the car to view the land. Moosehead Lake lay 800 feet below us, and Mirror Lake off in the distance. Then Hayden Lake, Ruth Lake, and Trial Lake off in other directions. Across the valley stood Hayden Peak, and to the south of it, Mount Agassiz. A spectacular view. From the top of Bald Mountain, about two-dozen lakes are visible. Three drainages have a headwater at Bald Mountain Pass: from one spot water flows into the Bear, Snake, and Columbia rivers, then the Pacific Ocean; from another into the Green and Colorado rivers, and on to the Gulf of California; from yet another, into the Jordan River and the Great Salt Lake—one of the last vestiges of the ocean that once occupied much of the Great Basin.

"Are there snakes here?" Gloria asked.

"No, not this high up," I said.

"What about lions?"

"Mountain lions? Sure, some, but we're fine. They avoid humans and won't bother us."

"Ay!" she exclaimed. "Then I wait in the car."

We pitched a tent Near Mirror Lake, pumped up the air mattresses, and spread out the sleeping bags. But Gloria was ill at ease: uncomfortable in a sleeping bag on the ground and worried about creatures that might lurk outside. She was horrified after a forest ranger stopped by and advised us to keep our food cooler locked up in the car trunk at night—*even our toothpaste*—so bears wouldn't smell them and rummage the campsite. The giant, fierce mosquitoes kept her in the tent or car most of the time. She wouldn't hike the trails.

Gloria didn't understand what drew me to the wilderness. She found it a threatening, inhospitable place.

From then on, I went solo.

Gloria almost always viewed my excursions into the wilderness, and my need for solitude, as a rejection of her. Or worse. Her first husband had been a stoner. Her youngest brother was an alcoholic and a druggie. She feared I might have been out smoking pot—*why else would I wander off into the mountains alone?* She sometimes looked into my eyes for a marijuana-induced glaze when I returned. I didn't do drugs, yet she worried. In fact, I had not smoked pot for years. I'd had a five- or six-month trial period with dope during my student activist days in 1970, but discovered that regular use only muddled my mind. I'd quit using it.

At other times when I'd return from the mountains, she'd be cold and distant.

I returned one Sunday evening. Gloria was watching a rerun of *The Lawrence Welk Show*.

"I'm back!" I announced. She didn't look away from the screen or greet me.

I leaned my head around the wall into the living room. "Hey, I'm back."

"Did you have a nice time?" She kept her eyes on the TV. Missy and Bobby danced and smiled at the screen while the Champaign Orchestra played in the background.

"Yeah," I answered.

"That's nice."

Then silence. The dance routine ended. *Wunnerful! Wunnerful!* said Welk, applauding and smiling into the camera, ready to announce the next act.

I left the house and retreated to the library. Our juvenile behavior slowly developed into alienation.

TV dramas were Gloria's escape from the harsh world of workplace politics and the anxieties of life. She spent several hours a night watching TV movies and programs. I hated television, and didn't understand her need for escape any more than she understood my need for solitude. I often went to the Marriot Library at the University of Utah to study and write. Gloria construed that, too, as rejection.

While at the library, I fell in love with art. I had gone to the Western Americana reading room to search for some rare books by Byrd Baylor about the connection and fragile balance between land, spirit, and native peoples. On the way, I passed through a small exhibit of surreal and fantasy-laden paintings—I didn't know the name to give them. A replica of Hieronymus Bosch's *In the Garden of Earthly Delights* hung on one wall. Salvador Dali's *The Temptation of Saint Anthony* hung on another, and replicas of the Mexican muralists Diego Rivera, David Siqueiros, and José Clemente Orozco on yet another. The paintings absorbed and fascinated me. Why were they exhibited together? I wondered. So different, though they all had a surreal quality to them, and an overpowering element of—what? Realistic fantasy? Fantastic realism? I didn't know what to call it. I later spent hours poring over hefty art books that contained color plates of their paintings. Fascinating worlds inhabited them: beauty and ugliness; death, suffering, and redemption; greed, pain, and temptation; misshapen and distorted images of Christ on the Cross; the grotesque and the sublime all thrown together and mutually intertwined. I had not known art could be so powerful.

At home, Gloria browsed through some of the plates. "Why do you look at this stuff? It would give me nightmares."

Gloria did not understand my visits to the library—especially during periods when I was working and not attending the University—any more than my trips to the mountains. We shared little by way of common cultural or intellectual interests. We went to Mass at the Catholic church on occasion, though not often. Our marriage had no spiritual foundation. Instead, it became clear, it was founded on mutual need.

10

A Softening
of Nature's Edges

GLORIA and I made a Thanksgiving trip to Mantua, Utah, a small farming community surrounded by wide-open country in the northern Wasatch Mountains. We had been married just under three years and our marriage was crashing on the rocks. We hoped time away from routines might do us good. We chose Mantua because Gloria's sister, Hortencia, had just given birth to her third child. She lived on a dairy farm with her husband, Joe. Gloria planned to help with the household chores for a while. I wanted to feel the earthiness of farm life and enjoy some time alone out of doors. I planned to steal periods of solitude whenever I could.

On Thanksgiving morning, Joe invited me to join him with morning chores, to feed and milk the cows, then shovel and clean their stalls. I welcomed the chance; it had been over a decade since I had spent time on a farm. We rose at 3:30 a.m. After a cup of coffee, we went out into the night. At an elevation of 5,200 feet, the cold November air stung our faces. Our breath rose as we walked to the barn, which felt warm by contrast, the bodies of farm animals giving off heat. Inside we loaded bales of hay into a large wagon, using baling hooks to grasp, lift, and move them. We pulled the loaded wagon out of the barn by tractor, and tossed the bales out into the adjoining field. After half an hour, my back began to ache. *How did Joe do this day after day without break?* Farm animals take no days off, so neither did Joe. Later, we drove the cows into the barn for milking. I felt invigorated from working in the quiet darkness. There is a curious urge deep inside the primate brain that resonates with the elemental powers of nature. I first experienced that resonance as a boy when arising early to go on hunting or fishing trips.

I experienced that early morning comfort on the farm in Mantua. Joe did, too. "Without this quiet," he said, "I couldn't hack the hard work. Gives me time to think." He didn't mind waking early.

After morning chores, we returned to the farmhouse for breakfast, then a short nap to catch up on lost sleep. Gloria and Hortencia caught up on family talk and began the Thanksgiving preparations: turkey tamales made from scratch, a day-long undertaking. I had several choices before me: watch television, play with the children, read, help the women in the kitchen, or go for a walk in the brisk November air. I put on my coat and boots, grabbed a note pad and pen, then called to Gloria, "I'm going for a walk. I'll be back in a while."

I knew from her sidelong glance that she took my "be back in a while" with skepticism. She still disliked my solitary forays into nature, still considered them a sign that I didn't want to be with her. We did not understand one another's motivations and needs well. She preferred the domestic sphere, while I gravitated to open spaces, to wilderness. It called me. And on this Thanksgiving Day in the northern Wasatch Mountains, there was open country just beyond the farms, and I wanted to observe and know it up close.

It was late morning, around 11:00 a.m.

The fields lay fallow, partly blanketed in snow. The grayish brown of the hills alternated with intermittent streaks of snow. I walked across the mown hayfields, reduced now to yellow stubble, toward the tallest hill overlooking the valley, Perry Peak (elevation 8,200 feet). The snow's surface had melted slightly from the sun the day before, and then had refrozen during the night, forming a thin crust. It had not yet re-thawed, so the snow crunched with each step, while the dormant hay and stubble gave a feeble and slightly crackling resistance to my boots, yielding to my weight. Its give satisfied. I walked to the end of the fields, to the fence circumscribing the last farm, almost a mile from the farmhouse. Beyond the fence, the land began to rise toward the hills, gradually for about two hundred meters, then steeply. The lower slopes were vacant but for scrub brush. I looked back to the farms. *Should I turn back?* The fence line would be a logical place to do so. I hesitated a while, then climbed the fence and walked out and away from the farmland.

The land returned to its natural ruggedness. Low-lying vegetation—sagebrush, wild grass, rabbit brush, cattails near the lake, a few stunted willows—grew uncultivated. Cottonwoods lined the creek that fed the lake. Scattered conifers and willows populated the upper portions of the hills. Gullies formed by the flow of water, and narrow ravines created by the natural folds of the earth, made scars on the hillsides. As I left the boundary of the domesticated world, a hollow space grew inside me, as if I had passed a threshold into the gates of no-place, subject to neither law nor custom. A chill breeze whisked across the open space, unimpeded by trees, houses, or silos. The cry of birds pierced the air. No other sounds vied for my attention, beyond the scrunching of my boots on the semi-frozen ground. I began to climb, a hundred meters, two hundred, then more. My heart rate increased. I breathed in the cold air, rhythmically, deeply, as my leg muscles pulsed and stretched and flexed. My mind livened. After about twenty minutes, I stopped to catch my breath and look out over the valley.

The Mantua valley cradles a small lake surrounded by farms. The shape of the valley—the relation among the lake, the town, the farms, the surrounding hills—came into view. I could see Joe and Hortencia's farmhouse in the distance, set in a cluster of box elder trees.

I vacillated again between continuing on or returning to the farmhouse, to companions, to the ordinary tasks of living that make us feel secure in a known world. I imagined Gloria and Hortencia in the kitchen.

They have just put the turkey breast in the oven. They stand together at the counter, forming the corn *masa* into dough that they will wrap around the shredded turkey after it marinates in red chili sauce. They swap stories: the joys and tribulations of children and husbands; news of their brothers in Mexico; and comparisons of their adolescent dreams to their current lives. The children run in and out, laughing, squealing, and squabbling. When they begin jumping on the furniture, Hortencia shoos them outside. Between chores and naps, Joe sneaks in to snatch a bite of food before Hortencia can swat him playfully with a stirring spoon.

A part of me wanted to be within the warmth and conviviality of that kitchen. The pull of the familiar and domestic was strong. But I didn't have the knack for engaging in its conversations well, or for long. The stronger pull of the mountain and solitude kept me going.

The hills surrounding the Mantua valley, and what lay beyond them, hinted at the unknown. I knew from experience that after wandering far into uncultivated space, a yawning emptiness would open up before and around me. That disquieting emptiness formed a sort of invisible barrier that proclaimed "no trespassing." And the no trespassing referred not to entry into private, domesticated land, but to the wild and nameless, to something mysterious and possibly dangerous. Perhaps the empty spaces beyond the fence were like those oceans on medieval maps with drawings of monsters, accompanied by a warning sign: "Beyond here lie dragons," denoting a dangerous and unexplored land that one ought not enter unprepared. Stay on *terra firma*. I experienced it as a lure just strong enough to keep me going, though the dragon's power was raw and unmediated out there. I walked on cautiously and attentively, determined to make the top of Perry Peak. I wanted to behold the high peaks of the Wasatch Mountain range stretching southward to the horizon. To the west, I would see the Great Salt Lake, one of the last vestiges of the great sea that once covered half of Utah and much of Nevada.

From halfway up Perry Peak the farmhouses appeared like small boxes with smoke rising from toy chimneys. The small lake, shaped like a human embryo in its early stages, shimmered in the early afternoon sun. Thin ice formed on the surface of its shallow edges. In a month, thick ice would cover the entire lake. Forced to zigzag across slopes of a steep grade, I stopped frequently to catch my breath, beholding the landscape in silence. The breeze carried faint echoes from far distances—like when it weaves through deep, hollow rifts in the earth—hinting of mystery and of a brief journey into a primordial world of quiet, into an experience of the raw power of nature.

No trees blocked my view, and I took in the entire valley: the dormant fields waiting to be awakened when the seasons cycled back around; the farmhouses with smoke rising from their chimneys; cattle in the fields; the hills circumscribing the valley; the restfulness of the lake, shimmering in the afternoon sun; and the pure blue sky uninterrupted by clouds. Unfiltered sunlight gleamed through the landscape, bringing all into harmony and oneness, into unity. A sacred light seemed to permeate the whole. The different objects— field, lake, farmhouse, sky—existed only as manifestations or bearers of it. *All things are kin within the mind of God*, I thought. I saw it all in one synoptic sweep.

Years later I would stand before a painting of Claude Monet's *Haystacks* at the Art Institute of Chicago and remember vividly this very place and time, where boundaries between self and environment merge into—not an undifferentiated identity, as in pantheism—but a differentiated and intermingling unity in which the being of all individual things—the hills, the sky, the fields, the lake, my self—participate in the Being of a transcendence that vastly exceeds its immanent manifestation in the particular. Impressionist painters like Monet tended to dissolve the face of nature, allowing the viewer to experience the being of the whole, especially the all-suffusing light. Instead of using local colors, Monet used "universal" coloring that pervaded the painting and grounded the total environment of the canvas. His *Haystack* series is an example of just such a use of light. Art historian William Seitz describes Monet's *Haystacks* this way: "Inert and porous, set in the midst of neutral or snow-covered surroundings, the masses of piled hay are vitalized, and become one with their background, through the momentary permeation of a unifying light. They are passive modulators of a wholly immaterial life."

Modulators of a wholly immaterial life. Immaterial, immeasurable, intangible, yet real. Something beyond the ordinary shows itself through the ordinary. The unifying light permeates all; absorbs and unites all things into itself. At the same time, the haystacks remain haystacks; the fences are distinguishable as fences, the fields as fields. They are not abolished in an undifferentiated unity, yet they surrender the hard edges separating them from a reality that shines through and envelopes both them and the viewer. All things merge into a differentiated unity. Was this elemental reality not the true subject of Monet's paintings, whether or not he conceived of it as such? Certainly, the American impressionist painter George Inness sought to elicit the spiritual depth of the natural world in his later landscape paintings, knowing we have withdrawn from communion with nature, forgetful of its beauty, power, and holiness. Unlike Monet, Inness often placed a small, enigmatic human figure, barely visible, in the fields beyond the farms, going to or fro within the mist of nature's softened edges, the distant horizon aglow with sunset or sunrise.

I continued up the mountain. Soon I came across an abandoned sheepherder's cabin. Part of the roof had caved in and its single door had fallen from the frame. Willows grew high and untrimmed around the walls and through the broken windows—nature reclaiming its hold on the land. Wood planks, fallen from the frame, lay scattered about. Now-yellowed grasses poked through the blanket of snow, indicating once good pasture for sheep grazing. I remembered the trips to sheep camp with my friend John and wondered whether sons once accompanied their fathers into these hills. Did they play here, fish in the lake below, hunt quail? Did they sleep in the cabin, or under the stars? I wanted to poke around the cabin for interesting artifacts, to find remnants of the stuff of life: perhaps an old wine bottle (what vintage?); spent bullet casings (what caliber?); remnants of a mattress (what filling?); a worn and musty book from the old country (in what language?); a child's wooden toy (hand carved or bought?).

Instead, I continued the hike. The day was growing late and I wanted to see the Great Salt Lake whole and from on high. I climbed slowly, another half hour, perhaps forty-five minutes, until I reached the top. The lake, seventy miles long and twenty-eight miles wide, glistened in the afternoon sun. The snow-capped peaks of the Wasatch stretched to the south, and the Oquirrh Mountains extended southward from the lower end of the lake. The town of Perry was directly below me, Interstate 15 skirting its western edge. Willard Bay lay just beyond that, and Promontory Point at the tip of a peninsula reaching southward from the northern end of the lake. Far to the west of the lake lay the white salt flats, larger than the lake itself, extending all the way to the Utah-Nevada border, almost one hundred miles away. When most of the sea drained away, only its salty sediments remained. And on this clear day, I could see—I was sure of it—the curvature of the earth across the salt flats.

I sat on a boulder to rest and contemplate the boundless vista of landscape and geological history along with the shimmering presence, emanating from all around. The sea was once vast enough to cover most of the Great Basin, its waters a thousand-feet deep and teeming with great fish. Wildlife drank and preyed and became prey along its shores. Native tribes fished along its banks and hunted in these very hills. Then the great sea disappeared abruptly in a cataclysmic event fifteen thousand years ago when a land breach in southern Idaho caused most of the sea to drain away, leaving only this salty lake unable to support life save for a few brine shrimp. I thought about the Humboldt River snaking its way through Nevada, disappearing into an alkali flat.

I stood and stretched. I didn't know how long I had been there, but the sun was on its downward arc in the late November sky. It was late afternoon, so I began my descent. As I pictured what the Great Sea looked like before it drained away, a sudden motion off to my right distracted my reverie. Across a narrow ravine, something moved. Moved? *What was out here but me?* It was not the shadow of a cloud—none were in the sky. Only my breath, as it met the cold air, resembled a cloud. But I had sensed motion. I looked in the direction of the movement. Nothing. I kept my gaze fixed in that direction, focusing not on anything particular, but the area as a whole. Then it moved again, trotted twenty feet across the hill, stopped, pawed the grass, and sniffed the ground. A coyote. Its grayish-brown coat and the whitish bands under its neck and belly blended perfectly into the background. Had it not moved, I would not have picked out its distinguishing features. Then it saw me, too. We looked long at each other; neither of us moved. I became wary. *Was it alone or running in a pack?* I had seen many coyotes in the western U.S. and they usually hunted alone during the day, and in packs of half a dozen or more at night. A solo coyote would not bother a grown man, but a pair or pack, if hungry, could find me an opportune meal.

Now I stood directly across a ravine from one, staring into its eyes. I could not run to safety or get help. I kept my gaze on the coyote while looking for movement in my peripheral vision. He could not cross the ravine easily, but if he and his pack mates had seen and stalked me earlier, some of them might have already circled around. Would I have time to run back to the abandoned sheepherder's cabin, where I might improvise a weapon? Perhaps an old board with a nail sticking through it. Or at least something to use as a club. I could stand just inside the old doorway with the club and fight them off, assuming there were no gaping holes in the dilapidated building through which they could come at me from the back or sides. I had not told anyone where I was going, had not even brought a pocketknife. I looked slowly to my left and right to discern movement. Then back at the coyote. Then again to both sides. There were no others. This was a loner, probably raiding chicken coops or just drinking at the lake or hunting small mammals.

The coyote and I continued to hold one another's gaze. Each of us turned our head occasionally, but soon re-engaged. Then I surprised myself. I gave out, in my best coyote imitation, a shrill *yip yip yiooo!*, with the latter syllable rising to a high, elongated pitch, then falling. The coyote's ears perked up. Its leg muscles tensed. He looked around, trotted about ten meters up his side of the ravine, then stopped and looked at me again. I raised my hands in the air and began to jump. *Yip yip yiooo!* I yelled, then ran ten meters up my side of the ravine. I knelt down to pick up a handful of snow. I formed it into a snowball, then bellowed out another "*yiooo!*" before hurling it across the ravine at him. The snowball didn't even reach the other side, but his ears and head perked up all the more. He barked one solitary, dog-like bark, perhaps in playful response or, more likely, annoyed warning. He pawed the ground, trotted a ways, then stopped.

Well, I thought. *Have we got something going here?* Was he taking to this game? Coyotes are closely related to dogs. Were they as playful? Should I hurl him a stick across the ravine, to see if he'll pick it up? No. That wouldn't work. I couldn't hurl a stick that far. I looked for something with more heft, a stone half the size of a baseball, say, that might make it across. I searched around some of the brush until I found one. When I looked back across the ravine, the coyote was casually trotting away into the brush. As he did so, a shadow skirted across the hillside, drawing my attention. Where did *that* movement come from? I looked up, surveying the sky. A small cloud had formed low in the southwestern sky, floating in the wind, casting its shadow over a now-luminescent yellow hillside. The sun had sunk toward the hilltops; I had to return to the farmhouse before it grew dark. I had no flashlight, and coyotes do hunt in packs at night. I then remembered Thanksgiving dinner. Gloria and Hortencia and Joe and the children would be waiting, and looking for me. I had told Gloria I was going out for a walk and would be back in a while. *A while.*

Seven hours after I left the farmhouse, I returned. The last light of dusk was receding in the west. As I approached the yard, Joe met me outside.

"Where the hell've you been, man? We were about to call the sheriff. We thought a mountain lion killed you."

"Sorry about that. Didn't realize how late it was. I went for a long hike up the hillside over there. It's beautiful out here. You really found a great spot. No mountain lions. I did see a coyote, though. Is dinner ready?"

He paused before speaking. "Yeah, about two hours ago."

Crap! I thought, *I've thoughtlessly worried everyone. Dinner is waiting. Everyone is waiting.* How was I going to explain this to Gloria? That I lost track of time? That I'm sorry? She'd heard it all before. What could I say? I rummaged for words to articulate the day's experience. Joe and I stood momentarily beneath a large box elder tree, near the threshold to the back door. I could see only his silhouette because of the darkening shadows. Behind him, the barn and a cluster of trees merged with the dusk. Above, the upper hills still reflected a light amber glow from the sun's waning light. Could I tell them I was detained by a softening of nature's outlines and its mergence with the divine? That I was in a place where nature tends to dematerialize and spirit tends to incarnate? *How would I articulate that at the dinner table?* At the time, I could not articulate it to myself.

I repeated my feeble excuse. "Sorry. Lost track of time."

"Well," said Joe, "Gloria's upset. Just so you know."

We walked through the doorway into the house, into warmth and the smell of tamales. I kissed Gloria and said, "Sorry I'm late." She didn't reply, but did look intently into my eyes for signs of a fading high, a far-away glaze. I was used to this.

We sat down to dinner. Hortencia asked about my day. I told them about the sheepherder's cabin and asked if sheep still run in the hills around there. I mentioned the coyote and asked if they are a problem for the farmers.

"Yeah," said Joe. "They raid the farms all the time. A pack of them brought down a calf last spring. Mountain lions are even worse. Much more crafty, and they come around only at night. Coyotes are dumber, kind of like dogs."

Gloria was silent throughout the dinner. Later, when we lay in bed after everyone else had fallen asleep, she asked, "Why do you go off alone like that, where no one knows where you are?"

"I don't know. I guess I just need solitude and lots of space sometimes. It's invigorating."

"Weren't you afraid out there? That beast could have killed you." *Beast*, she said, her way of translating *animal salvaje* (wild animal) into English.

Beasts. Dragons. No-trespassing signs. The beast is raw spiritual power. It stalks you if you cross the border to the outlands.

"I'm a little afraid at first, but after I get used to it, it's fine. It's really quiet and beautiful. I feel at home there."

"But not here?

A Softening of Nature's Edges

"Yes, here, too."

As always, Gloria took my desire for solitude as rejection. I, on the other hand, was inclined to Rilke's understanding of marriage. Marriage, he said, is not created "by tearing down and destroying all boundaries, then merging with one another body and spirit, but rather a good marriage is that in which each appoints the other guardian of his solitude. . . . All companionship can consist only in the strengthening of two neighboring solitudes." Yet, that was too stark, too selfish. There must be *some* softening of boundaries into what—a differentiated union?

Haystacks remain haystacks, people remain both individuated and merged. A unifying light permeates all without producing homogeneity. How do two people accomplish that successfully? It required a balance Gloria and I could not reach. Although I didn't then conceive of it this way, I resonated with those solitary human figures in George Inness's late landscape paintings—like *Winter Evening, The Gloaming*, or *Home at Montclair*. They walk contemplatively away from the farmhouse into the fields, forests, and hills—with an alluring horizon in the background—then return at dusk to hearth and family. Neither Gloria nor I had the maturity to understand the dynamics pulling us apart.

After a pause, she asked, "What were you doing out there all day?"

I shrugged. "Just hiking. Enjoying the view. Thinking."

"Thinking about what?"

I shrugged again. "I don't know. God, I guess."

She turned away, lying in silence for what seemed eons. A ravine separated us, one so wide you couldn't hurl a stone across it. Finally, she said, "I don't understand you."

Then go out there with me, beyond the last fence, I wanted to say, but I knew she wouldn't.

11

A Home for the Spirit:
The Land of My New Ancestors

I N LATE 1979, Gloria and I prepared to separate. We had been married for nearly three years. I had to find out what the Spirit wanted of me. I had encountered God in the natural world and in solitude, but that alone only led to shipwreck. I had dropped in and out of college, unable to settle on a major that satisfied my curiosity. I was still lured by a vague, indeterminate calling, still searching for an elusive wholeness. I had to make a break.

I still dreamed of being a writer. I had never stopped journaling, even during the dark and hollow years before and during psychoanalysis with Dr. Greene. Journals were piled on the floor next to my writing table. Now that our marriage was ending, I wanted to give writing my full attention, to see if *that* was my calling. I'd have to quit my job and live on the cheap for an extended period. Like Bellow's Eugene Henderson, Updike's Rabbit, and Twain's Huck Finn, I felt trapped in the stasis of suffocating social expectations, with little possibility of fulfillment. I was aching to head out for "the territory." The territory was Mexico, where the cost of living was low.

Gloria asked what I planned to do there.

"Write a novel," I said.

"What kind of novel?"

"About the individual quest for self-actualization."

"Why?"

"I don't know. I have to."

She didn't want to continue living in Salt Lake City, so she made me an offer.

"I haven't been to see my family in Apatzingán for six years. I know a place you can go in Michoacán. A clean little town in the mountains called Coalcomán. Apatzingán is only forty miles away. You can drop me and Kenito off on your way."

We sold our house and stored our furniture in the basement of my sister's house. Just before Christmas we drove to Mexico in my used Volkswagen sedan, five-year-old Kenito either sitting or sprawled napping in the backseat. We spent nights in Tucson and Guaymas before continuing on toward Teacapán, Lake Chapala, and Gloria's hometown.

Once in Mexico, we noticed armed military troops stationed at regular intervals along the Pan-American Highway. Signs posted nearby read "Tourist Auxiliary Services." The troops were out in force during the height of tourist season: Christmas and Easter. At one gas stop, Gloria asked a soldier why they kept guard.

"To assist tourists if they have a flat tire, or their car breaks down," he answered.

Yeah, right, we thought. To change a tire, they need military rifles. American tourists do sometimes disappear, though.

After a night in Guaymas, I planned to spend a night in the town of Teacapán, a small fishing village on the tip a narrow peninsula by the same name, where I had spent several days camping eight years earlier. Only one road led in; the same one led out. There were no houses or buildings, or even reflecting lights along the highway. Darkness surrounded the car's light beams as we drove south on the peninsula. Ahead, we saw a large bonfire near the road. A group of men stood around it. As we neared, they walked onto the road and waved us to stop. I slowed to a crawl. Gloria perked up suddenly.

"Don't stop!" she shouted. "*Son bandidos!*"

I had a millisecond to react. I pressed the accelerator to the floor. The engine revved. The men jumped out of the way as we sped by. They hurried to their cars and began chasing us. I kept the accelerator to the floor: 80, 90 miles an hour. Their headlights shone in the rearview mirror. I increased the distance between us and them, and we made it into Teacapán safely. The bonfire bandidos didn't follow us in.

But it was late, and we couldn't find lodging. Every inn we stopped at turned us away. The proprietors looked at us with suspicion. Their coldness and unfriendliness gave Gloria the creeps. With no place to stay, we had to return along the same highway. We went to the local police station to seek help. We told them what had happened on the drive in.

"Pinche ladrones," said one officer, shaking his head slightly, indicating he was familiar with the bandits' tactic. Three officers escorted us out of town to Tepíc. We drove behind a paddy-wagon with two armed policeman standing on small platforms at the back of the wagon, grasping a handle with one hand and a rifle with the other.

The bonfire bandidos did not reappear, and the fire had been put out. As we approached Tepíc, the nearest city, the police stopped in the middle of the road. Two officers approached us, rifles in hand. They said they'd need some money for the gas they'd used escorting us. I gladly gave them a $20 bill.

Once we were lodged in a hotel in Tepíc, Gloria showed her displeasure.

"How did you find a place like that? Why do you go to such dangerous places?"

Two days later, I dropped Gloria and Kenito off with her brother and sister-in-law, then continued on.

Coalcomán sits in a remote area of the Sierra Madre del Sur in southwestern Mexico, about half way between the volcanoes of Colima and Paricutín, both active. In 1979 the town was accessible only by a winding dirt road through the mountains. I left the hot and arid *tierra caliente* behind, and ascended into pine forests. The air felt cool and fresh. The top layer of the road was a fine, powdery dust that seeped through the cracks in the worn seals of my car doors. Dust drifted throughout the cabin, covering every square inch of the interior, my clothing, my hair.

Coalcomán had a pleasant climate. Its streets were cobblestone and well kept, and its adobe buildings were painted white or one of several pastels: blue, yellow, or pink. I rented a room at the former Hotel Martinez, now a boarding house (*casa de huéspedes*) facing the town's central plaza, opposite the Catholic church. The Martinez was a rectangular building with bedrooms and hallways opening to a central garden courtyard. Room and board cost ninety dollars a month. I budgeted an extra thirty-five dollars for spending money each month. I lived comfortably. My room was spare: a double-sized bed, dresser, small table, and chair. On the table I set my Smith-Corona electric typewriter. I wrote in notebooks during the mornings, seated in the hotel courtyard or on a bench in the town plaza across the street. I typed the manuscript in the afternoons.

Doña Agripina Godinez, or Doña Pina as everyone called her, ran the boarding house. She was a small, frail woman about fifty years old. Her seventeen-year-old son, Enrique, also lived there. He attended the local *colegio*, or preparatory school. Doña Pina also cooked and, for those willing to pay extra, did laundry. Boarders received two full meals a day: eggs, tortillas, coffee, and beans for breakfast, and meat, tortillas, and beans for dinner. Occasionally she threw in some vegetables, such as chili peppers or fried prickly-pear cactus.

A small yard behind the hotel had a few orange and lemon trees, a dozen chickens, several concrete laundry basins for the boarders, and a clothesline. I washed my clothes by hand, scrubbed them with a bar of laundry soap, rinsed and wrung them out, and hung them on the line to dry. Occasionally, Doña Pina let me use her old electric wringer-washer, also stationed in the backyard.

A ten-foot-high brick wall separated the backyard from an open sewer. The wall kept the odors out of the yard, for the most part, but didn't discourage the rats that scurried across the top of the wall at night and into the yard. Doña Pina stuffed rags in the gaps around the kitchen's back door, but the rats came over the roof into the central courtyard off our rooms. We stuffed rags or wood wedges into the cracks of our bedroom doors to keep them out. That kept the rats and mice out, but not the scorpions.

Scorpions hid in the cracks of the overlapping clay roof tiles during the day and emerged at night. They dropped from the tiles onto the floor or, sometimes, onto the bed, making a muffled thud just loud enough to awaken me. My first night in Coalcomán, I'd woken in panic, jumped out of bed, and groped in the dark for the light switch. I looked around for something to use as a club—the heel of a hard-soled shoe or boot. Scorpions have tough, thick bodies, like a piece of rubber hose, so I had to whack each one multiple times to kill it. After two nights of dread and little sleep, I rigged up a mosquito net around my bed. That kept the scorpions off, but I could still hear their soft thud as they dropped from the netting and hit the floor. I learned to inspect the inside of my shoes before putting them on in the mornings.

The country around town was rugged and wild, broken up by cattle ranches and farms. Mountain lions prowled the hills and poisonous snakes abounded. Most townspeople were wary of wandering into the country. Even worse than wild animals, the *marijuaneros* ran plantations in the remote mountain areas. Armed men guarded the roads into the plantations, which were isolated, inaccessible, and easy to defend from outsiders. Even the *federales*, it was said, were reluctant to invade their territory.

Coalcomán was similar to Álamos in size and in the colonial Spanish architectural style of its buildings. There was one other similarity: an abundance of strikingly beautiful women. The town's slogan was "*la tierra de hombres ilustres y mujeres bellas*," the land of illustrious men and beautiful women. One of those young women was María de la Luz Acevedo Chávez, who played a key role in my entrance into the Catholic Church. On January 6, I attended a public procession through town for the *Fiesta de Los Tres Reyes*, the reenactment of the three wise men entering Bethlehem. The procession ended at the house of a local family who hosted a communal dinner and dance in their backyard. Someone from the boarding house introduced me to María de la Luz (at her request), an eighteen-year-old student in the *colegio*. Maria had long, wavy, black hair, large brown eyes, and fulsome breasts and hips. We danced, then chatted. She flirted a while, then asked, "May I ask you an indiscreet question?"

"Yes."

"Are you married?" The question, preceded by flirtation, indicated she might have a romantic interest in me, but she wanted to clear the air right off. I caught the drift, and bit.

"Yes, but my wife and I are separated. We're in the process of getting divorced," I said with a certainty of conviction that did not yet truly exist. My words satisfied her; I sensed it. And I went right along, anticipating where the flirtation might lead.

This moral unevenness plagued me for decades. My religious and moral conversion was far from complete. God's moral law had not yet taken fully hold of me. Spirituality, no matter how rich, disconnected from a religious tradition with a strong moral foundation, does not prevent one from committing immoral actions, as was the case with my illicit marriage to Gloria. I did not commit adultery with María de la Luz, but I did lead her on while keeping the flirtation a secret from Gloria, who thought I had gone to Coalcomán to write. Though my marriage was seriously on the rocks, I was still married and not free to pursue romance. I knew in my heart that what I was doing was wrong, but rationalized it by pretending that my marriage was more doomed that it really was at that time. I was responding to this young lady as if I were single and free. How easily we deceive ourselves! How easily our passions out-flank our moral compass if we have not been well formed in a moral tradition! Perhaps Gloria had intuited early in our marriage that I wouldn't stay around, and for that reason did not want to have a child by me. I couldn't blame her.

I had, in fact, gone to Coalcomán to write a novel and completed a first draft. The novel dealt with a quintessential American theme: the individual's quest for self-realization by breaking away from a stultifying social order, and searching for a new land unencumbered with social obligations, where his full intellectual and artistic potential could flourish. Like many canonical American novels, my "enlightened" and rebellious protagonist had no desire or plan to return to society and take a responsible place in it once his adventure was completed. It was a novel of escape in the individualist tradition of Emerson, Thoreau, Twain, and Bellow, the hero dreaming of a perpetual childhood or adolescence free of adult commitments. I was living out this theme of escape, without thought for the moral obligations to my wife and adopted son, or how those obligations had been breached.

The opening passage of the novel came easy: "I slept the first twenty years of my life and woke up in a desert! My words had no ancestors, my deeds no lord. I was a wild man, a savage, without memory or name. Alone and disoriented, I called out into the vastness, but there was no response, not even an echo. The desert void engulfed all. Night came and darkness crept into the void." It seemed such an apt metaphor for my life before the hunting accident and my wilderness conversion.

In the novel, I flee family responsibilities and a bourgeois life, travel to a Mexican village where I meet a wise man, Carlos, an expatriate American and former Jesuit priest who lives among the peasants along the banks of a river opposite a colonial Catholic monastery. Carlos agrees to be my teacher, and instructs me in philosophy and the hidden mysteries of sacred reality, drawing on religions both native and highly developed intellectually: Taoism, Buddhism, Christianity. He also admires Teilhard de Chardin—whom he met and studied with in the 1940s.

The river—a dry arroyo much of the year—separates Carlos's house from the monastery. The monastery has a deep well and the monks have installed a faucet outside their walls for townsfolk to draw on during dry seasons. Carlos's own well runs dry during droughts, forcing him to obtain water from the monks' faucet. He doesn't like having to rely on them, though, and begins to dig deeper for his own well. I help him. We spend a few hours each day at it, and after a month we reach an aquifer. It bubbles up uncontrollably and spreads out over the ground, and under the foundation of the house. We are not prepared for such a volume of flow and cannot channel it. The water cuts under a section of the house. Eventually, the well hole caves in and a section of Carlos's house sinks into the ground, too.

I don't remember if the novel even had a plot, or if it came to a conclusion. I remember only that it was bad art, and I abandoned it after leaving Mexico.

Opposite the plaza from the Hotel Martinez where I boarded, stood St. Thomas Catholic Church. Two bell towers adorned the front corners of the church, topped with cupolas. I regularly attended Sunday evening Mass, the town's central event of the week. I brought along my writing journal to take notes for later incorporation into my novel—a disrespectful act in the midst of a sacred ceremony, but I was an observer—an artist—not a participant, not at first. Over time, though, the richness of the liturgy affected me. In Elko, I had found Mass tedious. Here, at St. Thomas Church, I was struck by a sacred power as soon as I entered. Inside, vaulted arches rose to a central dome. High stained-glass windows filtered sunlight and transformed it into many-colored light beams. The space engulfed me. When the church was empty, footsteps on the stone floor reverberated in the silence, then diminished through a long tonal decay. So, too, with the lowering of kneelers hitting the floor. Sound ricocheted off the walls, giving them a sort of voice that had years of wisdom to tell, I thought. Decades—maybe centuries—of incense permeated the wood pews and even the stone walls.

Neither theology nor doctrine played a role in attracting me to Catholicism. Instead, I was taken by the way Catholicism pervaded all aspects of Mexican life: their liturgies and rituals; baptisms and confirmations; births, marriages, and deaths. Religious festivals marked the seasons and the calendar, and religion knit families close together, something I had not known, not even in my marriage to Gloria. And, most of all, the people had such a welcoming spirit. The alienation I had always known in America, I did not know here.

During Mass, I jotted notes in my journal:

> The Church is like a container for the sacred. No, the sacred can't be contained—God is everywhere. Maybe the Spirit inspires creative believers to fashion and build a suitable home for itself, where it can be less diffuse—more like a concentrated vein of gold than microscopic flecks diffused over a broad area. A gold-like glow shimmers through things made of earthen materials: flames from beeswax candles, light through stained-glass windows, paint

depicting the halos of saints, and burnished chalices holding bread and wine. Bread and wine, fruits of the earth and made by human hands, which become spiritual food and drink. A home where the sacred dwells and rests and breathes itself into worshippers—and they're supposed to take that with them into the world outside. There's something about the recitation of prayers, the bowing and kneeling, the incantation of hymns, the flow of the rituals, that focuses the mind yet holds my analyzing, critical faculties in abeyance. Sacred power envelops me when I'm here. It's different from wilderness, but similar, too. Is this what I've been missing all these years?

I remembered the backpacking trips to the Jarbidge mountains; the rainbow colors glistening through water droplets sent flying when trout jumped out of the water to catch an insect. A similar incandescence gleamed in the sanctuary, and not for a moment only.

Spirit returned gently, like cool evening air. No lightning bolts of ecstasy this time, just the easy unfolding of dusk into dawn within the soul.

In Catholicism, material things are used as aids in human sanctification, by transforming them into signs of God's presence. Through the sacraments the Church sanctifies the major stages of our lives: our birth through the sacrament of baptism; the passage from childhood into adulthood through the sacrament of confirmation; the joining of a man and woman into one through the sacrament of marriage; the taking of holy orders by priests, monks, and nuns; the transformation of the fruits of the earth into the body and blood of Christ through the sacrament of the Eucharist; reconciliation with God through the confession of sins; and the anointing of the sick for those near death.

The Church, especially in Third World countries, has elaborate rituals that often seem bizarre to the educated classes of America and Europe. I witnessed some of these rituals years earlier in Álamos during the *Fiesta de la Virgen de la Balvanera* and *Las Posadas*. Similar rituals and feasts formed an integral part of the cycle of seasons in Coalcomán, even outside the regular calendar of religious feasts.

One pleasant, sunny Saturday morning in mid-February, the church was overflowing with worshippers. Those unable to enter stood in the street and plaza, listening to prayers on a loudspeaker.

"What's going on?" I asked Doña Pina.

"Because of the drought," she said. "They are praying for inter- cessions to end it."

Serious drought had left the fields and crops of Western Mexico desiccated, and drinking water was scarce. The town authorities turned on the water pumps for only half an hour each morning, and the townspeople hurried to fill as many containers as possible to get them through the day.

The priests brought a statue of San Heriberto, the patron saint of rain and drought relief, to town and organized a prayer service, fol- lowed by an elaborate procession to the top of a nearby mountain. Priests and deacons took turns carrying the statue. Hundreds of townsfolk and *campesinos* from the surrounding region partici- pated: they prayed the rosary, chanted prayers, and pleaded for the saint to intercede, to coax God to send rain. They slowly ascended the mountainside. Four men, two on each flank of the procession, carried rifles to protect against wild animals such as mountain lions and boars. I followed along as an observer, hanging back a ways, writing notes in my journal from time to time. *Great material for my novel!*

Our ascent lasted over two hours, with a fairly steep climb during the final stretch. As we ascended, the air cooled. Clouds gathered in the west, then darkened. Soon, thunder rolled in from the distance. Just before we reached the summit, rain began to fall, steadily. I was incredulous. *O, come on!* I thought. *The priests must have gotten a weather forecast!* The common people didn't have access to phones or televisions, or even radios, but the priests did. At best it was a fortuitous coincidence. The *campesinos,* however, had no doubt that San Heriberto had interceded for them. They rejoiced and contin- ued to the top of the mountain, singing hymns of praise. *Holy, holy, holy Lord, God of power and might! Heaven and earth are filled with your glory.*

Filled with glory, indeed.

On another occasion, the priests brought in a statue of the Virgin Mary for veneration. On three consecutive days, from around noon until 10:00 p.m., the statue was on display in front of the church altar. Over those three days, thousands of pilgrims from the surrounding countryside came to venerate the image of the Virgin. Near the front door of the church, a cardboard box held thousands of wallet-size photographs of the statue. The faithful picked up a photograph, then took their place in a long line of believers shuffling slowly down the central aisle of the church. They waited patiently to touch and venerate the holy statue. When they reached it, they knelt to pray. They kissed the Madonna's feet. They rubbed the photograph against the statue for a moment, in expectation that its healing power would transfer onto the photograph. They then took it home in hopes its radiance would bring blessings to their families.

I was astounded by the sheer number of people who visited the church: a steady stream from the outlying districts, young and old, mostly *campesinos*. On the first night of this three-day event, I sat in a pew, observing people venerate the statue, and jotted notes in my journal about this curious ritual. On the second night, I took my place in line. I did not believe the statue had miraculous powers, but there was something primal and appealing about this passionate folk religion, and I wanted to participate in it—even if vicariously. Religion permeated every aspect of communal life here.

The rituals—both simple and elaborate—the chants, processions, the ceremonies—the whole of it—had a profound effect on me in ways not readily open to rational analysis. I began praying in church more often, not just during Mass. One Sunday I arrived at Mass early and sat alone in a side chapel to meditate. A large statue of St. Joseph stood in the back. Lighted votive candles filled several shelves below a glass-encased painting hung from the wall opposite me—an icon of Christ Pantokrator—the Cosmic Christ, Ruler of the Universe, I later learned (I did not then know enough to even wonder what a Greek Orthodox icon was doing in a colonial Spanish church). The Christ's large eyes gazed directly into mine. Light from the candles reflected off the glass covering the icon, and I saw my own reflection, too, made dim and distant by the overpowering look of those penetrating eyes.

As Mass began, I moved back into the pews, near the center aisle. Throughout Mass, I felt moved by a divine presence. Somewhere near the end of Mass, the beauty and power of the liturgy overpowered me. Or maybe it was those eyes. Tears began to flow; they streamed down my face. I knew my spiritual journey had been leading me here, to this religious tradition. My life had been a chaotic mess for years, with no focus or goals. Even my spiritual conversion at the age of twenty-one in the Jarbidge Mountains—and throughout the subsequent summer and fall in the hills surrounding Elko—was unruly and without direction. I had the certain realization that I had found, or been led to, a new home for the spirit, where different ancestors—spiritual ones—held fellowship with the living, and framed a context for their lives. I belonged here! I had been lost and now was found.

The choir sang Psalm 122, "*Qué alegría, cuando me dijeron, vamos a la casa del Señor. Ya están pisando nuestros pies, tus umbrales Jerúsalen!*": "What joy when I heard them say, let us go to the House of the Lord! Already my feet are crossing your threshold, O Jerusalem!" I experienced an overwhelming catharsis and sense of wholeness.

When Mass ended, the congregation got up to leave. I remained seated. People stared at me as they passed by; they must have wondered at this strange American weeping in church, oblivious to the spectacle he was making.

The next day, María de la Luz and I met in the town plaza. We made small talk, and then she said, "People say you cried in church yesterday. Why?"

"I don't know. I was kind of overwhelmed by the presence of God, I guess."

"You should become Catholic, you know."

"Yes, I know," I said without hesitation. "I've been thinking about that."

"Then I will introduce you to the priest."

And she did.

The next day she accompanied me to the rectory of the church to meet with Fr. Juan, a priest at St. Thomas Church. Fr. Juan asked preliminary questions.

"Have you been baptized?"

"No, Father."

"Did your parents instruct you in Christian doctrine?"

"No, Father."

"Why do you want to join the Catholic Church?" He looked at me, then at María de la Luz, then back at me. I could tell what he was thinking: Did I want to marry this girl because I'd gotten her pregnant? Would her parents not allow marriage because I was not Catholic? I had presented myself as a candidate for baptism, accompanied by an attractive young woman of marriageable age. How could he not wonder if we were planning to marry? Marriage was not at all on my mind, though I was sure María de la Luz had it on *her* mind. She was ripe. Her fulsome hips and breasts—just shy of voluptuous—her flirtatious eyes and smile, the lush red lips, exuded desire and sensuous love. I could imagine a fortunate young man in her arms, absorbed in her warm flesh, cooperating with her fecundity. I imagined her surrounded by a passel of children. I could not imagine her going on to university, even though she was attending preparatory school; could not envision her as a professional, a teacher, a scientist. A mother: yes. She reminded me of those Pre-Columbian figurines of earth mothers, of matronly goddesses—a Catholic earth-mother. A man would be happy to come home from work to her embrace. But that man would not be me.

Why *did* I want to join the Catholic Church? I struggled to formulate my answer and translate it into Spanish. I did not have a cogent theological reason. Nor did I hold the belief that Catholicism was the one and only true religion; in fact, I had spent many afternoons in Coalcomán reading the *Tao te Ching*, a book I loved for its spiritual insights. I suppose my reasons were more personal and aesthetic: I had observed the cohesiveness of Catholic families—both in Mexico and of my Basque friends in Elko—and longed for that; and I had been moved by the richness and power of the liturgical rituals, and the fervor of the people. There was no way I could summarize my spiritual journey in a few sentences, so I blurted out something like, "because it's the original Church, the trunk that all the other churches branched off from."

"Éso es!" the priest agreed. "That's right."

We proceeded with the catechism, a very brief one. Fr. Juan wanted to baptize and confirm me at the upcoming Easter Vigil Mass, about a month away: much too short a time to become familiar with the teachings of Catholicism. I read a few rudimentary catechetical pamphlets, so my introduction to Catholicism was quite shallow. Fortunately, while meeting with Fr. Donovan in Elko, I had read some detailed catechisms and documents from the Second Vatican Council, so I already knew the basic elements of the faith.

I spent time each day in prayer at the church. During Holy Week I participated in the *Via Crucis*, which re-enacts scenes from Christ's last days: his condemnation by Pontius Pilate, the scourging by Roman soldiers, his long and torturous walk to the mountain top carrying the cross that he would be nailed to, and his crucifixion and death. There are fourteen stations along the way. It is one of the most popular Catholic devotions in the world and, along with Good Friday and Holy Thursday, a core ritual during the season of Lent. The ritual was performed in public. A young man was chosen to represent the Christ figure and given a cross to carry up a nearby hill. The priest read from scripture at each station and the faithful recited prayers. I followed along, writing notes in my journal.

> *Christ is condemned to death.* For his selfless commitment to God and his love of neighbor. Yes, love of neighbor. Can *I* say that— anything even close to that? Or is my love of God selfish? Seeking self-actualization. What does that mean? Am I still a self if alone? He came to fulfill the Law, not abolish it. The Law says love God with all your heart and mind. It also says don't commit adultery.

> *We adore you, O Christ, and we bless you.*
> *Because by your holy cross you have redeemed the world.*

> *Christ carries the cross on which he will be crucified.* Thorns pierce and bloody his head. Suffering. He does this for us. For *me*, though? Why?

Kenito cried when I dropped him and Gloria off. "No, daddy! Don't go!" he pleaded. "Please don't go!" I walked to the car. Gloria had to hold him back as he tried to run after me. "Daddy, don't go!" I felt a stab in my heart, but went anyway. Why would Christ sacrifice himself for someone so selfish, who had done such a thing to an adopted son?

> We adore you, O Christ, and we bless you.
> Because by your holy cross you have redeemed the world.

Jesus falls the first time. Oh, God, how we stumble through life without knowing which road to take. We wander aimlessly. Yet, I've tried to follow you faithfully. And failed. How about some help? Is Christ *really* my help? How can that be?

Jesus falls the second time. Screw up after screw up. Stumbling, stumbling, unable to carry the burden. Will I learn?

Simon helps Jesus carry the cross. Would *I* do that—in public? Or would I lurk behind the crowds, not wanting to be seen, like Peter, denying that he even knew him.

He is comforted by a group of women. Where were the guys? Denying and abandoning him, though he called and saved them, forgave them though he knew in advance they would desert him. He chose them for a mission, in spite of their spineless unworthiness. I wonder if any of those women had been whores? Probably. Sinners were drawn to him. They drew strength from him and one another. Got their act together. Why? He forgave and healed them—those who would be healed—and told them to sin no more. *Sin no more,* those eyes said from out of the Christ Pantokrator's image: sin no more. I'm not doing so good with that one.

Jesus falls a third time. The young man representing Jesus in the *via crucis* lies on the ground as if collapsed under the weight. I try to imagine Jesus on the ground, broken. His brokenness makes *me* whole? A surrender that gives *me* life?

They nail him to the cross. He feels abandoned by his Father, and his shriek of dereliction pierces the sky: *My God, my God, why have you forsaken me?* "No Daddy! Don't go! Daddy!"

We adore you, O Christ, and we bless you.
Because by your holy cross you have redeemed the world.

He dies. From Leonard Cohen's song *Suzanne*: "Jesus was a sailor /
when he walked upon the water / And he spent a long time watching / From his lonely wooden tower / And when he knew for certain / Only drowning men could see him / He said 'All men will be
sailors then / Until the sea shall free them' / But he himself was
broken / Long before the sky would open / Forsaken, almost
human / He sank beneath your wisdom like a stone."

Should I trust him, since he's touched my soul with his perfect,
radiant mind?

The sea shall free them? The Ocean that is God? Must I drown in it
before I live?

They lay him in the tomb. Silence. Darkness. The place of phan-
tasms and malign presences and terrible loneliness. And insanity.
The Abyss.

What follows the abyss?

At the age of twenty-nine, during the Easter Vigil Mass of April
1980, I was officially received into the Catholic Church—baptized
and confirmed on the same night. My godparents were Doña Pina
and her son Enrique. We stood on the left side of the altar, a statue
of the Virgin Mary behind and above us. I was baptized along with a
dozen newborns, held in their mothers' arms.

I left Coalcomán a week after the baptism and confirmation, for
two reasons. First, I had been in Coalcomán for about four months
and had completed a rough draft of the novel. I needed a break
from the writing. Second, my relationship with María de la Luz was
wrong, and I had to end the pretense that we had a future. It was
best to make a clean break. I did not leave, though, before seeing her
one last time. The night before I left, she invited me to her home to

meet her mother. We walked through the narrow streets together. I had not been to her house before. We had met only in the central plaza, furtively. Now that I was a Catholic, it was permissible for her to be in my company. María's mother greeted me graciously. She knew I had been received into the Church—the entire town knew—and she spoke to me warmly.

"So, you are the man my daughter is so fond of! I see you often in town or in church."

"It's an honor to meet you," I said. "Your daughter is the one who persuaded me to become a Catholic."

"Oh, well then, she has at least done some good," she said, teasingly, with a sidelong glance at María de la Luz.

"Yes," I said, "she has."

Night was falling. The streetlights came on and shone against the soft pastel hues of the adobe houses. As we talked on the porch outside her home, neighbors walked by and greeted us. A man on a burro, carrying a load of sticks to be sold as firewood, passed by on the cobblestone street. Laborers were coming home from the fields. It was mid-April and spring filled the air. The Sierra Madre Mountains were alive with life. The amber sunlight of evening's golden hour shone against the higher mountains. Yellow porch lights reflected off the colored houses, creating soft, radiant colors that shimmered with warmth and comfort. A sense of new life filled the air. I breathed it in.

When I said goodbye to María de la Luz, she handed me an envelope, and asked me not to read the contents until after I had gone. I no longer have the letter, and do not remember what it said, except the last line that read, "When you say goodbye, kiss me gently on the cheek, and promise you will never forget me."

Sadly, I had not said anything poetic to her, though she had played a key role in my decision to become a Catholic. I did not have any contact with her after that night, but I have not forgotten her. How could I forget someone with a name so beautiful: Mary of the Light? As a gift for the baptism and confirmation, she gave me a copy of the Holy Bible in Spanish. I still have it. It has an inscription from her on the title page. It is strange how God can work even through an improper relationship to bring grace to a sinful man. I might have continued to drift along spiritually, without a home, had it not been for her catalytic words: "you should become Catholic, you know"—which in their simplicity caused years of searching to coalesce around a great religious tradition.

Before returning to the U.S., I stopped in Álamos and remained there for two months, revising the novel. I rented a room in the home of friends rather than stay with Hal and María. Hal's family life was fraught with tension. Several months earlier he had awoken from sleep and gone to the kitchen. He heard noise in María's room and went to see what was happening. He discovered her in bed with a younger man, who quickly got up and fled, carrying his clothes in his arms. After this incident, Hal had begun locking María's bedroom door from the outside so she couldn't get out, and no one else could get in. The situation was too awkward for me; eight years earlier, I could have been the young man who fled.

Hal had become visibly frail. Alcohol would have all but destroyed his liver by then, and he knew it. While I was working on my novel revision, Hal arranged to visit to the United States to see a daughter from his first marriage. I had the sense it would be the last time I saw him, and it turned out that I was right. I would return to the U.S. before Hal came back to Mexico, and I would never hear from him again.

While in Álamos, I met a group of seminarians from a newly established monastery on the outskirts of town. I met with the abbot of the monastery to talk about my sense of spiritual calling and uncertainty about what path to take. He heard my first confession and told me to be patient with God, who would show me the right path in His own good time.

A few days later, during evening Mass at the Church of *Nuestra Señora de la Balvanera*, I quietly prayed following communion. The sacristan tapped me on the shoulder to get my attention. I looked up. He whispered, "Father Abbot would like you to go up to the altar and join him."

I was not prepared for this, but what could I do? I walked hesitantly toward the altar, looking at the abbot. He signaled me with his hand to come forward. Once there, he asked me to turn to the congregation, whereupon he introduced me to the congregation as a newly baptized convert and asked everyone to welcome me into the faith. The assembly applauded.

After that, I was known and greeted all over town. On one occasion, I went to the pharmacy to fill a prescription for tranquilizers, written by a doctor in Coalcomán. The pharmacist told me the prescription wasn't valid in Sonora, that I needed a new one from a local doctor. Just then the proprietress entered, looked at the script, and said, "He's a good Catholic; fill the order."

A day later, while crossing through the Alameda, the outdoor market, I passed a group of young men loitering, drinking beer, and playing kickball. One of them approached me, his eyes bloodshot and glazed. He reeked of liquor. He placed his left hand on my right shoulder. I thought for a moment that he was going to pick a fight.

"You are a good man," he said. "I am very bad."

"Why do you say that?"

"Because you are! I am a sinner."

"We're all sinners. I'm no exception."

"But I've done something that I cannot confess."

"What is it?" He clearly wanted to talk to someone.

"Sometimes I usher at the church. I pass around the collection basket. I have stolen money sometimes to buy beer. I am very bad." A soccer ball rolled our way; he kicked it to his buddies.

"You are not bad, but you should confess this to a priest," I said.

"I can't. Everyone knows everyone here."

"Can you go to a church in Navojoa (a city 50 kilometers to the west), and confess it to a priest there?" I asked, not knowing whether or not that was an appropriate suggestion.

"I can't," he said, "but you are a good man. I am very bad."

As he walked back to his drinking buddies I thought, *if only he knew what a whitewashed sepulcher I am.* From that exchange I realized how important it is for someone with a guilty conscience to confess, to unburden the soul from the weight of sin, from the guilt of wrongs committed, and of right actions we fail to take.

I now had a home, a context for my journey; a connection with people everywhere, including the spiritual ancestors known as the Communion of Saints. Entrance into the Church was not a culmination, but the beginning of a lifetime project that I still had no blueprint for. I did not think of joining the Church as a conversion, per se: the experience during the summer of radiant colors in the Jarbidge in 1972 was that. In this case, the Spirit of God led me to join the Catholic Church—the renewal and continuation of a quest begun years earlier, only this time within the framework of an ongoing religious tradition. A new beginning.

I had gone to Mexico to escape a broken marriage, adulthood, and a conventional life; and to try my hand at writing fiction. Fiction turned out to be another dead end, but I found my way, instead, into a new home with its rich history and tradition, its deep sacramental life, and its varied and sometimes bizarre rituals and cults; its boisterous and contentious schools of thought; its deep and abiding wisdom; and, as I learned later, its rotting walls, its sometimes stifling stasis, its too-worldly and, in some cases, morally degenerate priests—all jumbled together within its solid and deep spiritual rootedness. It was time to set about exploring the contours of this spacious new mansion, with its admixture of classical, byzantine, baroque, gothic, and modern elements—an exploration that has taken up the remainder of my life.

12

Transitions

I CROSSED the border into the U.S. as a returning citizen, but, as a
newly baptized Catholic, I had just begun to claim citizenship in
a new homeland: an ancient tradition spanning the globe and
stretching across millennia. Before I could set about becoming
assimilated to its culture and traditions, I had to learn what my citizenship papers meant. They meant, first of all, trying to set my life
in order and resolving the mess that was my marriage to Gloria. By
the time I had been baptized and confirmed at Eastertime, Gloria
had returned to the United States and moved to Reno. She did not
approve of my joining the Church.

Our marital situation remained problematic. Even more so since
she was still canonically married to her first husband, though legally
divorced from him. That had not meant anything to me previously.
At one point after my return from Mexico, we tried to stitch our
marriage back together, to give it one more try. I encouraged Gloria
to file for an annulment of her first marriage. She reluctantly
agreed, and submitted the paperwork to the local diocese in Reno.
Several weeks later she received a notice from the diocese stating
that they would look into the case in accordance with established
procedures of canon law. The letter also requested a fee for process-
ing the paperwork. It was not a large fee, but the request infuriated
Gloria. Her past resentments against the Catholic Church—what
she saw as its corruption, its money-grubbing ways, its frequent dis-
regard for the poor in favor of the wealthy—rose to the fore.
Although the letter stated the diocese would waive the fee if she
could not afford it, she refused to request a waiver or even to continue the process. That ended any possibility of the Church recog-
nizing and blessing our own unorthodox and secular marriage.

From the Church's perspective, we were living in sin, though I disliked expressing it in those terms. We had not intended to be sinful, and our marriage brought a good deal of healing to both of us. We helped each other to our feet following dark times. Even so, the relationship just wasn't right; it was missing the mark, and was not of a nature to bring us into communion with God. We shared few common values, beliefs, or life goals, and we had no shared love of learning to speak of. I still wanted to pursue higher education, and was especially determined to go, full bore, into this new phase of my spiritual journey. Baptism had re-energized my religious longing and re-awakened something from the depths. Once the Spirit has seized you, you are claimed. It haunts and pursues you all the days of your life. You can attempt to flee it or repress its voice, but it will persist, condemning you if you do not turn, listen, and respond. Consider what happened to Jonah. I was ready to respond. There was no way to make the marriage succeed if it was not founded in a common religious bond.

In October 1981, we divorced. I was thirty-one.

The divorce created no small moral dilemma for me. I was, in essence, forsaking my wife and adopted child, even if our relationship had been a messy and illicit one from the beginning. I did not leave them destitute—Gloria had a well-paying job—but it was an emotional abandonment. In spite of the messiness of our marriage, Gloria's life and mine had become intertwined and dependent, bearing mutual obligations. I rationalized the divorce in part by drawing on Emerson, who writes, "no law can be sacred to me but that of my nature. Good and bad are but names readily transferable to that or this; the only right is what is after my constitution; the only wrong is what is against it." Carl Jung writes that one who has received a vocation must follow the "law of [his] being" and break from the social fabric if necessary. I was following that law, but there were consequences. Gloria and Kenito were devastated. How does one balance the strong pull from opposing directions? The literature I was reading at the time did not address moral decision making when one is confronted with such dilemmas.

Transitions

I had years before discovered that watching television de-centers the soul—at least my soul—and I rarely turned it on. Yet, one Saturday night I was up late watching it. During a commercial break, an odd advertisement appeared—audio only, no video—for a new liberal arts college just then being founded in Reno. Reno? *Philistine Reno?* A male voice spoke from the blank screen:

> *"Join us at Old College School of Humanities! A liberal arts college that focuses on the great thinkers and ideas of Western civilization and the Christian intellectual tradition; on connecting the sciences, humanities, and philosophy into a comprehensive whole."*

Did I hear that right? The words went straight to the core of my being. A single visual image appeared at the end of the advertisement: an address and phone number to contact for more information. I wrote down the information. I called first thing Monday morning and matriculated in Old College in January 1982.

Old College School of Humanities was founded in 1981 by Father John Leary, a Jesuit priest and former president of Gonzaga University. Fr. Leary had become disillusioned with American higher education, including Catholic higher education. America's great universities had become secularized, and he foresaw Catholic universities going swiftly down the same path, losing sight of their core mission: to form character, sharpen the intellect, pursue truth and wisdom, and integrate spirituality into the center of intellectual life. Catholic colleges had begun to mimic secular institutions, allowing their core liberal arts curriculums—focused on the great works of literature, philosophy, and theology—to fragment into a host of specialized academic disciplines with little coherence. Fr. Leary considered that a great loss, and he had a vision to establish a number of small colleges grounded in traditional liberal arts education, even while incorporating contemporary knowledge and insights from other cultures. In 1971 he founded New College of California in San Francisco; and ten years later, Old College School of Humanities in Reno.

At first, the College rented space in a then-closed parochial school connected to the Church of St. Thomas in downtown Reno.

The classrooms were still furnished with old elementary school desks and chairs. Our first assignment as students was to move them to a storage room and scavenge for adult-sized chairs from empty offices and hallways. We were at the ground floor of a new, exciting, and implausible endeavor: the creation of a new college. I took courses in Early Christian Theology, the Reformation, and the Philosophy of Education; in the Pentateuch, Liberation Theology, and Psychology and Religion.

Fr. Leary taught the Philosophy of Education course. He was in his late sixties, an experienced educator and administrator. We read John Henry Newman's *The Idea of a University*, Jacques Maritain's *Education at the Crossroads*, John Dewey's *Democracy and Education*, Karl Jaspers' *The Idea of a University*, and Questions V and VI of Thomas Aquinas's *Division and Methods of the Sciences*. The class had only eight students, and Fr. Leary met with each of us individually once a week to discuss questions we might have that didn't come up in class. His office was the former school principal's office— same wood desk, tall metal file cabinets, probably second-hand government issue.

I had recently come across the Aristotelian concepts of *entelechy* and *teleology*, and wanted to discuss them. Entelechy is the vital principle that guides the development and functioning of an organism or system. The entelechy of an acorn, for example, is to grow into an oak tree. The fully formed oak dwells, in potential form, within the acorn. But its growth can be impeded by being planted in poor soil, or by unfavorable climate conditions such as lack of rain or sunlight. The goal of the arborist is to remove those obstacles so the acorn can develop according to its inner potential, its inherent "instructions" for development. I wanted to know if the concept could be applied to education.

"O, yes," said Fr. Leary. "Think of each student as a seed. The goal of education is to unlock the potential of each student, to lead them out of their latent state into fully developed persons who comprehend life as a whole, the goal being possession of *wisdom*." Everyone has a unique inner self that seeks to sprout, grow, and flourish. The goal of the educator is to help lead that inner vital principle (the word *educate* comes from e-ducare: "to lead out").

Teleology is a closely related concept: the idea that nature is directed toward an end or shaped by a purpose immanent within nature itself, as contrasted with merely mechanistic explanations for the workings of nature. I treasured those words—entelechy and teleology—and drew on them frequently. I looked for occasions to use them.

Fr. Leary kept a quotation from John Henry Newman on an eight-and-a-half-by-eleven-inch placard on his desk:

> *All knowledge forms one whole, for its subject-matter is one; for the universe in its length and breadth is so intimately knit together, that we cannot separate off portion from portion, and operation from operation, except by a mental abstraction; and then again, as to its Creator, though He of course in His own Being is infinitely separate from it, yet He has so implicated Himself with it, and taken it into His bosom, by His presence in it, His providence over it, His impressions upon it, and His influences through it, that we cannot truly or fully contemplate it without in some main aspects contemplating Him.*

The College had only five or six fulltime faculty members at the beginning; the others were adjuncts from the community. Julius Rogina, a practicing psychologist and former Jesuit priest, taught the Psychology and Religion course. We read Sigmund Freud, Carl Jung, Abraham Maslow, Carl Rogers, Lawrence Kohlberg, and Erik Erikson. We discussed our own psychological and religious development in light of the theories developed by these authors. At last I began to have a context for the psychological and spiritual conversion—and torments—I had experienced years earlier. We read books by Jung and others on the interpretation of dreams. I dug out the old dream journals that I had kept when consulting Dr. Greene in Salt Lake City. Dreams that had made no sense to me earlier suddenly were full of meaningful symbols.

Encouraged by my readings of Jung and others, I began to record my dreams again. The tenor and direction of the dreams began to change. They were no longer beset by invading armies or ghoulish presences. One dream represented an important turning point in my healing:

I am traveling on a small motorcycle in a remote area of the country. It is winter. The ground is covered with a thin layer of snow. The motorcycle runs out of gas. I abandon it and begin to walk. I come upon a frozen lake. There's a path along the lake's edge and I follow it. A crack appears in the ice of the lake, and water trickles forth, slowly at first, but increases in volume and strength until it becomes a stream. I follow it downstream into an abandoned town that has been long forgotten and buried. I enter a building and descend some stairs into a basement. The river flows underground through the basement of a once strong building, cleansing old walls stained with years of grime. The walls are still solid, though, capable of bearing up. The stains remain on the walls, but the flow of water is strong, cleansing away the mold and excrescences. I step into the river and feel its power.

A trickle grew into a stream; the stream increased in volume, forming a river, flowing strongly, and cleansing the long buried depths of my soul.

Professors at Old College gave me ample room to expand, even soar. My faculty advisor at Old College, Daniel Norton, gave me the freedom to write a senior thesis on as broad a topic as I wished, as long as I drew on historical facts, made sound arguments, and cited appropriate, reputable sources. I attempted to apply Teilhard's evolutionary vision to the history of western civilization (small topic!). History is but an extension of the evolutionary process, displaying the same tendency toward gathering ever more multiplicity into increasingly complex unities, with each higher unity possessing a higher level of consciousness. As each higher level arises, greater multiplicity coalesces into more complex and unified wholes, and, ideally, this leads to more internal freedom of human individuals. If not, a government becomes crystallized into an inorganic, despotic entity that seeks to maintain the status quo through oppression. History possesses its own entelechy, and human social arrangements display a struggle to get this unification right. Like all evolution heretofore, the evolution of human society has progressed through experiments, mistakes, progress. There does not always appear to be progress toward freedom and unity; instead, history is full of degradation and suffering. Over time, however, one can see a gradual increase in more complex social orders, increased connectivity and, in the more advanced societies, greater internal freedom. The thesis was ninety-five pages. I am amazed, and embarrassed, to this day that I had the temerity to present an evolutionary theory of western history in a mere ninety-five pages! I was even more surprised, and grateful, that my advisor allowed me to conduct a study on a topic so broad, though he did warn me that I would never be allowed to write on a topic this broad in graduate school. I would never have been able to do this in a mainstream college. Both Old College and I resided outside the mainstream, at the margins of academia. The implausible educational venture that was Old College— in the heart of a pagan and philistine city—lasted only seven years. But I finally had a bachelor's degree. My desire for God was joined to a love of learning. They arose from the same impulse: an *eros* for God and for understanding all things *in relation to God.*

I graduated from Old College in June 1983, at age 33, with two dozen other students in an informal and intimate ceremony. Fr. Leary gave me the plaque with the Newman quotation as a graduation gift. I have hung it in my study spaces ever since.

I cannot give an account of why it took so long to discern the exact nature of my life's calling, but it was this: help heal the rupture between spiritual and intellectual life in Catholic universities; help overcome the divide between nature and spirit, between secular academic disciplines and theological insight; trace the divide back to its source and reestablish their integral link drawing on ancient, medieval, and modern thought. Is such a call not grandiose and quixotic—meriting incredulity and even mockery—yet also noble, at one and the same time? Yes, it is. But it was *my* call and I had to respond to it or find myself in the belly of the beast, as did Jonah. But how? I would need to learn and appropriate the scholarship: the history, theology, and philosophy of higher education. That would require years of intensive major-league study and I was a bush-league scholar, at best. I didn't have a scholar's mind or temperament. I recoiled from too strong a focus on analysis of narrow slivers of reality; I preferred synthesis and mythopoesis. I'd have to get through a series of gatekeepers: graduate school admissions committees, advisors, a dissertation committee, editors and publishers, and then, if I became a professor, tenure and promotion committees. How could someone with an unorthodox and renegade disposition and a failed academic past get through all that? Moreover, I feared graduate school would dry up my renewed spiritual life with its narrow focus on intellectual, left-brained activities to the neglect of interior movements of the soul. I could lament with Wordsworth:

> Our meddling intellect
> Mis-shapes the beauteous forms of things:
> We murder to dissect.

Yet, I had to try.

I consulted Fr. Leary about my misgivings, told him about my lack of ability to speak in public, my introversion. He understood and, in fact, had recognized early on that I was a diffident young man. He said, "When the Spirit calls, you don't get to carry out whatever project you like, as if it were a career choice. Sometimes you get goaded into a vocation against your preferences, to a task that you have no special talent for. Look at Moses. He was called to confront Pharaoh and to tell him to let the Israelites go free. But Moses was hesitant."

Fr. Leary took a Bible—the Latin Vulgate—out of a desk drawer and opened it to the Book of Exodus. He found the passage, and translated. "Now, listen to Moses's protest: 'I'm too inarticulate, Lord! I lack the power to influence others. The Israelites themselves, who I'm trying to help, have not even listened to me, so why should the Pharaoh take any notice of such a poor speaker?' But God was unmoved and sent him anyway. He gave Moses his brother Aaron to speak on his behalf." Fr. Leary wrote down some names on a sheet of paper: Jeremiah, Ezekiel, Jonah, Gideon. "Read the stories about their call from God, and how they hesitated and protested, and then see how God responded. God brooks no excuses. He doesn't care if you're not qualified. It's not a matter of talent or charisma, but of calling. If he's really sending you to do this, you have to do it. God will find a way."

Fr. Leary presided at daily evening Mass some days at the Church of St. Thomas, and I attended on occasion before my evening classes. He sometimes gave brief sermons about the saint whose feast day it was. A common thread wove through many of his sermons: what made these men or women—ordinary human beings like the rest of us—saints at all? They weren't perfect, they had weaknesses and flaws. Fr. Leary's answer: *they single-mindedly followed God's call in spite of discouragement and overwhelming odds against success. They kept at it.*

And that's what he told me when I sought his counsel. "Follow your call single-mindedly and a door will open. Your work will come to fruition, sooner or later, and in ways you can't anticipate. It might even come to fruition after you're dead," he said. "Your duty is to do what the Holy Spirit guides you to do, and not worry about the outcome. That's in God's hands."

Old College survived less than a decade, but what I learned there launched me into a career in the Republic of Letters. Sometimes things happen at just the right time and in a way that can only appear providential. I am thankful to Father Leary's vision, initiative, and wise counsel. May God grant him rest.

I had a degree in the humanities and was ready for graduate school. Old College had received provisional accreditation from the Northwest Commission on Colleges and Universities, enough to make it credible to some of the nation's best graduate schools. I applied to and was accepted into the University of Chicago, the University of Notre Dame, the Graduate Theological Union at the University of California, Berkeley, and Catholic University of America.

Two of the institutions—Notre Dame and the Graduate Theological Union—were at first hesitant (with good reason, given my unorthodox journey through college over a fifteen year time span). The chair of the Theology Department at Notre Dame contacted me for clarification—my grades at Old College were excellent and my professors had given me very strong recommendations. But the admissions committee was puzzled by my earlier convoluted academic record (A's, B's, F's, incompletes, and withdrawals). They asked for an explanation. I told it straight. I had been wild and muddled when young, without focus and without goals. I had lacked the discipline to make it through college. Only after years of working, traveling, a failed marriage, and finally, finding a spiritual home in the Catholic Church, did I gain the mental focus to see my studies through to completion. The response satisfied them and they admitted me, though without a scholarship. I would have had to pay the entire expenses myself, which I was unable to do.

The Graduate Theological Union (GTU) at Berkeley admitted me with a caveat: if I intended to pursue doctoral studies after completing the Master's degree, there would be almost no chance I'd be accepted into the doctoral program, regardless of how well I did at the Master's level. The reason, they explained, was that applications to the doctoral program have to be approved by scholars at the University of California, Berkeley, with whom the GTU was affiliated. The professors at Berkeley would never accept someone with such a checkered academic past. I appreciated the honesty. In fact, I was delighted that *any* graduate school was willing to give me a chance. My past academic record was so unorthodox and puzzling, who *wouldn't* hesitate?

I accepted a scholarship at the University of Chicago from the MA Program in the Social Sciences, a separate department for students who looked promising but did not quite have the academic background necessary to pursue advanced studies in a standard academic field. The idea was to familiarize them with a broad range of methodologies and theories in the various social science disciplines so that they would be ready for advanced graduate work following one year of preparation in the MA program.

While at Chicago, I drifted toward courses in the Divinity School: "Modern Religious Thought," "Medieval Mysticism," and "Modern Social Science and Theology." At that time, the Divinity School at Chicago was considered one of the best in the country. Scholars such as Mircea Eliade, Langdon Gilkey, Bernard McGinn, David Tracy, and Martin Marty taught there. The academic program was rigorous and the standards high. It was exhilarating and, at the same time, disappointing. Disappointing because intellectual and spiritual life had been severed from one another. Even Theology had become a separate academic "discipline," a "science," an analytical, left-brained activity with its own jargon and specialized methods of inquiry—not an integrative, all-encompassing study of, well, *everything in relation to God*, as I had naively hoped. Theological study was devoid of personal religious development and formation. For one with a contemplative orientation and synthetic view of the world, this distressed my soul.

After a year at Chicago, I transferred to Catholic University of America (CUA) in Washington, D.C., where I was offered a teaching assistantship in the School of Religious Studies. Perhaps there I could couple higher learning with ongoing spiritual formation, the life of the mind with deeper initiation into the mystical life. Surely, I thought, I would find that opportunity at a Catholic University. *Wouldn't I?*

I had been claimed by the Spirit and when that happens, your horizons expand. Never again do you see the world in the same way. My conversion began in the Jarbidge Mountains in 1972, where I realized that the natural world is not just material; it is suffused with spirit. The Logos of God is at creation's core, giving it coherence and intelligibility, and guiding its unfolding. All things—living and non-living—are connected to one another, imbued with divine presence. I viewed everything through this new lens of interconnectedness and wholeness, and that constituted the basis for my long discontent with university life. Throughout my struggles to complete a degree, I had intuitively recoiled from the narrowness of academia, with its tightly defined fields of study and focus on only small slices of reality.

The road in pursuit of this calling was less chaotic, though no easier or less meandering than the one I had already traveled. Fortunately, I did not have to go it alone this time. When I entered the Church, I began to understand that Spirit dwells in communal life, too.

13

The Country of
Sacramental Marriage

TOWARD the end of spring semester 1985, I met Elizabeth Watkins just outside the graduate student dining hall at Catholic University, accompanied by a friend from my dorm, Scott. Elizabeth was a graduate student in the School of Music. She had long brown hair with the sides curled outward. She wore thick-rimmed glasses and a camel-colored dress. She had two armfuls of belongings: a satchel full of music scores, a purse, her flute, and various books. She attempted to balance them, shifting the satchel from hand to shoulder, the flute case from one hand to the other, and wedging the loose books between her arm and body in an attempt to get the balance just right. She was flustered and self-conscious about her awkwardness, but had a sincere humility about it that was endearing. Scott introduced us. She smiled and shook my hand. Her books fell to the floor.

As I helped Elizabeth gather her books, I noticed blue eyes behind those thick lenses. She wasn't a beauty, but attractive in her own way. Not sexy—a bit on the heavy side and awkward—but pretty. She was friendly and open, with a naiveté and good-heartedness that were both charming and winning. I knew that Scott was not interested in her romantically, so I looked for ways to be around her more frequently. She had a spontaneity and enthusiasm for life that sparked my own, which was normally reserved, if not inhibited.

Her roommate, Rose, whom I dated on occasion, invited me to a surprise birthday party for Elizabeth. A mixed age group attended: fellow graduate students, older women with whom she worked at the School of Music, as well as her middle and high school flute students and their parents. At first, the guests, not knowing one another, gathered in separate groups. Elizabeth moved from one group to another, hugging, thanking, chatting, and laughing. I leaned against a wall near the kitchen and watched her as she introduced people to one another, got conversations going. People obviously liked being around her—they had made the trip from different parts of the Washington, D.C. metro area to be there.

After Elizabeth and I began dating, I noticed how she sympathized with grocery store cashiers or store clerks who were having a rotten day. She listened to the sad incidents in their family lives, or about their heartless bosses; she talked to them, encouraged them. The cashiers felt a bit better after she left. She showed patience with her flute students who sometimes just needed to talk: about the pressure of an upcoming science fair, about another student trying to displace her from first flute in the school orchestra, or about a boy she liked. Elizabeth listened sympathetically while gently and skillfully steering them back to the task at hand.

It turned out that Elizabeth and I had much in common. She, too, was a convert to Catholicism, having had no religious upbringing whatsoever. In fact, her parents were very anti-religious and fancied themselves atheists. It further turned out that both Elizabeth and I had been baptized and confirmed into the Church at the same Easter Vigil Mass in 1980—she in Spartanburg, South Carolina, I in Mexico. We met five years later outside the CUA dining hall.

She, too, came from a troubled family. Her father, an architect, was an abusive alcoholic, her mother a classic enabler, trapped in a thorough dependency on her husband. As her father's alcoholism had progressed, Elizabeth watched her family become increasingly dysfunctional and withdraw from social relationships. Her parents spent their last several decades as virtual shut-ins in their own house, without friends, contributing nothing to society, nursing their self-imposed wounds. Elizabeth's younger sister turned wayward and wild as a means of escape from the family life. I believe Elizabeth's naive optimism and natural spirituality spared her that course.

After a short courtship, we were married in Caldwell Chapel at Catholic University in December 1985, just three weeks before my

Ph.D. qualifying exams. I was thirty-five, she twenty-six. As graduate students, we had little money for a honeymoon, so we rented a cabin for a week in the Blue Ridge Mountains of Virginia. The dead of winter had descended, with temperatures often well below zero, so staying indoors near the fireplace worked out well for studying. I'm sure my study infused the atmosphere of the cabin with romance: "Hey! Did you know that Heidegger says there is a direct intellectual path from medieval scholasticism to the dualism of Descartes?" Such words I spoke. Surely they hung aloft in the air, glowing in the firelight, pregnant with romance. Surely.

Our marriage was founded on a common faith and common values. Having both come out of the desert of agnostic indifference or doctrinaire atheism into the light of spiritual awareness and promise, we were finding our home in a religious tradition and a community thousands of years old.

Elizabeth gave me a deeper love of music, especially classical music. We frequently attended classical music concerts at the Kennedy Center for the Performing Arts in Washington, D.C. The Kennedy Center manager occasionally asked Elizabeth to turn pages for the piano accompanists of soloists like James Galway, Janet Baker, Itzak Perlman, and Yo Yo Ma. As payment, she got a free ticket for me. We went to folk music concerts at The Birchmere in Arlington, Virginia, and musical theater and concerts at Wolf Trap. We attended concerts by John Renbourn, The Seldom Scene, and Peter, Paul, and Mary.

I shared my love of nature with Elizabeth, and we fed off of one another's passions. We went frequently to the country on day trips or week-long vacations. We hiked the trails of the Blue Ridge Mountains and camped at Douthat State Park in western Virginia and New Germany State Park in western Maryland. We biked the rural country roads of Maryland and Virginia.

New Germany, in the Allegheny Mountains, a hundred and twenty miles west of Washington, D.C., became an especially favored spot. On our first anniversary, we rented a small cabin there for a week during Christmas break. One night we put on boots and coats and walked out into the falling snow. We came to a small stream—Poplar Creek—and followed it. Ice had formed around the stream's edges, and snow had settled atop rocks in the still-running water. A large tree had fallen across the stream many years earlier, forming a log bridge. The stream flowed underneath, but the log caused some of the water to back up, creating a small pool about three feet deep. We wanted to get to the other side of the stream and enter the forest, so we walked gingerly onto the log that was wide enough to serve as a bridge. The view from the middle of the log was serene: moonlight shone on the snow and bounced off the water. Pine trees towered above us. We stopped, embraced, and kissed passionately; then lost our balance and fell into the pool. *Holy shit! It's so cold!* We sucked in deeply as we rose, then laughed and shivered as we hurried back to the cabin, snow crunching beneath our feet.

Whenever we went on out-of-town trips, we took our bicycles. One of our favorite biking areas was the farm country near Middleburg, Virginia—a country of horse farms and seldom-travelled roads. During one trip, after biking all afternoon and evening, we drove back toward Washington, D.C. on a series of back roads. The countryside alternated between farm fields and woods. The windows of farmhouses glowed as night descended. As we passed through some woods and entered an open field surrounded by a ring of trees, a full, orange moon rose above the tree line to the east. We experienced a brief moment of awe, but before we could enjoy the beauty of the scene we were out of the field and into the next set of trees. We looked at each other.

"Did you see that?" I asked.

"So beautiful," said Elizabeth. "Was that real? Can we go back?"

I stopped the car, put the engine in reverse, and backed up until we had a full view of the moon. I parked along the edge of the road and turned off the engine. The moon was large and luminous. In the distant trees, on three sides of the field, sparkles of green phosphorescent light moved about, flickering off and on. Thousands of fireflies flitted about in the night, performing a ritual dance of courtship during their short season on earth. We stood on the side of the road, leaning our backs against the car, speechless in the orange glow of the moon. Elizabeth then reached into the car and pulled out her flute, which she took everywhere, as if it were a baby. She spun out a series of Debussy pieces: *Syrinx, Clair de Lune,* and the prelude to *Afternoon of a Faun*. The music twined around the rays of moonlight, floated across the field, filled the air with mystery and sonic beauty. After the final notes of Debussy drifted away, she paused and looked around. Her eyes gleamed in the moonlight. Then she began playing an Irish jig. I began to dance; we danced together in the night, beneath the moonlight, unaware of the world around us.

Car lights reflected diffusely off the leaves of distant trees, and we heard the hum of tires. Elizabeth lowered the flute, and we quickly walked back to the car. She set the flute on the front seat and I began adjusting the cords on the bike rack. The car pulled to a stop beside us. The driver rolled down a window.

"Anything wrong? Need some help?" asked a voice from inside the car.

"No, thank you," I said. "The bikes came loose. I'm just tightening them down. I appreciate it, though."

"Okay, have a good night."

"Thank you. Same to you!"

The car drove off. Elizabeth and I caught one another's eyes, then laughed. What an odd spectacle we would have made, two adults dancing in the road under the moonlight. She reached her arm out to me, beaming with a smile, inviting me to take her hand. We walked out into the field and lay together in the sweet-smelling grass, gazing at the moon and the fireflies. I don't remember how long we stayed in that field because time stood still. It seemed an eternity. *O God, how wondrous you are!* We felt God's love and, together, loved him back.

Slowly, through the country of sacramental marriage and the country of western Maryland and Virginia, the life of spirit grew strong.

After two years at CUA, I had completed most of my graduate coursework, but did not know for sure what area of religious studies I wanted to specialize in (my aversion to focusing on just one narrow spectrum of reality still impeded my path). Nor did I have a dissertation topic. Religion and Science? Too broad. Spiritual and

Psychological Development? Too broad. I took a one-year leave of absence in hopes I might gain some clarity about a dissertation topic, and found a job at the National Endowment for the Humanities (NEH), a federal agency that awarded grants to scholars in the humanities. The job served me well and later opened up many possible university administrative positions for me. And it afforded me time to think and write.

Elizabeth and I wanted to start a family, but not in Washington, D.C. In 1988, after having spent three years at the NEH, we moved to Spearfish, South Dakota, at the northern end of the Black Hills. I took an administrative job at Black Hills State College, a small public college with around 2,300 students.

Spearfish was a laid-back town with welcoming people. Townspeople greeted one another and strangers alike. When driving on a country road, a rancher driving a pickup truck from the opposite direction—a complete stranger—would wave with the "South Dakota wave," that consisted in raising the index finger off the steering wheel, pointed straight up, in greeting. One returned the wave with the same gesture. In Washington, D.C. drivers also frequently raised a finger, but a different one.

We felt at home in Spearfish right away and could not imagine ever leaving, in spite of the severe Dakota winters. Car batteries froze; cars would not start. At twenty below, your face and hands hurt when you go outside, no matter how well wrapped you are or how short the time. Cold penetrates everything. Car heaters needed about ten minutes to warm up. When townspeople went to the grocery store, they left their engines running in the parking lot, so that the car would be warm when they returned. The town was small and safe, so people didn't worry about their cars getting stolen. After living in Washington, D.C. for four years, where you dare not leave anything unlocked, this took some getting used to.

There was wide-open space around Spearfish: the Great Plains extended east and northward; the Black Hills to the south; and the rugged tablelands of Wyoming and Colorado stretched to the west and southwest. Country to explore. We made trips to Devil's Tower and the Bighorn Mountains in Wyoming; a two-week camping trip to Yellowstone and Grand Teton National Parks.

The Country of Sacramental Marriage

One evening we took a drive north of town to explore the country. On the side of the road we noticed a small, marshy area with colonies of red-winged and yellow-winged blackbirds flying to and fro among the tall marsh grass and cattails. We stopped to observe. The birds cawed defiantly at one another, flitted from one branch to another, bluffed and challenged one another over territory. We were on a desolate stretch of highway 85; no other cars passed by. Twenty miles to the southwest rose Crow Peak, the northernmost point of the Black Hills. To the south lay Terry Peak, rising over seven thousand feet above sea level—one of the highest mountain between the Rockies and the Pyrenees of Spain. Directly to our east, another twenty miles away stood Bear Butte, alone and isolated, a volcanic intrusion of igneous rock into the Great Plains. Bear Butte, unlike the Black Hills proper, was not covered with pine forests, but with low brush and prairie grasses. Only a few scattered pines had gotten a foothold.

The blackbirds continued to squawk and squabble over territory, making a great din. Even the din was a sort of music, absorbed by the atmosphere into a sassy serenity. The sun had set and night began to fall. We walked back toward the car, but before we got in we saw a bright orange glow on the side of Bear Butte.

"Look," said Elizabeth. "It looks like a fire."

"Maybe a brush fire on the side of the mountain," I said. I had seen brush fires in Nevada. The land there got so dry that the least spark or lightning flash could start a range fire that would burn hundreds of thousands of acres of sagebrush and cheatgrass. One year the fires came so close to Elko that we could walk to the edge of town and see Graystone Hill burning orange in the night. The orange glow on Bear Butte looked similar. We leaned with our backs against the car, watching the blaze. Then the orange glow grew larger.

"There aren't forests on the side of the mountain, are there?" I asked, puzzled. The glow was now too large to be a brush fire. Tall trees must be burning. But how could that be? There were too few trees to cause a forest fire. The glow increased in size again, and soon we noticed a defined curvature to the glow—not a fire, but the full moon rising over the horizon, big and orange. Bear Butte stood in a direct line between the moon and us. The world—this silent, serene world stretching out in all directions to the horizon—was suffused with glory. We stood in awe.

John Two Bears, the director of admissions at Black Hills State, invited me to join him on one of his recruiting tours of South Dakota Indian reservations: the Pine Ridge, Rosebud, and Crow Creek. I gladly joined him. John was a tall Yankton Sioux from the Crow Creek Reservation, a member of the Mdewakanton Band (People of Spirit Lake) of Sioux. John stood six-foot-six, with long black hair bound in a ponytail. He always wore blue jeans, a long-sleeved white shirt, and a bolo tie. He knew of my interest in Native American spirituality and gave me tips on books to read: James Welch's *Fools Crow,* Leslie Marmon Silko's *Ceremony,* John Niehart's *Black Elk Speaks,* and Frank Waters's *The Man Who Killed the Deer.* John was a painter in his spare time, influenced by the artist Oscar Howe, a famous Sioux painter from the same reservation as John. Elizabeth and I were admirers of Howe and had bought small reproductions of *The Wood Gatherer* and *Origin of the Sioux.*

Our first stop was Red Cloud Indian School on the Pine Ridge reservation, a school run by the Jesuits. Before meeting with students and parents, John stopped in a small chapel at the school. We both went in. John dipped his finger in the holy water at the entrance and made the sign of the cross before kneeling to pray. This surprised me. *He's Catholic?*

I asked him later if he had been raised Catholic. "No," he said. "Not until I went to St. Joseph Indian School in Chamberlain. Just like you, I'm not Catholic from birth."

"So," I asked, "do you still carry any of your Sioux spiritual traditions alongside Catholicism?

"Oh, sure," he said. "The Holy Spirit came to my people, too, even before Christianity came here. It reveals itself through our land, and in my people's sacred ceremonies. In fact, the word for *Life*—capital L—in some Indian languages means 'a breathing into.' You know where the word *spirit* comes from, right?"

"Yeah," I said. "From *breath.* God breathed into Adam and gave him life. After the resurrection, Jesus breathed on his disciples and they received the Holy Spirit."

After a pause, John said, "Oscar Howe was both Episcopalian and Sioux. He learned native culture and spirituality from his grandmother, and Christianity from his devout mother. He tried to harmonize both sets of beliefs and it shows in many of his paintings. In fact, if you want we can go see his *Indian Christ* behind the altar at St. Joseph chapel when we go to Crow Creek on Wednesday."

"Sounds great," I said.

I knew that the Black Hills were considered sacred ground for the Sioux and that it had been taken from them after prospectors discovered gold in the nineteenth century. I asked him what he thought of the sculpture being carved out of a mountain in memory of Crazy Horse, one of the great Sioux war chiefs who had fought and defeated George Armstrong Custer at the Battle of the Little Big Horn. The Crazy Horse monument was conceived by the late sculptor Korczak Ziolkowski to honor Native American leaders, as a kind of counter to Mount Rushmore's immortalization of white American leaders.

"I hate it," John said. "It's a desecration of our land. And the worst of it is, they'll never finish. It's a tourist trap, just like Mount Rushmore. Korzcak's descendants make their living off selling souvenirs and giving tours, so they have no motivation to complete it. They work at a snail's pace so it never gets finished."

Native American spirituality appealed to me. It taught the unity of earth and spirit, of the harmony of mankind and its unity with the spirit world. I was glad native cultures had begun to recover their traditions and religious rituals after having them all but wiped out by conquest and forced assimilation into American society. In fact, Oscar Howe had been taken from his family as a child and sent to an Indian school approved by the Bureau of Indian Affairs. He was not allowed to speak his native tongue nor learn his people's traditions and culture. Fortunately, because of a long illness, he had to leave the school and live with his grandmother for a long time. She taught him the beliefs and traditions of the Sioux, and he later integrated those traditions into his artwork, sometimes incorporating them into Christian themes.

Even so, I did not want to romanticize Sioux spirituality and culture. Elizabeth and I had observed some Lakota Sioux rituals at graduation ceremonies at Oglala Lakota College, and had been moved, but I had been called to a different religion. If I'd grown up in the Far East, I might have been called to Taoism. I loved Catholicism as one of the "Religions of the Book," and had settled into it as well as I could settle into anything: awkwardly and liminally, one foot in, one out. Like Judaism, it had foundational texts dating back over 3,800 years; lengthy commentaries and interpretations had been written on those texts; highly sophisticated theologies and forms of literature had emerged in an attempt to elucidate its meaning in new and varying contexts; rich and diverse spiritual paths had sprouted over the centuries to live out its teachings; and magnificent music and artwork had been created to capture—in sound and image—its central stories. I loved that tradition, in spite of its many and obvious flaws. Native religions, as rich as they might be, just didn't have that history or fecundity.

John Two Bears and I drove for three days over long and desolate highways between speaking and recruiting engagements. We skirted the western edge of the Badlands, the scenery as bleak as a lifeless planet from *The Twilight Zone*. We spent hours each day in the car, but I spoke little. On the second day, John said,

"You're sure a quiet man, Ken. You would have made a good Mountain Man."

Yes, I thought. I would have. From that point on, John began greeting me affectionately as "O quiet one." As in "Good morning, O quiet one," or "Have a good weekend, O quiet one." It fit. If I'd had an Indian name, that would be it: *Quiet One.*

Our short time in Spearfish was one of the happiest periods of our marriage. Our first child, Meghan, was born there in deep winter, December 1989. The temperature at night dropped to twenty-five below zero (fifty-seven degrees below freezing). During the day, it rose to around ten below. I had prepared to drive Elizabeth to the hospital at a moment's notice, except for one thing I hadn't known to prepare for: the effect of severe cold on the car's engine. We did not have an attached garage, so the car was exposed to the full force of the Dakota winter. Before bed, I ran the engine for ten minutes to warm it. I set my alarm clock for 2:00 a.m. each morning, then went out to warm it up again, fearing the battery would go dead and the engine wouldn't start. Many of the local residents used engine block heaters, but we were newcomers to this climate and didn't think—or know—to install one.

About four o'clock on the morning of December 20, Elizabeth awakened me. "It's time to go," she said. I had slept through the 2:00 alarm; I had hit the off instead of the snooze button. I rushed to get my winter clothes on.

"Are you sure? O, my god!"

I stumbled as I dressed, then rushed to start the car—I had to warm it up before Elizabeth got in. I turned the key. Urr... Urrrr..., it droned. I tried again. Its droning faded to a barely audible *whirr*. "Oh, shit!" I stepped on the accelerator a few times to force gas into the carburetor. Again, I turned the key. Urr... Urrrr... Vroom! It started. Thank God! I rushed back inside. Elizabeth had her handbag with a change of clothes and toiletries, ready to go.

When Meghan came into the world, she was covered with whitish goo, her head shriveled and wrinkled. She looked deformed. My mind quickly went back to my dissolute youth—had my genes mutated through drug use or venereal disease? Had my past sins caught up to me? *My daughter was deformed and misbegotten. God help us.* The doctor assured me that all babies come into the world covered with cheesy white slime. She was a strong and healthy girl.

We took Meghan home on a surreal night. The air sparkled with frozen ice crystals—a frozen, light fog. The wind howled. The sign on the local bank indicated it was twenty-nine degrees below zero. The wind chill drove it down to minus fifty.

When we arrived home, the house smelled of baked lasagna, hot in the oven, courtesy of a gracious friend. But the garlic! So much garlic! She must have used five cloves in the sauce. The house reeked. It whacked us when we entered. What would those stinging garlic molecules do to our daughter's fragile lungs? Suffocate her? Cause her to have seizures? O, God! I opened some windows. Freezing air rolled in like a Chinook wind. O, God! What will that cold air do to her? I closed the windows. Now what? God help us.

Our first child.

Elizabeth was hired at Black Hills State as an adjunct flute instructor, had a home studio with a passel of flute students, was an occasional guest performer with the Rapid City Symphony, and played in the local community band that performed in surrounding communities. Her favorite venue was the annual Fourth of July parade in nearby Deadwood. The parade consisted mainly of fire engines, ambulances, politicians in convertibles, a float or two, cowboys and sheriffs on horses, and the community band.

Elizabeth walked to the parade gathering spot as I took a place along the street among the crowd, waiting for the band to march by. As the parade began, I could hear music in the distance but couldn't see the band. The sound of Sousa's *Stars and Stripes Forever* grew louder, the high notes from Elizabeth's piccolo solo rising distinctly above the other instruments. Still, no band in sight. An old John Deere farm tractor passed, then the town mayor in a Mustang convertible, holding a bucket of candy that he tossed to the children. A large truck with Johnson Cattle Company signs on the doors rolled around the corner. Long horizontal slats, about eight inches apart, framed the bed of the truck. The musicians were within. Elizabeth caught sight of me in the crowd and called my name. She lowered the piccolo, waved through the slats, and shouted, "Wahoo!" She then belted out as deep a "Mooo," as she could. Her eyes and face beamed with happiness through the opening in the slats. "Moooo!" she called again. The cattle mooing caught on and some of the other musicians lowered their instruments and joined in. Others continued the Sousa piece.

At the parade's end, the Johnson Cattle Company truck pulled into a parking lot adjacent to an amphitheater at the edge of town. The cattle-musicians disembarked with their instruments and climbed on stage, where they performed more music. The amphitheater had no seating, so the audience members sat in their cars and pickup trucks, as if at a drive-in movie theater, windows rolled down. At the end of each piece they honked their horns in approval.

As we drove home that night, Elizabeth said, "God I love this place! It's like a little 1950s town. I never dreamed we'd live somewhere like this!"

On moonless nights, Elizabeth and I drove a few miles out of town on a dirt road, and sat on the hood of the car with our backs resting against the windshield. From there we gazed at the stars. South Dakota skies are clear and dry, like in Nevada, and the stars shine bright. Elizabeth had never really seen the Milky Way galaxy before. She had lived in cities on the East Coast all her life, and had never been to the dry climates of the west. We lay in the nighttime silence, transfixed. Occasionally we could hear the howl of a distant coyote, but nothing else. No din of traffic, no hum of motors, no buzz of electric lights. Just the night sky and us.

Elizabeth said, "Look how bright the stars are! I've never seen so many stars! Why don't we see as many in the East?"

"There's no city light here to compete with the starlight. And no humidity—no water particles in the air to absorb and filter out the light. There's nothing between us and the stars."

"What's that whitish cloud across the sky?"

"The Milky Way." Its four hundred million stars formed a continuous bright trail across the sky.

"Our galaxy! Wow!"

"The Shoshones call it the Trail of Ice Crystals."

"How can we see our own galaxy as if it were way out in space when we're inside it?"

"I don't know. I guess because we're at the edge of it, and the rest of it extends away from us."

We marveled at being two tiny creatures on a small planet that revolves around a smallish star at the outer edge of one small-sized galaxy that is but one of billions of galaxies hurtling through the cosmos. And it was *our* galaxy stretching across the sky; we were part of it. Our infinitesimally small bodies (by comparison) were made of galaxy dust, of stardust, of earth dust. Physicist Ani Aprahamian says "each constituent atom of our bodies has been processed through many generations of stars, numerous supernova explosions, or thermonuclear reactions in binary star systems or the interiors of massive stars before they were ejected into space and eventually condensed to form us." Those atoms had been processed and condensed right here in our solar system, on this planet, and here we were, under the night sky in South Dakota, looking back up at the stars.

Galaxy and star dust. Yet we are creatures of spirit, full of wonder at this immense cosmic spectacle, knowing that although we are but tiny specks in the great universe, the human mind is capable of knowing and understanding and loving it. The measure of our mind and spirit is equal to the measure of the cosmos. And we knew that something out there—something infinite—loved us back, immeasurably.

Even as I experienced this, Elizabeth by my side, I felt, somewhere deep inside, a restless spiritual eros. The galaxy dust that forms us is not inert. The urge of the cosmos has direction. Spirit inhabits the basic stuff of the universe and gives it a barely discernible tendency. The movement is neither random nor straight and clear. Like a ship that sets sail across the ocean, it may be blown off course, in one direction and then another. It may temporarily be forced backward. It zags and zigs its way across the water. If an observer from space looked at a brief period of its voyage, and contrasted its direction to the direction of another time period, he or she might conclude that the ship wanders aimlessly. Over time, though, viewed from a broad and long enough perspective, its overall direction emerges into view. Eventually, it crosses the ocean to a port. So it is with evolution: a seemingly aimless wandering that, over time, moves in a certain direction. So it was with my life, made of the dust of galaxies and stars and earth, each speck of dust containing a bit of the cosmic urge. My body enfleshed a myriad of monads from the stuff of the universe that vaguely remembers, through some ancient haze, a former wholeness, an ocean of Spirit, and my being trended with the cosmos toward it, restively. I intuitively knew that the Spirit was not done luring me, that my idiosyncratic and implausible calling had not yet been fulfilled. Sooner or later, the Spirit would summon me elsewhere.

For now, though, underneath the night sky, in the silence of a vast uninhabited space, we were at peace. Elizabeth spread her arms and hands out toward the sky, as if to encompass the whole of it, and asked, "How could anyone look up at these stars and not believe in God?"

14

A School of Love,
Patience, and Forgiveness

MY RELATIONSHIP with Elizabeth had almost ended a month prior to our wedding. That's when I told her about the herpes. We had driven to downtown Washington, D.C. We stopped so she could run into a store. "It won't take long," she said. "I'll be right back."

As I waited in the car, a suppressed memory rose, and I knew: *I have to tell her.* She has a right to know, had a right to know a long time ago.

I watched Elizabeth emerge through the sliding exit door and hurry back to the car. She stashed her purchase under the seat and fastened her seat belt.

"I have to tell you something," I said.

"Yeah? What?"

I hesitated a moment. "It's not good."

She unlatched her seatbelt and shifted to face me. "Well, what is it?"

I glanced down, then stared out the windshield, avoiding her expectant gaze while I figured out how to say it, tried to measure what the consequences might be, wondered why I was such a weird, private person, keeping everything inside. Not to mention an ass.

"Do you remember I told you I was pretty wild when I was young?"

"Yeah?" She said with an elongated diphthong that rose into a question.

"I should have told you this before," I said glumly, to prepare her.

"What *is* it? Just tell me."

"I caught genital herpes when I was young. It erupts now and then."

She paused. "Oh." She shifted in the seat, looked straight ahead. Silence.

"I'm really sorry. I should have told you a long time ago." Now I watched Elizabeth while she looked into the distance.

She pressed her bottom teeth against her top lip, shook her head affirmatively, almost imperceptibly. She paused again, then asked,

"How bad is it?"

"It erupts now and then. Maybe twice a year."

That was true. While married to Gloria, I had seldom experienced eruptions, and she never contracted the disease.

I had no idea where I'd caught the virus. Maybe at a brothel. Perhaps from María in Álamos, or from any number of easy-lay girls who came in and out of the parties my friends threw, girls whose names we never knew. Some who willingly pulled trains, as the saying went, one guy after another. We waited in line. Who knows what germs and viruses sloshed around inside a girl after such nights, or who deposited what, and who it got transmitted to. We were all easy lays, wallowing in life's mire.

Herpes never goes away. When it subsides, it's not dead; it just goes dormant, sleeps deep within the nerve cells until it rouses from slumber again and goes wild, forming blisters.

For several days, Elizabeth and I did not see each other, or speak. She needed time to process the information and make a decision.

I've never known for sure why she went ahead and married me. Had she been just a bit too weak to call it off? Or did the joy and love and hope we shared outweigh the disappointment and worry, enough to go through with it? Through the years, I've asked from time to time. She kind of stares into space, shrugs, and says, "I don't know. I loved you."

When Elizabeth and I married, I had not been sexually active for years. But on our honeymoon, flaming red blisters, many of them, burst forth. Burning, itching blisters. New ones appeared almost as soon as others subsided. Fifteen eruptions in eight months—the first eight months of our marriage. It seemed there was no end to them, until a new drug, acyclovir, came on the market. The drug doesn't kill herpes, but keeps it from rousing from slumber and infecting others. Now the virus sleeps in my nerve cells. Elizabeth has not caught it, or at least has had no symptoms. One family doctor, the one who delivered our third child, Diego, said there's no way the virus is not in her body, that her immune system must be strong enough to keep it in check. She has not gotten tested. Maybe she doesn't want to know.

That was our first deep wound, a wound always open and ready to enter any argument and assert itself. Not a one-time wound, inflicted then forgiven, but a forever wound that underlies and feeds many of the petty, one-time wounds couples inflict on one another over the years. From time to time, when we argued, when she lost her composure, she reminded me of it. A month before the wedding! Invitations had been sent, plans made, bridesmaid dresses bought and sized, a venue set.

Along with the harm I did Gloria and Kenito, not telling Elizabeth sooner about the herpes is the thing in life I regret most.

After leaving Spearfish, we moved to Frostburg, Maryland, where I took an administrative job at Frostburg State University. Our second daughter, Katie, was born there. She grew up with a quirky interest in words and their combinations. She wandered around the house saying "plaid nightgown," "National Geographic," "important documents." Later, "melodious banter" and "twisted hologram," that she worked into sentences and conversations with imaginary playmates. She wore clothes that clashed and socks that did not match. During pleasant days, her favorite pastime was to lay on a blanket in the back yard, draw pictures, write poems, and stare up at the trees. She loved thunderstorms, but cried when a violent storm snapped our silver maple tree in half. When we drove past an area where the city had cut down old trees to widen the street, she wept.

Our first son, Diego, was born two years after Katie. Later, after we moved to Indiana, two more children arrived, Mary and Michael. A rich natural and spiritual fruitfulness surrounded and infused our lives, and it was good. Our home was full, and the fullness absorbed the wounds, the disagreements, and the misunderstandings.

Elizabeth and I began incorporating spiritual practices into our family life. We prayed the Liturgy of the Hours—vespers—several nights a week, learning its arcane organizational structure as we went. The Liturgy of the Hours has been the prayer of the Christian faithful from ancient times to the present, celebrating and praising God each day, and fulfilling Christ's precept to pray without ceasing. Constant prayer is a common biblical theme: "In the morning I offer you my prayer"; "In the evening I will call on you"; "Late at night I will rise from sleep and thank you"; "Seven times a day I will praise your name." The Liturgy includes the antiphonal chanting of psalms, the Magnificat, the Canticle of Zechariah, the Our Father, and short readings from the Church Fathers. We gathered in the living room, four children, Elizabeth in the rocking chair with Michael in her lap, I in another rocker. Mary sat upright in the sofa, legs straight out, feet not quite reaching the front edge. The children jockeyed for positions, picky about who sat next to whom. Mary refused to sit next to Diego.

"He keeps poking me!" she protested.

Katie wouldn't sit next to him, either. "He's gross! He farted on my pillow this morning."

Diego, for his part, refused to sit next to Meghan. "She burps on purpose!"

After the pre-liturgical negotiations and shuffling of seats, we began the prayers and chants. The squabbling ceased.

We began going to Mass several mornings a week before I went to work at the university. We parked the mini-van across the street from church and unloaded the children. We carried Mary and Michael in our arms and made the others hold hands as we crossed Main Street. Traffic stopped for us at the pedestrian crosswalk. *Make Way for Ducklings.* On weekdays, we were the only non-grayhairs at church. The elderly worshippers huddled in the back pews. We claimed a pew near the middle.

We wanted our developing spiritual life to take root in our children. We prayed over one another before bed. The children grew to love these home rituals. When Elizabeth and I got overwhelmed with work and neglected the Liturgy of the Hours, the kids asked for them, or some other form of prayer. "Can we pray over each other tonight?" Diego sometimes asked. He liked the way we prayed, a hand of each of us on the head of one, offering spontaneous prayers as they came to mind.

Focused family time became sacred. We wanted our children to wonder and explore and experience the beauty of the world, to have the kind of spiritual awareness and nurture that we both had lacked as children. Our new religious tradition was no stranger to the world's wonder and beauty, as the Psalms proclaim: "The heavens show forth the glory of God and the firmament declares his handiwork." And St. Paul wrote, "The invisible things of God are clearly seen since the creation of the world, being understood by the things that are made."

We tried to point out God's beauty to the children.

We also wanted our children to have a defense and a guide against the encroaching secularism, neo-paganism, and anti-Christianity of the surrounding culture, a protection from the raw sewage that much of American culture now swam. They would encounter enough of it as they grew, but we wanted them to have at least a strong spiritual foundation and moral guideposts when they did.

We invited friends from church to our home on Sunday evenings to pray the Liturgy of the Hours, followed by a communal potluck dinner. People brought guitars and hammered dulcimers, and after the meal we had song-fests. We hosted parties and gatherings at our house: summer barbecues, Christmas parties, and baptism receptions, often through my initiative (that was something new!). Neither of us came from families that socialized, but Elizabeth was a natural. I had to feel my way into this new communal world.

When the children were young, I seldom went to the country alone. Our lives were as full as the household. God's presence came through marriage and children. I had once known the overwhelming grace of ecstasy in the wilderness; now I knew the subtle but powerful grace of an infant falling asleep on my shoulder. Elizabeth and I bought mom and pop rocking chairs at an antique store shortly after the children started arriving. Elizabeth rocked Meghan to sleep while I rocked Katie. She squirmed and wriggled on my shoulder. I rocked and sang lullabies. *Hush little baby, don't say a word, Papa's gonna buy you a mockingbird.*

The girls fussed and squawked some more. Elizabeth sang. *Hush-a-bye, don't you cry, go to sleep little baby.*

Eventually they let go, surrendered themselves, and sleep overtook them. In the same moment, grace overtook me. I surrendered. *And a baby when it's sleepin', has no cryin'.* I could barely hear and feel the breath of my sleeping child, so soft was it, like the easy unfolding of dusk into dawn within the soul.

Could anyone who'd experienced an infant falling asleep on his shoulder not know something of God?

As the children grew, we vacationed often at New Germany State Park in western Maryland, where we rented a cabin. The children swam in the lake, caught crawdads from under rocks in the stream, and learned to fish. I relaxed in a chair alongside Poplar Creek, near the log that Elizabeth and I had fallen from years earlier. I read the works of Wendell Berry, Annie Dillard, and Marilynne Robinson. I wrote. We hiked the trails together and we grew rich.

About a mile downstream from the cabins, a small, unnamed streamlet flows into Poplar Creek.

"Where does it come from?" asked Meghan.

"It must come from a spring up the mountain," I said. "There's no snow up there right now, so it has to come from a spring."

"Can we go see where it comes out of the ground?"

"Sure, let's hike up to find the source."

Katie, who loved words and trees and thunderstorms, waded in the streamlet, then asked. "Daddy, why doesn't it have a name?"

We left the trail and followed the streamlet. Up and up—straight up McAndrews Hill. We walked in the stream when the brush got so thick we couldn't walk alongside it. The stream was only ankle deep.

About half a mile up, we came to a fence separating state forest from private property. We climbed through and continued on, a few hundred yards more. We heard the din of machinery in the distance. The sound intensified as we ascended. We sloshed in the stream through some thick brush, then came into a broad clearing. The sound of machinery grated and groaned. Loggers were clear-cutting the forest: *all* the trees over many acres were down. Toppled trees covered and blocked the stream; we couldn't continue, couldn't make it to the source.

"Why are they cutting down trees, Daddy?" asked Katie, anxiously.

"For lumber," I said, "but they're doing it wrong. They should cut only every third tree, and leave the rest alone so that the forest will regenerate itself. With clear-cutting like this, scrub brush and bramble will grow thick and trees will have a hard time growing back." *Greedy, thoughtless bastards!* I thought.

I remembered a line from a Wendell Berry poem, "There are no unsacred places; / there are only sacred places / and places that have been desecrated." In that clear cut, loggers had desecrated a piece of the forest, thoughtlessly. Yes, *desecrated*, I thought. Nature is a bearer of Spirit and should be treated with respect. We are called to be good stewards of the earth, which is a gift and sacrament of God. But humans treat the earth as if it were just inert matter, of only utilitarian value, with no integral link to Spirit.

Katie held my hand as we descended the hill, tears in her eyes. *Why doesn't it have a name?* she had asked.

"From now on," I said, "we'll call this little stream Katie Creek." And we did.

Children have a way of changing and deepening one's views of life. I was already well aware of the sacramental dimension of the natural world. When our children were born, I gained a keen appreciation for the sacredness of human life. When one of the children moved in Elizabeth's womb, she took my hand and placed it on her belly, so I too could feel the baby kicking. I accompanied her to the clinic for ultrasounds: we saw a small baby on the computer screen, with arms, hands, and feet; a head with eyes, lips, and a nose; a chest with a rapidly beating heart. *My God,* I thought, *this is an entire human life, not fully developed yet, but entire.* This had a profound effect on me. Up to that point I had always been vaguely against abortion, but hadn't really given it much thought. After the births of my children, I knew from direct experience that the small lives growing in Elizabeth's womb were unique individuals, loved by God. They had not been just "globs of protoplasm," "fetuses," or "tissue." They were Meghan, Katie, Diego, Mary, and Michael—five irreplaceably unique children, full of vibrancy and spirit and mischief (and in one case, heartbreak).

As I watched the ultrasound screen, I thought, there have been so many tiny human beings—images of God—growing in their mothers' wombs who have been desecrated. The same mentality—a lost awareness of the integral link between nature and Spirit—characterizes both abortion and environmental degradation. *Why,* I wondered, *are environmentalists and pro-lifers not on the same side, working together to protect the sacredness of all life?*

Our marital fruitfulness produced five bright and beautiful children. Unfortunately, some of our genes did not mix well: three of our children—Meghan, Diego, and Mary—developed epilepsy. Diego's showed up first when he was three. The left side of his face went into spasm for thirty seconds. Meghan's showed up next, when she was twelve. She and Elizabeth were baking bread in the kitchen. Meghan suddenly lost her balance, fell sideways, and hit her forehead on a doorjamb. She seized up and her eyes rolled inside their sockets. Her limbs twitched and kicked. A grand mal seizure. We tried to awaken her, but the seizure continued. We called an ambulance.

Our youngest daughter, Mary, later developed the same condition as Meghan. Neither Elizabeth nor I had ever had seizures and there was no family history on either side. Some of our genetic material must have gotten tangled in transmission.

A School of Love, Patience, and Forgiveness

Diego's form of epilepsy was the mildest, and yet, he was the child who gave the most trouble. Elizabeth and I wondered if his early bout with epilepsy contributed to his behavior. Epilepsy, said the neurologist, is an "electrical storm in the brain." Chemicals that stimulate neuron activity run amok, become erratic, and over-whelm a portion of the brain. In other cases, chemicals that temper the stimulants are deficient. Balance is lost.

The electrical storm metaphor rang true.

Each night we read and sang to our children until they drifted off to sleep. But Diego couldn't get there; his brain churned on and on.

Midnight came: "I can't sleep; will you sing me more songs?" A child's endearing plea. I sang more songs.

1:00 a.m.: "Will you read me another story?" His brain would not shut down. On and on it whirred.

Diego impulsively destroyed the things he handled. He unraveled and ripped up cassette tapes, dozens of them. We had to lock the stereo cabinet. He tore pages out of books: reading books, school books, magazines. Elizabeth was disturbed. I tried to convince her that he was just being a boy. Elizabeth had no brothers with whom to compare. "You just don't understand boy energy," I said.

"Maybe," she said, "but there's something dark about his behavior sometimes." And that was true enough. He argued incessantly from the moment he awoke. *Wash your hands for dinner,* evoked an argument; *brush your teeth before bed,* yet another. Not just a child's normal whine or protest, but full-throttle argument. We couldn't reason with him. He always had a comeback, even as a child. There was indeed something dark.

While we were struggling with our difficult son, Meghan was approaching school age, with Katie close behind. There were two elementary schools in Frostburg, and we talked to other parents and assessed the quality of the schools. We met with teachers and princi-pals. The schools were decent, but mediocre. The local school sys-tem faced the same bureaucratic problems as all others. Our friends Richard and Maria LaRocca, who had both been public school teachers until Maria gave up her job to be a full-time mother, home-schooled their children and encouraged us to look into that. At first we were reticent: isn't homeschooling what Fundamentalists do? We eventually looked into it. We read several books by homeschooling parents: David Guterson's *Family Matters,* Nancy Wallace's *Better than School,* and David and Micki Colfax's *Homeschooling for Excellence.* The logic behind homeschooling was compelling, especially the ability to adapt the curriculum to the individual needs and abilities of each child. You can allow the children to follow their natural interests wherever they wanted to go, and fill in other topics around those interests. What finally clinched the deal for us was when the local school district bestowed its annual Teacher-of-the-Year award. The local news report noted the teacher's innovative methods, including taking students to Chi-Chi's restaurant during Mexican Culture Week, where they got to wear straw sombreros, were given free tortilla chips, and played the piñata. This, the award certificate noted, gave students a unique feel for a foreign culture.

We knew we could do better.

To meet our children's socialization needs, we joined other homeschool families for activities. The group we belonged to was a mixture of secular, Catholic, Unitarian, and New Age families, all dedicated to keeping our children out of the confinements and conformity of schools and educating them ourselves. A new phrase had arisen among some homeschoolers and "unschoolers": *free-range kids.* We liked and adopted it. We didn't want our children cooped up in schools, sitting at desks all day, governed by school bells and state-mandated lesson plans. We went on group camping trips and hikes, on joint field trips to museums, zoos, and nature parks. We organized quarterly music recitals. The children built birdhouses and doghouses from scratch as a team; they formed soccer and baseball teams and volunteered occasionally during the summers on an organic farm, the hub of a sustainable farming cooperative.

Homeschooling was easy during the children's early years: reading, writing, and arithmetic. And science. For arithmetic, all you need is a pencil, paper, and Cheerios, and later, multiplication and division tables. Read to children daily, and again before bed, until they develop a love for stories. Include poems and nursery rhymes so they develop an appreciation for rhythm and rhyme. Then you supply them with good books and let them read.

For science, grow one garden in the sun and another in the shade; part of it in topsoil, part in sandy soil. Water one garden well and the other ... not so well. Write down your methods, record your observations. Read about photosynthesis and transpiration. Stick an electrode in a potato and another in a lemon to see if one generates more electricity than the other. Go to museums of science and technology. Throw in some music lessons, dance lessons, and sports to develop the mind and body, and you've got a curriculum for the early grades. We were weakest at the more advanced math and sciences, so it would not have worked for us to homeschool into high school. We have never regretted educating our children at home. We believe it is the best environment for learning, at least up to a certain age.

We didn't have a rigid formula or plan for home education, nor a timeframe for how long we would homeschool each child. We made up curricula as we went and re-assessed each child's progress and needs year by year.

We liked Frostburg, liked the location. The town of 7,500 sits on the eastern flank of Big Savage Mountain in the Allegheny Mountains, surrounded by forests and farms. Frostburg State in the early 1990s had around 5,400 students. I had a spacious corner office on the fifth floor of the library with a view of the mountains, and I was valued by the senior administration. On two occasions, when other universities attempted to lure me away with job offers, Frostburg State made me attractive counter-offers. Yet, while working there, I experienced a bifurcation between spiritual life, on one hand, and the general intellectual life of the campus on the other. I worked well with the scientists and education faculty, but had an uneasy relationship with the humanities faculty, who knew of my Catholic beliefs. Postmodernism and political correctness, like on most secular campuses, were ascendant at Frostburg State in the 1990s. A kind of radical, politically correct madness dominated many departments, I thought, and infected the university in general. Traditional works of Western civilization—especially those of dead, white, male, Christians—were routinely disparaged. I was not politically conservative, but was not a doctrinaire liberal, either. Years earlier, I had found even the study of theology at Catholic University to be highly politically charged. It mirrored the conservative/liberal dichotomy of American culture. Even so, not long after we began homeschooling Meghan, I decided to complete my doctorate and re-applied for the doctoral program at Catholic University, primarily because it was the closest Catholic university. With my supervisor's blessing, I drove to Washington, D.C. one day a week for graduate seminars. I arose at 4:00 a.m. and drove to the capital, a thermos of coffee and a sandwich on the seat of the minivan, and returned to Frostburg in the evening.

I had homed in on a dissertation topic: the severance of spiritual and intellectual life in Catholic universities—how had it happened and what could be done about it? Was there *a viable theology of Catholic higher education adequate to the times?* I read widely on the topic, but found mostly fruitless debates over liberal vs. conservative takes on whether or not theologians had the right to dissent from official Church teachings—an important topic, to be sure—but not quite what interested me. I wanted to explore whether there was a theological basis for scholars to pursue the relation between their field of study—whatever it might be—and spiritual insight. I daydreamed of working at a Catholic university and *helping convert it back to the life of Spirit.* Grandiose vision? Yes, and it energized me.

After six years in Frostburg, a job opportunity arose at the University of Notre Dame in South Bend, Indiana. *Hmmm.* Notre Dame: a leading Catholic university. *Could that be a place for me?* South Bend, elevation 692 feet above sea level. Flatland. Cornfields. No vast horizons. *Hmmm.* Didn't sound like hospitable geography for a mountain man. I mulled it over. The timing wasn't good—I had only three more courses to complete at Catholic University. But I assumed—without confirming that it was so—that I could take the remaining courses at Notre Dame and transfer them to CUA.

I showed Elizabeth the job announcement to get her take on it. She read it, shrugged, and said, "Go for it."

A School of Love, Patience, and Forgiveness

I was a bit surprised. I'd expected resistance—I'd dragged her around the country enough, and she was tired of it. She wasn't unhappy in Frostburg. But she gave me the green light. Perhaps she hoped a change would alter Diego's behavior.

I was forty-five.

At Notre Dame, I was a mid-level administrator in the Institute for Scholarship in the Liberal Arts. Notre Dame was an emerging research university and a trend-setter among Catholic institutions. If I could have some influence there, I thought, perhaps my calling would come to fruition. But how? I was a shy, introverted man with a quiet demeanor, a helpful and kind disposition, but no skill at persuasion. I didn't even know how an organization with entrenched interests *could* be changed. I knew I had to do *something*, to see where the call took me, to do what I could, even if it came to naught. I didn't even have the doctorate yet, and had to discontinue the Ph.D. program at Catholic University. I could not commute to Washington, D.C. and my advisors were not willing to accept courses from Notre Dame. I didn't have the credentials to be even credible at Notre Dame, except in my administrative job.

I went on faith. What is faith but a moving forward with hope and trust that you're doing what you *must*, because summoned, even when it seems implausible. When the Spirit beckons, it gives you hope that the impossible *is* possible. You don't, however, get to carry out whatever project you like, as if it were a career choice. Sometimes you get goaded into a vocation against your preferences, to a task that you have no special talent for.

I remembered Fr. Leary's talks about Moses and Ezekiel, reluctant followers of God. The Lord, for example, had commanded Ezekiel to prophesy to the rebellious Israelites: get your lives in order, or else. And if the reluctant Ezekiel failed to deliver the message, well, he would be just as responsible for the ills that befell Israel as were the evil-doers. Then, after giving Ezekiel instructions on what to do, God said to him, "Go and shut yourself in your house. Son of man, you are about to be tied and bound, and unable to mix with other people. I am going to make your tongue stick to the roof of your mouth; you will be dumb, and no longer able to reprove them, for they are a tribe of rebels."

Ezekiel the introvert, locked within himself, unable to mingle well with people, not given the skills to articulate his vision, yet commanded to do so.

What's with God calling semi-autistic oddballs and inarticulate introverts to deliver messages? Had that call from the whirlwind and that primordial urge from galaxy dust really been leading me to *this? Why me, of all people?*

I bade my time at my new Notre Dame job, holding tightly to my calling and wondering if it would be fulfilled. Year after year, I waited for an opportunity to arise. Evangelical hope requires that we not despair; that we continue our work regardless of how futile it may seem; that we follow our calling no matter what the consequences. Man proposes, God disposes, said Thomas à Kempis. So, too, the author of Proverbs: "In his heart a man plans his course, but the Lord determines his steps" (Prov 16:9).

After five years in South Bend, I transferred into the doctoral program in Notre Dame's Department of Theology while still working full time and helping raise children. Notre Dame accepted most of the credits I'd earned at Catholic university, but stipulated that I complete six more courses. I took a course each semester and one each summer. After work, I joined the family for dinner, then went to the university library to do research. I woke up early and stayed up late to study and write research papers. I spent less time at home. Family prayer time fell away, gradually. Elizabeth supported my doctoral work, yet lamented the effects my virtual absence was having on the family. She was dismayed over the slide away from family cohesiveness that prayer life had given us, and she laid much of it at my feet.

"You need to be the leader of this family," she said. "We don't pray together anymore. You don't go to Mass as often. It teaches the kids it's not really important."

It was true. There was a contradiction in what I was doing: while studying theology I neglected the commandment to pray—though I did consider study a form of prayer, but that form, unfortunately, did not convey to the children.

"I know, I know." I'd say, "But I'm doing what God's calling me to do. I have something important to say and hardly anyone else is saying it. I don't *want* to be doing this—I'd rather be writing literature or fishing or building a summer cabin in the woods—but I have to," I said. "It's not as if I were drinking away my paycheck and falling into an alcoholic stupor every night. I'm here at home almost all the time when I'm not working. I'm a good provider!"

That was true, but my words angered Elizabeth; she knew my references to drinking away the paychecks and alcoholic stupors was an unsubtle reference to her father. A cheap shot.

Then there was Diego: the other reason contributing to the fraying of family cohesiveness. He was a difficult child, and the trouble was constant. We had sent him to school in third grade because he disrupted the family so much that Elizabeth couldn't homeschool Mary and Michael. His behavior didn't improve in a school setting; he was always in trouble. He stole from classmates, lit matches and burned paper in the back hallways, and fought with other boys. He sassed his teachers. Most of my free time and extra energy—what little I had left over from work and doctoral studies—went into dealing with him, and it stole time from the family as a whole.

15

Diego and Our Lady
of the Wilderness

I OFTEN wonder what will become of my son, Diego, and if someday the two of us will meet as friends. So many things went
wrong, and the causes will always be in dispute between us.
Diego's and my accounts of incidents diverge dramatically. If he
read this memoir, he would call it a lie. No, he would say it's
bullshit. If in a charitable mood, he might call it fiction. But this is
how the events have congealed in my memory during this, the final
season of my life. As I age and my memory fades, events that
occurred separately sometimes fuse with one another. If I've not
remembered each detail precisely, I'm convinced the overall por-
trayal is accurate.

I lost count of the times I wanted to throw Diego out of the
house; lost track of the times I wanted to see the back of him, to be
free of the emotional storms that raged daily, free of the lies, the
stealing, the way he dragged down the family and drained the sap
from us. I even considered committing him to a state institution.
But I hesitated, clinging stubbornly to the hope things might
improve.

Diego had been a beloved first son, playful, bright, and gregari-
ous: a greeter of strangers in restaurants, in church, and on side-
walks in neighborhoods both familiar and unknown; he reached up
to be held, climbed onto people's laps, often to our dismay. He
lacked inhibition. At the age of three he ran onto a soccer field
amidst a swarm of ten-year-olds and kicked the ball as it rolled
toward our sideline. And more: he ran after the ball into the melee
of boys converging on it, oblivious to danger or impropriety. I

remember how the sunlight filtered through wisps of his sandy-brown hair, and the joyous look on his soft face. The refs had to stop the game. I carried him off the field over my shoulder, unable to suppress a smile, though I wanted to be stern. He was both charming and mischievous. Yet he was not like other children, not by a long shot.

Perhaps we were too permissive, or too strict, as parents. Maybe Diego needed more discipline or, instead, an expanse of wild country to grow into, a place that could absorb the wounds he inflicted. We tried counseling, alternative schools, medications, appeal to his reason, and half a dozen books on how to handle "the difficult child." And, every summer from the time Diego was nine, I took him on trips to the country, to the forests and mountains, hoping the outdoor experience and close interaction might help me reach him, help find a way to channel his dark energies. Elizabeth encouraged these trips. Perhaps experience of the wild would enkindle a flame able to leap across dormant synapses in Diego's brain and turn his darkness to light. Just as it had for me years earlier. The astute questions he occasionally asked suggested something might be fermenting in his mind.

"Why do so many Catholic churches and colleges named after Saint Mary have lakes and mountains or streams in their name?"

We had just gotten out of Mass at Saint Mary's-on-the-Highlands Church in western Maryland and were about to drive to New Germany State Park where we had rented a cabin for two weeks—one of our excursions into the natural world. Diego was then twelve years old. His sandy-colored hair had turned brown but his face retained its boyish softness. He wore a T-shirt and long, baggy shorts that hung sloppily to half way down the shin—shorts designed to make boys look stupid. I hated those shorts, but had given up trying to persuade him not to wear them.

"Probably because they're built near lakes and mountains or valleys," I said.

"No, that can't be why!" he protested immediately. "Everything's built near *something*, but other churches and colleges with saint names don't have lakes and mountains in them! How come?" The tone of his voice told me that he was in a mood for argument. *Some churches might,* I started to say, but realized he had a point. Many Catholic colleges bear the names of saints, but I couldn't think of any that had a natural feature attached to its name. If it did the sound of it wouldn't ring true. But the association of St. Mary and nature seemed, well, natural—so much so that it didn't seem remarkable.

The question lingered. Why *do* Catholic institutions so often attach a natural feature to Mary's name? I had never thought about this question, even in relation to my own employer, whose official name is the University of Notre Dame du Lac—Our Lady of the Lake. There is a Mount Saint Mary's College, a College of Saint Mary-of-the-Woods, and a Saint Mary of the Lake Seminary. There are a number of Marymount colleges throughout the country. The Florida Institute of Technology has a resident hall for Catholic students named Mary Star of the Sea. There are parishes, too: St. Mary's-in-the-Valley, Our Lady of the Harbor, and St. Mary's-on-the Highlands, from where we had just come.

Mary and nature. What's the connection? I mulled over Diego's perceptive question. Mary, through whom infinite, divine power was born into human measure, paired with the raw power of nature, of wilderness—serene, awe-inspiring, and sometimes deadly. As I had learned as a boy.

At age eleven, I joined twenty other Boy Scouts on a backpacking trip up a narrow, glacier-scoured valley in the Ruby Mountains of northeastern Nevada to fish in the stream coursing through the high mountain meadows and to camp overnight. The trail was rugged and the oxygen grew thinner as we climbed, so we stopped frequently to catch our breath. Half a mile before reaching the meadows, the valley narrowed to a thirty-foot wide flume carved out of solid granite. The water below rushed violently. Forest rangers had carved a trail in the slope above the flume, but we had to cross cautiously.

Once we reached the meadows, our muscle fatigue dissipated. The July snow, not far above us, fed the stream that meandered through the meadow. Above the brush and tree line rose the solid rock formations of the mountain peaks, jagged and imposing. Wind and snow had eroded the face of the rocks, leaving rock debris and boulders along the steeper slopes. We explored the glacial moraines, fished in the stream, and slept under the stars. The glory of nature abounded.

The second day opened out to a splendid morning, cool and fresh. Dew covered the grass and the sky was a deep blue—not a trace of cloud. We fished up some breakfast and pan-fried it over the fire. Around noon the scoutmasters returned to the main camp with a group of ten scouts, leaving the rest of us under the charge of Byron Perry, an Eagle Scout. Byron was a resident of the state boy's reform school, the state prison for juvenile offenders. We knew he had some kind of criminal record, but we liked and trusted him; he had a calm presence.

About mid-afternoon the sky suddenly grew dark and fierce. Lightning flashed and thunder clapped simultaneously. The clouds opened and rain poured in sheets. The stream rose rapidly, overflowing its banks and turning the meadow into a lake within minutes. As we gathered our soaked gear, we heard shouts from boys on the opposite side of the stream; they were trapped by the flood waters. Byron acted quickly; he tied one end of a rope through the handle hole of a cast-iron frying pan and the other end to the lower branch of a tree, six-feet high. He hurled the pan side-armed, Frisbee style, to the scouts on the other side. "Tie the rope tight to that tree, just above the first branch," he yelled. "Then grab the rope with both hands and work your way over." They did so, one at a time. The rope bowed with their weight. A younger scout lost his grip, fell into the current, and was swept away. He flailed wildly. There was little time to react. *What could we do?* Byron didn't hesitate; he sloshed through the water, dove in, struggled against the current, and pulled the boy to safety.

The trail had been washed out, so we descended the mountain cautiously, Byron in the lead. Then the rain turned into hail the size of golf balls, falling furiously. Having no shelter, we walked on, covering our heads with backpacks while our bodies were pummeled. The ground was slippery with mud and ice. Large boulders from the mountainside had lost their moorings and tumbled down into the lake. One crashed against another boulder no more than twenty feet from us. We were in the path of the boulders, so we had to keep moving.

When we arrived at the flume, only a muddy, icy slope straight down to the granite walls and raging water remained. Hail stones jutted out from the mud like the tops of small ice-cream cones. *What now?* Byron tied three ropes together, tightly, one end around his waist, the other around a tree. He unfolded his spade and began digging a new trail across the slope—thirty yards until he reached flat ground. There he tied the rope around a boulder that rested on flat ground, pulled it taut to about four feet above the ground, and yelled. "You guys grab the rope and cross over one at a time. Hold on tight and keep your feet planted on the trail. Be careful! It's slippery." We crossed over one by one, clutching the rope.

Thank God for Byron Perry's smarts.

As we slowly descended the mountain I wondered, in the inchoate way an eleven-year-old does, how utter beauty and serenity can co-exist in a continuum with unrestrained power and violence.

How does one prepare for such unbridled power?

Nothing had prepared Elizabeth and me for the tempestuous and ungovernable storms that came daily from Diego. He was always in trouble at our parish school: he fought with other boys, stole pens and money from their backpacks, and told lies. He was expelled, then fared no better at public school. We tried military school, hoping strict discipline might make a difference. Week after week his barracks leader called with increasingly frustrated updates on his behavior. Diego accumulated so many demerits in one month that it would take years of good works to wipe them away. After seven weeks, they kicked him out.

Diego stole habitually: from my wallet; from his mother's purse; from his best friend, Andrew Riley. Andrew had invited him for a sleepover one Saturday night. The next day Andrew's mother called, with hesitation in her voice, to tell Elizabeth that Andrew's wallet, with fifty dollars in it, was missing. She had seen the wallet at their house the day before, when Diego was there. We asked Diego if he knew anything about it. "No," he said.

Later that afternoon, Elizabeth found a beige canvas wallet under the couch, empty. It did not belong to us. She called Mrs. Riley and described the wallet. It was Andrew's. When we confronted Diego, he denied it vehemently, saying Andrew must have left it the last time he was over. But Andrew had not been at our house for at least two weeks. No way it got here unless Diego brought it. We searched his room for the money, but could not find it. Elizabeth later returned the wallet to the Riley's house, with fifty dollars from our savings.

"Can you imagine how embarrassing that was?" she said. I knew her shame. I had returned stolen baseball mitts and knives to the homes of other boys. I had returned measuring weights filched from the school science classroom. Diego didn't own up to any of it.

His charm and affability wrestled with his defiance, compulsiveness, and dishonesty, and always lost. He bullied, manipulated others, and argued incessantly. Each day we awaited the storms, and they came, relentlessly.

There were hopeful moments, too, like when he built a dollhouse for his younger sister Mary. The pieces for the house came in a kit from Norway. It had hundreds of interconnecting pieces—over 700—with instructions translated poorly into English. The house had two stories, multiple rooms, balconies, and staircases—a complex design. Diego spent hours at a time, over several weeks, assembling it—a work of love that he presented to Mary at Christmas. He was then ten.

Seeing his pleasure in woodwork, we bought him a set of woodworking tools and enrolled him in a local class. He surprised me one day with a walking stick made from a fallen branch of our maple tree. He had engraved my name into it and carved a spiraling helix from top to bottom. At the top he chiseled a primitive face with sunrays flaming out from it. He highlighted the grain with wood stain and finished it with two coats of polyurethane. I propped it against the desk in my study, pleased with his gift. It was a bit too thick and heavy for a walking stick, but I used it whenever I took him to the country.

Mostly, though, he made bats and mallets to bash and break things with, indoors and out. Indoors, to smash light bulbs, toys, and stored-away Corelle ware, leaving debris throughout our basement; outdoors, to whack downspouts and fence panels, or to smash insects. And animals. One evening when I returned from work, he greeted me at the door, excited.

"Dad, I killed a raccoon with my bat!" Elated, he took me out to show me. A baby raccoon lay dead on the ground. We had seen a sow around our back yard in recent weeks, followed by five kits. This one must have become separated from the mother. Diego looked up at me, eyes bright, looking for approval. Elizabeth came out to the yard, agitated.

"He just beat and beat that poor thing," she said. "I asked him to stop, but he just kept doing it. Now he's so proud of himself. It's just sick!"

"It's just a dumb animal, Mom," Diego yelled. "What's sick about that?"

Elizabeth looked to me for backup.

I hesitated for a moment, remembering the times my brothers and I prowled the outskirts of town with BB guns, shooting birds and squirrels; and the times my high school buddies and I shot groundhogs along the railroad embankment outside town. The groundhogs basked in the late afternoon sun just outside their burrows; mile after mile of them. Fat, easy targets. We picked them off one-by-one with our .22 rifles; watched them squirm and flail uselessly before they died; then moved on to the next ones. Did Diego's heartless killing of the baby raccoon differ in kind from what my friends and I did? Not in the results (dead animals); not in experiencing the fun of it; not in the callousness. Yet, there was a qualitative difference that I could not then put my finger on. A dark energy resided inside him.

"Diego," I said, "it's cruel. It was a baby."

"That's bullshit!" he said, and stormed into the house, furious for not getting a positive, or at least neutral, reaction from me.

Diego's counselors and psychiatrists used a number of labels to categorize his condition: oppositional defiance disorder; conduct disorder; attention deficit disorder, and—a word almost whispered to Elizabeth and me by one psychiatrist—psychopathy. *Psychopathy!* The word lingered in the air, the susurration of the first and last syllables trying to soften the harsh accent on the second, without success: sī-Kó-pa-thē. The meaning filtered slowly into our minds, then locked in. We looked at each other as a deep and formless sorrow descended.

"We don't use that term for children under eighteen," said the psychiatrist. "We call it 'conduct disorder,' but most of the symptoms are the same. Unfortunately, there's no cure."

"No wonder I'm afraid to have him in the house sometimes," said Elizabeth.

"There might come a time when you have to turn him over to the state," said the psychiatrist. "We can prescribe medications to help modulate his moods, but there's no guarantee they'll work. So far, they haven't."

Turn him over to the state? No way.

Yet, the idea did have a certain appeal.

Later, we looked up the symptoms of psychopathy in the *Diagnostic and Statistical Manual of Mental Disorders*: habitual lying; lack of remorse or guilt; habitual stealing; grandiose sense of self-worth; manipulative of others; glibness and superficial charm; failure to accept responsibility for one's own actions; impulsive; constant need for stimulation; cruelty to animals; emotionally shallow; lack of empathy. It was as if the authors had lived with Diego for two years, then wrote their list of symptoms.

Psychopathy is a loaded word, charged with undertones that suggest cold-bloodedness. Not all people with these traits, however, become killers; many become factory supervisors, drill sergeants, managers. They come from all walks of life. Still, the diagnosis unsettled us.

Diego was eleven the first time we called the police to our house. The bullying and arguing started before I arrived home from work. I entered a tense and charged atmosphere, Elizabeth distraught and near tears. Diego was bickering with his sister Mary over use of the computer, demanding first dibs, and pushed her away from it. Shouting and arguing ensued. I separated them and told Diego to go to his room.

"This is none of your business!" he yelled defiantly, "so butt out!" I knew from experience how this would go. I stood between him and Mary, and pointed to his room. *Go.*

"This is bullshit!" he shouted. As he walked away he mumbled, just loud enough for me to hear, "you worthless piece of shit." He always had a match ready to light the short fuse to my own reservoir of anger. He used it. *How dare you talk to me like that!* In silence I counted to ten, then twenty, trying to control my urge to slap his face. On other occasions I had not, and regretted it. This time I held back.

Storm clouds steadily darkened, Diego's wilderness a seething, humid jungle. Creatures stalked in the night; snakes slithered up trees in search of bird nests; panthers lurked in the brush, eyes glowing in the dark. I lost track of the disruptions, the number of times Elizabeth or I said "Stop it!," "Leave them alone!," or "Give it back." Whenever Diego walked into a room, screaming and recriminations ensued.

I'd had enough. Again I sent him to his room, but he refused. I took his upper left arm in my hands and walked him to his bedroom, as I had done many times. He resisted. These power struggles seldom ended well. He squirmed and pulled loose from my grip; said he was going back into the living room. I blocked the doorway. *No you're not!* He tried to squeeze past me. I barred his way. He lowered his right shoulder and thrust it into my ribs, pushing and screaming, *I hate you.* I could barely constrain him. He stepped back, then lunged forward with his shoulder to my midsection. Several times. On the third lunge I side-stepped, used his momentum to get him off balance, and pulled him to the floor where I pinned him down. He struggled, pushed, and kicked. Then struggled some more, maniacally, his face deeply reddened. *I hate you!*

Elizabeth called the police. The officer ordered Diego to sit on the couch, and gave him the options. "When you have your own house, you can do what you want; while you live in your parents' house, you live under their rules. Or you can go with me to the Juvenile

Justice Center and spend a couple of nights there. And believe me, it's not a place you want to be."

"Well, their rules are stupid!" said Diego. "And just because you're a cop doesn't mean you get to come in here and boss me around."

I didn't catch the policeman's exact words as he moved closer and stood over Diego, thumbs in his belt, speaking firmly. My thoughts strayed. Why *not* let the police take him away? We had not known peace in the house for years. Why not turn him over to the custody of Child Services? Let them send him to a foster home or a juvenile center. Sure, he'd end up angry and bitter and vengeful. So what? He was headed there, anyway, unstoppable. I imagined our home without him: no need to confiscate hunting knives and switchblades that he snuck into the house; no anxious fear when he prowled the house late at night when everyone else was in bed, searching for who knows what to destroy; no more finding remains of dolls dismembered, hammers with their handle broken off, ping pong balls crushed, CDs gouged with screwdrivers and strewn about. No more little piles of ashes; always ashes—the remains of burnt paper. He was a caged tiger, pacing restlessly, darkly. *What had gone wrong?* Perhaps key neurons in his brain were unable to connect, preventing him from feeling empathy or remorse. Perhaps I should never have lost my temper with him. Had I made the psychopathy darker, his moods angrier? My mind wandered back to my own childhood.

I am awakened at 3:00 in the morning to shouting and arguing in the hallway outside the bedrooms. I throw off the blankets, jump up, and open the door. My father is hitting my mother, pulling her hair, slapping her. She tries to defend herself. My brothers and sisters watch in horror. I force my way between my parents and try to push my father away. I yell at him, call him a jerk. Anger flares in his eyes and a sharp slap stings my face. More shouting. More arguing. More slapping.

A single memory of an oft-repeated event, one that haunted my dreams for decades. A dark violence lurked inside my father, just under the surface. I possessed it, too. Diego's in-my-face lies and defiance drew it out, on several occasions. He too felt that harsh slap to the face. I had walked him to his room, gripping his arm tight, threw him on his bed, and spanked him. Later I felt remorse and apologized, but some things cannot be undone. James Baldwin said, "when one slaps one's child in anger, the recoil in the heart reverberates through heaven and becomes part of the pain of the universe." He was right, and the recoil affects both father and son. *Yet, our other children weren't like Diego,* I reasoned, partly in self-justification, partly as undeniable fact. I had never been provoked to strike them. The reverse of Baldwin's point was also true: when a defiant child curses his parents and shows utter disrespect, that too, cuts a wound in the world. The universe could easily absorb our cuts, but Diego and I sometimes brought hell a little closer.

I remembered the many times Elizabeth had voiced her fear of going to sleep while he prowled the house and rummaged in the basement, afraid of what he might do. It would be good to live without that fear. Yes, the idea of sending him away had appeal. We had already filed two Ungovernable Child Complaints with the Juvenile Justice Center, just to have them on record. Just in case.

Absorbed in these thoughts, I didn't grasp what the policeman was asking me.

"Sir? Excuse me, sir."

Elizabeth stood nearby. Diego sat on the couch, sulking. I looked at the policeman.

"Do you want us to take him to the Juvenile Justice Center? You'll have to file delinquency charges."

Elizabeth and I exchanged glances.

"No," I said. "Thank you for coming, though. We're grateful."

We couldn't do it.

Half an hour after leaving St. Mary's-on-the-Highlands church, Diego and I arrived at New Germany State Park. Our plan was to hike the upper trail through the park, cross over McAndrews Hill, then descend to the Savage River. There we would rent a canoe and paddle to the Savage River reservoir, where we planned to fish and camp overnight on the shore. It was a three-and-a-half-mile hike to the boat rental. We found a walking stick for Diego—I'd brought the one he had carved for me—and started down the trail from the ranger station, our backpacks loaded. At the trailhead the rangers had posted a caution sign—Black Bear Warning!—followed by advice on what to do if you encountered one in the woods: back away; give it plenty of room; if it is close, talk to it in a calm but assertive voice; stay calm and don't run away—a bear can out-run you; remain in an upright position; avoid direct eye contact as it may perceive this as a threat; if it charges, don't run—it may be bluffing; back away slowly.

"Are there really bears here, Dad?" Diego asked.

"Some, yeah," I answered. "They were driven out of Maryland by the early twentieth century, but they're starting to come back. State laws protect them now. I've hiked the trails here for years and never seen one. We'll be fine."

"Could anyone really follow that advice on the sign?" he asked. "I mean, *come on!*" Then, after a pause, "Will you buy me a gun, Dad?"

"No. You don't need a gun."

We followed the trail along Poplar Creek for a mile or so, then took the upper trail that ascended McAndrews Hill by way of a series of cutbacks. From there it dipped into the Savage River drainage. The upper trail was seldom used, so the grass grew shin high. An occasional fallen tree obstructed the path. The rangers had not yet cleared them, and probably wouldn't until winter and cross-country skiers arrived. We high-stepped over or sidestepped around the trunks.

Diego did not say much. He wanted to be back at the lake where he could swim, fish, and catch crawdads from under the rocks in the stream below the dam. Something less boring than hiking. I hoped the forest and mountains might awaken something in him. A sense of awe, perhaps. Something profound that might shake up and rearrange the configuration of neurons in his brain. Something that would make the psychopathy go away.

We veered off the grassy path and hiked straight toward the top, avoiding the cutbacks. We ascended slowly and steadily, passing through groves of maple, birch, oak, and poplar. We skirted around the area near upper Katie Creek that had been clear-cut years earlier. Ugly scrub-growth and brambles choked the trees and made it nearly impassable. Once around the clear-cut, we entered dense woods again, with occasional openings populated by ferns. There was a slight breeze that gently swayed the tops of the trees. Some of the branches creaked and groaned, the only sound other than our footsteps and an occasional birdcall.

We had hiked at least two miles when we saw it. A black bear crossed our path about thirty yards in front of us, traveling on a course roughly perpendicular to our own. Its large shoulders and forearms had a ponderous yet elegant grace and power. I flung out my arm to stop Diego. We froze. As bears go, black bears are on the smaller side, but this one was nearly 300 pounds—large, but *too small to be a male*, I thought, and that was quickly confirmed when two bear cubs scrambled from a grove of trees not more than fifteen feet from us. The cubs raised their noses high in the air, then to the ground, sniffing about while waddling on their still awkward feet, trying to keep up with their mother.

A few lines from the rangers' notice raced through my mind. *Don't run. Back away slowly. Speak in an assertive but calm voice.* The rangers' advice did no good; there wasn't time. The she-bear turned her head and saw us. She didn't freeze, didn't stop to look. She *woofed*, pivoted on her haunches, and charged.

"Let's get out of here!" I shouted. "Drop your pack and follow me."

Diego didn't hesitate. We ran together down the hill toward the stream, jumping over fallen logs, weaving in and out of trees. My heart tripled its pace in no time; quadrupled. I heard the she-bear's heavy feet crashing through brush, in pursuit. As I ran I remembered what a Newmont geologist once told me to do if a bear charges while you are hunting. Position yourself on one knee, aim your rifle, not at the head (the bullet will likely glance off the thick skull), but under the throat, hoping to hit its heart. If that doesn't work, shoot straight into its mouth as many times as you can. If it continues to charge and reaches you, shove the barrel of the rifle down its throat so it can't bite, at least not right away. With luck, it may die before it paws the rifle out and mauls you.

This memory rushed through my mind in two seconds. Now, the only weapons we had were these five-foot long walking sticks. More seconds passed. We ran. *O, God, this can't be happening!*

"Stay with me!" I shouted, unnecessarily. Diego didn't fall behind; he kept apace. *Thank God.*

How many seconds had passed? Ten? Twenty? I didn't know. Was time passing? Or were we running fast enough to overtake eternity? I didn't know. Nor did I know how we got down the hill so fast. We seemed to be flying, two separate wings, moving without anything connecting us but fear. The bear gained ground. We heard her heavy footpads on the earth, the snapping of twigs. We reached the stream, shallow enough for us to run across. On the other side we entered woods again. Several seconds later, her paws splashed through the water.

She neared, a harsh *woof* in each breath. *We're done for.* Bears can run up to thirty miles an hour and we were over a mile from the ranger station.

"When it catches up to us," I said breathlessly, "I'll distract it. You run 'til you get to the ranger station!" I had no idea what I'd do. Perhaps I could jam the walking stick Diego had carved down its throat. It was sturdy and would not splinter. I'd stop when the bear was twenty feet away, turn, place my right palm on the thick end of the stick, hold the middle with my left arm extended, rush two paces and thrust it into its open mouth. Could I maintain the presence of mind to do that? If so, would it do any good? Perhaps startle and disorient it just enough to make it back off? Or would it make the bear even angrier? If the latter, would it maul me with more rather than less savagery? Three more seconds flashed by. We ran.

"Zig-zag with me through the trees!" I said. We made a sharp left, dashed a dozen paces, then made a hard right, zig-zagging from one clump of trees to another. This helped a bit; we could make sharper turns than she, creating, for a few moments, a bit more distance between us. Then I saw a small cluster of young birch trees growing close together in a jagged line, seven or eight of them, struggling with one another in an opening where sunlight shone through the forest canopy. There was just enough space between them for us to squeeze through and get them between us and the she-bear. She'd be too large to press through them, or so I prayed.

"Head to those trees," I said, "and get to the other side!"

O, God, let us get there! We ran. My heart pounded in my ears.

Diego and Our Lady of the Wilderness

Then we were there. We squeezed through. The bear arrived five seconds later. She stopped at the tree line, poked her head through. We backed out of reach, our walking sticks pointed toward her. She swatted the ground with her right paw; stood up against a tree, pushed on it, and *woofed*. Those were bluffing gestures, designed to threaten and scare. Maybe she wouldn't really attack. She was so close we could see the yellow of her teeth near the black gums. We could smell her hot, rank breath. She backed off and lumbered to the end of the jagged line of trees, then came around to our side. We slipped back through the trees. Diego jabbed his walking stick in her face as she poked her head through. He was grinning. I smiled at his bravado, half-approvingly. *The kid's got balls.* But the poking enraged the she-bear. She turned and scrambled down the line of trees, and back around to us. My approval went into reverse: *Why is he pissing her off even more? Idiot!* We squeezed back through to the other side. I breathed easier. We were safe. We could do this all day, until she tired of it. She'd have to get back to her cubs, sooner or later.

She prowled around the birch trees four or five times as we slipped back and forth, studying her movements. God, she was frightful, and so grand. And lovely with a mother's fierce determination to protect her cubs, a love that might destroy us.

"This is cool, Dad," said Diego. He wanted to jab at her some more. "Wouldn't it be great if we had a gun?"

"Stop taunting her with that damn stick!"

"Can we bring a gun next time we come here?"

"No." No way I'd buy him a gun. No telling what he'd do with it when his inner storms hit. At that moment he reminded me of the obsessed hunters in Faulkner's *The Bear,* unable to appreciate the grandeur of a magnificent creature and the wildness it represented, wishing only to kill it.

After about ten minutes of lurking, the she-bear trudged off to find her cubs. She stopped and turned occasionally to see if we'd left the cluster of trees. We waited around another ten minutes, staying close to the trees, watching intently in case she made a stealthy return. There was no movement anywhere, so we took off, crossed the stream to the main trail, and ran back to the ranger station.

We did not hike any more that day. Instead, we went for an early dinner at a nearby lakeside restaurant. We talked animatedly throughout the meal, reliving the bear encounter in every detail as each of us experienced it.

"Remember that fallen pine tree with the dead branches sticking out? I thought we'd get impaled. But it felt like we flew right over it in slow motion."

"Yeah! Did you see when I slipped on that rock in the stream and almost fell? I don't know how I kept my balance."

"Did you smell her breath? Whew! Imagine being a male bear kissing those lips. That's what happens when you don't brush your teeth."

"You sound like Mom."

As we got ready to leave and I paid the check, Diego said, "Thanks for bringing me here, Dad. This was an awesome day." The words came out true, in a way I couldn't remember hearing before, the sound of them golden.

"It was awesome alright. Maybe we won't hike that same trail tomorrow, though, eh?"

"Okay. Can we go biking on the old C&O Canal?"

"Sure. That'll be fun. I'm going to the restroom. I'll meet you at the front door."

When I returned, Diego was sitting on a bench in the waiting area, staring vacantly at the floor about seven feet in front of him. His posture reminded me of the night the policeman sat him on the couch. The restaurant manager stood next to him. He asked me if I knew the boy. *Yes, he's my son.* He told us to follow him to the office. I didn't need to guess what for. I'd been on this walk with Diego before: in the grocery store; at the farmer's market. I wondered one thing only: *what* did he steal? A waitress joined us in the office. The manager closed the door.

"This young man has something in his pocket that doesn't belong to him," the manager said. A customer had seen Diego snatch and pocket a five-dollar bill from one of the tables—the waitress's tip. Diego stared at the floor.

"You need to return the money and apologize," I said.

Diego pulled out the bill and handed it to her. His eyes would not meet hers. "Sorry," he said, flat and insincere.

It was left to me to say what needed said: that I'm really sorry for what happened, that I'm so embarrassed, that I have no words—a script almost memorized by now. The manager turned him over to my custody. As we walked away from the restaurant, I didn't hide my displeasure. "Dammit, Diego! What were you thinking? If you wanted five dollars, you could have just asked me for it."

"I didn't know it belonged to anyone! I just found it on the floor."

"Stop the damned lies!" I snapped. "I'm sick of hearing them. Just own up to it!"

"You never believe me! You always believe everyone else," he said. "That's the real problem!" and he hurried away.

We drove back to the cabin in silence.

That night I lay in bed reliving the day's events while Diego read in the loft upstairs, his bedside lamp on. From the sounds, I knew he was tearing out each page when done reading it, crumpling the paper, and throwing it across the room. Time and again.

"Diego, please quit tearing out the pages."

"I'm not tearing them. I'm just reading."

Lies. Petty ones, but always lies. Lies for all occasions, trivial and momentous.

Why had I even brought him here? Was he capable of a transformative experience? Hope said yes; experience replied no. Nothing we had tried—counseling, medications, alternative schools—had helped. *What else could we have tried, I reasoned, but the sacred as encountered raw in nature?* I had hoped that the experience of nature might open Diego to transformative spirit and set the cosmos ablaze for him. There had to be spiritual kindling somewhere in his darkness, waiting to ignite. In truth, I would have been satisfied with just a spark of empathy in him.

Diego got up from bed and came downstairs. "I can't sleep. I'm going outside for a while."

"Alright. Be careful. There's bears out there."

"Yeah, Dad. I know."

His question earlier in the day about Mary and nature floated into my mind. Why *is* her name so often associated with nature? Was it an analogy, perhaps for the mediation of raw spiritual power to our human condition, as a wilderness guide is to the unbridled power of nature? As Diego paced the cabin porch, whacking dead tree branches and sticks against the porch rail, breaking them into ever-smaller pieces, I remembered another question he had asked several months earlier. We had spent a day in Cape Cod following an academic conference I attended at Brown University. Driving through Provincetown, he noticed a sign on a small Episcopal church, "Our Lady of the Harbor, Where the Land, the Sea, and the Sacred Meet." He asked, "How can the sacred meet the land and the sea? What's that supposed to mean?" The question was rhetorically combative, yet cogent. I attempted an answer.

"I think it means that God's spirit kind of permeates nature, that there's more to the world than what we see. And if you meet the sacred it can change your life."

His eye movements told me he was trying to connect what I said to something he understood. Nothing registered. How could it; he was twelve? Yet his question suggested that something was percolating in his mind. I knew that if spiritual fire ever seized him, there'd have to be *some* spiritual tradition—with a damn good guide—to help channel its combustible energies. Perhaps an abbot Byron Perry, if one could be found—a wilderness guide with a past, now grown mellow and wise, someone not too close and not too conflicted, as was I.

I slept fitfully that night and woke early, well before sunrise. The cabin was silent. I put on a jacket and went outside for a walk around the lake. As I closed the door and stepped onto the porch in the half-light of dawn, I stumbled on the debris from Diego's breakage. Bits and pieces of tree branches—including the walking stick he had carved for me—lay strewn about. Amidst the litter I noticed a six-inch splinter of the helix near the door; chips with letters of my name scattered here and there; the sun-face at the bottom of the steps. I paused, leaned back against the porch rail, and surveyed the fragments. I then swept them up and laid them alongside the wood-pile near the cabin, for use as kindling, and continued on.

Continued on for five more years. Through more school expulsions, more trauma, more bullying. Through the theft of an heirloom wedding ring passed down to Elizabeth—a ring given to her great-great-grandmother during the Civil War.

Finally, two months before his eighteenth birthday, I threw Diego out of the house. We just couldn't take it anymore. Katie and Meghan were out of the house by then, but Mary and Michael were still at home, terrorized daily by Diego. Michael had become a nervous wreck.

"Pack your backpack with clothes and just get out!" I said.

Diego protested a bit, but realized I meant it. He went to his room, filled his backpack, then walked out the front door and disappeared into the night.

16

The Least of the Brethren

WHAT IF you are one of the many who are called, but not among the few chosen? What if you spend decades of your adult life trying to respond to a call from an elusive God who doesn't give clear directions? And who, knowing your frailties and shortcomings, is stingy with the grace that would enable you to accomplish the tasks implicit in the call, once you've finally discerned it? Would you consider it your own fault for not being up to the task, or conclude, in the end, that you were merely deluded all those decades? Would you curse God and all his empty promises as if he were some junior Satan in disguise, luring you into an abyss? Or would you stay the course because God has his hook in you with an irresistible lure that you cannot shake free of?

As I enter life's final season, I reflect on all the fruitless paths I've taken. Callings, or chimeras? I have been too introverted, too indecisive and unassertive to stride confidently toward a clear goal. I've made a decent living in a responsible job, supported my family and helped raise children in a stable environment—though the stability was fragile and the family bonds frayed at the edges. I earned a doctorate and published some books and scholarly essays. For most people, that would be accomplishment enough. Old friends have lived such lives. They raised children and taught them the basic skills and lessons of life, made a living, hunted and fished with their friends, gave back to their communities, and cared for their aging parents. They then retreated into pleasant-enough retirements.

Could I say my life had been spiritually fulfilled, after so much waiting for God? Waiting in the active sense, not merely passive expectation endured in boredom, as if you were in a doctor's office or a line at the grocery store. To wait also means "to search for," "to look forward with desire or apprehension; to continue in expectation of." No passivity there. The verb is active: searching; desiring aimed at the future; a continuing onward *in spite of it all.* My long waiting has been a long searching, often frustrating.

Thomas Aquinas claims that God would not plant a desire in the human heart unless it could be fulfilled; otherwise, he would have planted it in vain. I lost track of the times I wanted to call "bullshit" on Thomas's claim. God planted a seed. It grew and developed, though twisted and marred. It had not blossomed. I prayed for it to ripen. I waited, patiently and impatiently. Was I merely one of the many who are called, but not among the few chosen?

Four years after I kicked Diego out of the house, he began work at a manufacturing plant in Elkhart, Indiana, where he built recreational vehicles. Then he moved on to other jobs, one after another. He lived with his girlfriend for two and a half years, and had a son. They split up without marrying. We have not given up hope. We have helped with his living expenses, continued paying his cell phone bill, and given him rides when he needed one. Elizabeth has tried to keep in touch, and sometimes he responds.

Elizabeth sends me two pictures of Diego and his infant son. In the first, Diego sits in his bed, his back propped up by pillows. His son, Mattathias, is cradled on the inside of his right arm. The stocking cap from the hospital has fallen onto Diego's lap. Mattathias's thick, black hair contrasts with the white sheets. His dark eyes look up at his father, or whatever it is a newborn "sees." Something amorphous, probably, yet he knows where to look. Diego looks down at him. Their eyes engage.

In the other picture, Mattathias has fallen asleep on Diego's shirtless chest. Diego looks at the camera, contentment on his face, his eyes fully open and bright. A tattoo is emblazoned across the length of his upper left arm, in some crude Gothic script. Seen one way, it reads, *DEVIL;* flip the picture upside down and it reads, *ANGEL.* Appropriate, I think, but that's not what holds my attention. I'm focused on the gentleness of Diego's face, his eyes. Do I see a hint of amazement, of deep wonder? Or do I see my own hope? I want wonder and amazement slicing into the heart of him, into the immensity of his world, opening life up to its infinite depths for him.

These pictures hold hope, and I cling to it.

Diego's middle name is also Mattathias, named after the *paterfamilias* in 1 Maccabees. A warrior for God. I cling to hope, and pray: *What I couldn't do; what the wilderness couldn't do; let that sleeping infant enkindle in him. Channel Diego's wayward energies, O God. Give him purpose. And give his son a warrior's heart.*

I remember the pleasure Diego took in constructing the dollhouse for Mary, the walking sticks he made for Michael and me. Maybe he will show his son how to build, and will build things for him, like the treehouse I promised to build years ago for the children in the giant maple tree in our backyard, but then never got around to. The children and I gathered around the tree and measured its circumference: 143 inches, with an almost four-foot diameter. We talked through and developed a plan. Spiraling wood steps would lead to the first level, built in the fork where several large branches angle away from the massive trunk, about six feet up. We would build three-foot high walls with pine slats spaced about four inches apart, then large openings above the walls for a view. The ceiling would be the floor of the next level. A straight, 45-degree angle stair would lead to the second floor, in the crotch where other branches forked, another seven feet up. We talked strategy, tools, hardware. I bought a book on building tree houses. We were excited.

The doctoral program and God's relentless call sucked away my time and attention, and I never built the tree house. Perhaps Diego will build one for his son, or build it with him. He can use our sturdy old tree. I will help.

A month after Mattathias's birth, Diego sends me a text message. "Hey Pops, why don't we go out soon and have a dads night out?"

Let it happen, I pray. I say yes, of course, just name the time. But I get no further messages.

I cling to hope.

I came across another picture some years ago. After my father died, my older brother Brian came into possession of our father's photograph albums. Each picture was neatly framed in small cardboard corners glued to the page and labeled meticulously—except for one loose studio photograph of a young girl about fifteen-years-old. It had no label and no name on the back. The girl wears a dark dress. A black curtain in the background highlights her face. Her hair, too, is dark, with a wispy curl stylishly hanging down on her forehead. You would not call her beautiful; but if you were a young man, you would be taken by the mischievous smile and playful eyes, the rosebud lips, the high cheekbones. From the photograph you would not know she was a Russian Jew, nor that she and her family fled a Russian *shtetl* in 1904 to escape a wave of *pogroms*. All you would know from the photo was that she was attractive, and that young men would have easily fallen for her. Including, it turned out, my grandfather.

I did not know my paternal grandmother, not even her name. The space she occupied in family history was blank. No one mentioned her, not even in whispers. I later learned that she, a Jewish girl, had eloped with my grandfather, a Catholic boy, in 1917. They hopped a train to San Francisco where they planned to marry. Both sets of parents discovered the plan and intervened. They called the sheriff's office in San Francisco and had them arrested when they got off the train, only to learn that my grandmother was pregnant, a scandal for both families. The parents acceded to the marriage because of the pregnancy, but on condition the young couple return to Elko. They did.

My grandmother's maiden name was Katie Israel (formally, Katharine). I discovered information about her family's voyage to the U.S. from the ship's manifest.

The S.S. Köln sailed from Bremen, Germany on March 29, 1906 with eight members of the Israel family: the mother, Rachel, age 34, and seven children—Sara, 9, Meier, 6, Mosche, 5, Ester, 4, Krent, 3, Gedalia, 2, and Jankel, ten months. Common Jewish names, except *Krent* (female). That name stood out. The family landed in Galveston, Texas, on April 20, 1906. None of them could read or write. Their ethnicity/race: Hebrew. Provenance: Ziladorf, Russia (now disappeared from maps and historical records). According to the manifest, none of them were polygamists or anarchists (good to know). They had $20 dollars with them. They planned to join Tobias Israel, the head of the family, who had come to the U.S. earlier and lived in Denver.

Krent was the age Katie Israel claimed to be when she arrived in the U.S. Where did the name *Krent* come from and how did it get changed to Katharine, neither name (Krent or Katharine) Jewish? I consulted two colleagues, both scholars of Russian history and culture, and both natives of Russia. Neither knew the name Krent; it sounds like an English boy's name and is the German word for "currant." Neither had heard of Ziladorf—a very "un-Russian" name, though "zila" *could* derive from *Tsilia,* a common Jewish name, so Tsilia-Dorf *could* refer to a small village in the Russian territories (Ukraine or Belarus), where Jews had once lived. Moreover, the name Tobias, I learned from a Scripture-scholar friend, was unusual for a Jewish man, coming from the Book of Tobit—a noncanonical text in the Hebrew Bible. But, said one of the Russian historians, it *could* derive from the Yiddish "Tevye," and gotten Ellis-islanded (Galvestoned?) as "Tobias" upon his arrival in America. That's all speculation, intriguing as it may be.

I learned many years later that, two years after they married, Katie Israel left my grandfather and abandoned her son, my father. My father never saw her again. She did not communicate with him or seek him out. Ever. Surely my father would have wondered why, and would have known the hurt of that utter rejection; yet he kept her youthful photograph in his photo album, loose and detached. And surely he felt the sting of being considered a bastard by the townspeople. Growing up, I knew nothing of this history; I learned it only as I approached the winter of life, and it has helped me put my father's anger in perspective.

When my father died in 1977, I did not even attend his funeral. Only years later did I decide to say goodbye. I went to the cemetery in Salinas, California where he was buried. I carried flowers to place on his grave. I had not planned ahead, however, and found the cemetery office closed that day. I had no way to find out where he was buried among the thousands upon thousands of graves, except by search on foot. I searched for almost an hour, walking row after row of gravestones, but could not find his. After that much time I had canvassed about five percent of the cemetery. Emotionally exhausted, I was too weary to search more, and gave up. Before leaving, I laid the flowers on the grave of a stranger who, in death as in life, I never knew.

I keep a set of wallet-sized pictures of Meghan, Katie, and Diego in a desk drawer. Diego has now been out of our home almost six years. Meghan is married and attending graduate school. Katie has her own house, a job, and a daughter. Mary is in college and Michael still in high school. But the photos in my desk drawer are from years ago, taken in Frostburg just before we moved to Indiana.

Katie looks out from the middle picture, into the distance, with soft dreamy eyes. That look, I think, captures her essence—that gaze into the trees and sky. When thunderstorms rolled into South Bend, Katie and I sat on the covered back porch or in the attached garage with the door open, and watched the storm's darkening and changing moods. We quivered with excitement when it released its power; lightning flashed and thunder shook the house. Rain poured and streamlets ran swiftly in the gutters. Tree branches swayed, and sometimes broke.

When Katie was 12, she wrote this poem:

> Thunderstorm
> Daddy, do you remember,
> when we used to sit on the back porch,
> In green plastic lawn chairs,
> watching the thunderstorms?
>
> Soaking up the smell of
> wet grass, and
> rain, and thunder,
> and cleanness, and lightning.

The Least of the Brethren

When the late afternoons
would turn dark green.
And the temperature would cool
and humidity stick to our skins.

Rain would pound the earth,
just beyond reach of me.
I loved to be slightly chilled
by the freshness of wet.

But I was never afraid,
unless I stepped out into the lightning
from under the protection of the porch
and you.

Katie now has a daughter, Shenandoah, meaning "daughter of the stars." Katie's middle name is also Shenandoah. This baby, like Diego's, was conceived out of wedlock. Katie later married Shenandoah's father, but they are now separated.

Our family, in many respects, has been broken, gone astray in a world gone awry. The brokenness goes back three or four generations. Some of our children, like me, follow a crooked path, but I pray they will trend in the right direction amidst their drifting. Although Shenandoah and Mattathias were both born out of wedlock, they are nonetheless children of God, and Spirit shines through them. We will help our children care for them, in whatever way we are needed, for as long as we are needed, for as long as we can. All will be well enough. We pray.

I've encouraged Katie to become a writer. She has the gift of words. From time to time she shares her writings with me; asks for feedback. She doesn't share them with anyone else.

I split my universe into a thousand pieces. I cast the fragments of my life in a circle around me. I gaze at and ponder them, to learn how they fit together, if at all... I get lost in the vastness.

I love music, yet am saddened that I rarely have the time to pursue it. I feel safe and comfortable when I draw or paint, yet inadequate in my skill level. Writing mirrors my soul in a way that almost nothing else does, yet it invites others to see a part of me that is often painful. I am vulnerable.

During her teen years, Katie was active in the church, helped organize teen religious retreats, and planned to major in religious education in college. She found college too confining, and returned home after a semester. She rented an apartment with a friend and got a job as a waitress. Eighteen months later she was pierced, tattooed, and pregnant. During that same period of time, Mary and Michael began drifting from the faith. They refused to go to church—Michael even to be confirmed. Elizabeth and I wondered, *What the hell happened?* A typhoon blew through our family.

Around the time Katie and her husband separated, her writing grew dark and defiant.

> Forbidden fruit tastes better. Just ask Eve. She has a restless heart and knows the flavors of this world—the sweet, the bitter, and the decaying. She is a whore who lives in the satisfying moment of her sin, and wrestles the sting of guilt that follows with the bravery of a warrior...

> Mother Mary is beautiful. But is Eve not also? Is she any less loved? The beauty of Eve is an earthy beauty. A beauty drawn with blood and tears on a canvas of scars and stretch marks by an artist whose hands have murdered and crushed. It is a rough, pained, dark beauty, but still an expression of freedom, however imperfect.

> I am the daughter of Eve and I will never be able to hide the stain of forbidden fruit on my hands...

> I am Mary Magdalene ... and I cling to the sandals of my Savior. But I'm not sure if I will end up the woman that she became because I don't know if I'll ever let Him pick me up out of the rubble and the blood.

> There is a constant struggle in my soul between the need to be "good," "faithful," "submissive," and "holy," and the urge to be "wild," "free," "expressive," and "me." Do I allow my life to be a monotonous drone of lifeless motions and the constant repeating of things that *need* to be done—or not done? So that one day I can look at my past and say *I was a good person?* Or do I follow that

urge to expand beyond myself, to discover myself, to understand the wilderness within me?

If I allow the untamed breath in my soul to fully exhale, I risk losing the respect and love of others, and worse I risk my chance at eternal salvation. But if I permanently snuff that fire, I risk a life of not knowing, of ignorance, of never fulfilled desire.

I am the daughter of Eve.

I don't know where she got the idea that *free* and *expressive* are contrary to *holy* and *faithful.* Elizabeth and I have not taught such ideas. I tell Katie that they are not polar opposites. God himself is wilderness, untamable and utterly free. Artistic expression and joy in life is a participation in God's being.

Katie is not on a path gone wrong, but on a journey into deep, dark places that she will emerge from one day and do great things. The critical time is while she's in that dark place. What will happen there? Will she remain, or emerge scarred but strengthened? I don't know, but I cling to hope, and try to help. I encourage her to write, to develop her craft, as difficult as that will be with a young daughter. *Here*, I say, read *My Name is Asher Lev*, and Rilke's *Book of Hours*. I pile on the books: Augustine's *Confessions*; a biography of that little wild man Francis of Assisi. Teresa of Avila, Catherine of Siena, Sor Juana Inéz de la Cruz—women who brooked no nonsense from their peers and hierarchical superiors. *Read. Read. Read. And write.*

Six months later, she sends me an e-mail:

Dad, reading this book you gave me, *My Name is Asher Lev*, the more I read the more speechless I become. I have been moved spiritually, artistically, and deeply shaken in the assumptions I have of myself. I have rarely felt less confident in myself, and never reached the depth of meaning that this book breaches in a few short hours of reading.

I ask her why she feels less confident.

Because it's uncomfortable to have your own complacency pointed out to you. I have grown lethargic in my pursuits of anything. I'm an okay painter, an okay writer, I'm okay at designing clothes, I'm an okay cook, I'm an okay mom. I was an okay wife to an okay husband, and now I'm okay with that being over. Certain passages in this book have poignantly made me feel how pitiful it is to live with complacency, and that is uncomfortable.

I reply that her writing is anything but mediocre, but she has to develop her craft. There are ways to do that. Be patient and persevere, expect pain and suffering, follow whatever your call is—if you don't you will have to drink or drug your way into forgetfulness. And then your calling will still haunt you.

My children are on their own journeys, some rocky. They need guides. Perhaps an abbot Byron Perry, or an abbess Mary Magdalen, both with a past—a petty criminal and a whore; the least of the brethren, transformed into saints. Someone holy, like the man I did not become.

Sometimes the voice of Spirit emerges from the thunder and the whirlwind; sometimes it breathes through the quiet, hollow places of the world, or in the soft in- and exhalation of a sleeping infant. Occasionally, it arrives in the guise of a flowing stream. Whichever way it arrives—whether slowly and subtly, or swiftly and abruptly—from then forward you have to wait patiently for its return and its guidance, according to its own good time, as if you didn't have other things to do. It calls and lures, sometimes sporadically, at times frequently. You try to do what it wants, though the signals aren't always clear, or not specific. A voice inside says "Persist. Have faith."

I continue on.

17

Pilgrim River

"And lo, my stream became a river, and my river a sea"
—Sirach 24:30–31

YOU LEARN a lot from sitting beside a stream. The water flows without ceasing, gracefully and forcefully, but does not exert itself. It nourishes all things effortlessly. It forms its own channel even while conforming to it. It carves ever deeper, exposing the hidden layers of earth, revealing the buried secrets of things. The stream curls around and over jagged rocks, smoothing them down, carrying them away, particle by particle, to the sea.

I sit beside streams four weeks a year. In June 2013, I spend half a day clearing brush from my office clearing in the woods along Poplar Creek in Western Maryland, and from the log bridge that leads to it. Countless downed trees litter the ground in New Germany State Park and the surrounding Savage River State Forest, all of them uprooted and toppled. The extent of the destruction is unsettling. Thousands of trees per square mile, perhaps one in four, are down. Once-tall pine trees along a fifty-foot-high ridge above Poplar Creek hang downward at an angle of 135 degrees from their base, their roots ripped out of the ground. The root systems look like large brown-gray disks with twelve-foot diameters clutching dirt and rocks. The tree crowns have fallen across the trail and into the stream, several into my wooded office and onto the old log bridge. Park rangers have cleared the main hiking trails with chainsaws, but not yet the less trod ones, and certainly not my office alongside the stream.

I ask a ranger what caused the devastation. "Heavy snow and wind from Hurricane Sandy," he says. Sandy pounded the eastern seaboard in New Jersey and New York in October 2012. Heavy rains moved inland to the Allegheny Mountains, 150 miles west. There the rain met an unseasonable cold front that converted it to heavy, wet snow that fell for a full day. The autumn leaves of the hardwoods had not yet dropped, so snow clung to them. The swirling snow packed tightly into the outstretched arms of evergreen branches. The hurricane winds, though weakened after landfall, still blew with gusto. Branches broke and trees toppled, especially those that leaned, like the ones along the ridge above my office. They fell in silence—I imagine—the heavy crash of trees on the ground muffled by deep, soft snow; the prolonged groaning of roots as they ripped apart muted by thousands of thick snowflakes.

I call this clearing alongside the stream "my office" because I have come here to read and write almost every June for twenty-six years. I furnish it with a lawn chair and a small, folding end table that I set my books and writing tools on. The space is nondescript but spacious: about twenty-by-fifteen feet at the longest and widest points, shaped like a semi-circle with broad and irregular corrugations along the edges. To get to my office, I normally cross the old log bridge, which is now clogged and impassable. The log catches debris—twigs, small branches, pinecones, leaves—year round, causing the stream to back up and froth before the water curls around and under the log. I cannot come here without remembering that passionate kiss with Elizabeth and our tumble into the icy water. Tree crowns now obstruct passage across it. I take the long way around to my office, across a stone bridge near the ranger's office and down one of the hiking trails into the forest.

This office comes with a small stream, views on all sides, and is air-conditioned with shade and mountain air. It also has the virtue of being rent-free, except weekends, when I have to pay four dollars to get into the park. Over a four-week period, that's $32. It's a steal, and *I'm not giving it up*. The fallen branches will have to decompose elsewhere. I own the job of removing them.

I carry smaller branches to a spot ten meters downstream, but have to saw the large branches of greenwood, entangled as they are with one another and with young trees still standing. I drag them to the new debris pile outside the clearing. I have to moderate the exertion. I pace myself.

Several sawn tree trunks, too large and heavy to move, remain at the edge of the clearing. Small clusters of baby green needles lay atop them. I try to sweep them away, but they are moored—new shoots recently sprouted from the now dead tree. These logs still have life-generating sap in them. They push new life out from their own decaying corpses. Dozens of needle clusters, just atop the bark, spread out toward the sunlight. They find rich food in their mother tree. Are they *new* trees or the same tree regenerating and nourishing itself on its own remains? I jot the question in a notebook, to ask a botanist.

After three hours of work, I have cleared the debris from my office, except for small twigs and layers of pine needles that I leave in place. Beads of sweat drip from my body. My clothes are drenched, and the top of my balding head a mixture of skin oil, sweat, sap, and detritus from leaves and twigs. And bug bites. I remove my shirt and wade thigh deep into a quiet pool at the edge of the stream. The sunlight caresses my back and shoulders. I look down. The pool makes a glass-like mirror in which I see the reflection of my aging body, at first distorted by the shimmering water. I see a some-time scholar and a semi-autistic loner, a flawed man who has persistently sought the Holy. The Quiet One. The face remains the same through its permutations over the years, in spite of wrinkles, a balding head, a whitening beard, and a sinking eye socket caused by the weakening muscles around the prosthetic eye. I think of my marriages, my children, the sense of calling to both a religious and academic life, my meager success as a scholar, a father, and a husband. Have I done all that I could? Am I wizened, or just old?

Regardless, it is the season to retire. The rest is up to God.

I kneel and scoop cool water into my cupped palms. Again and again I raise water to my face, head, back, and arms, and feel refreshed. I stand in the stream and assess my work. The office is in good shape. The old log bridge is next.

Before this log fell, it was a massive pine tree at the edge of the stream. It fell years before I happened upon it twenty-six years earlier—how long before I don't know, but enough for both its outer and inner bark to have worn off. The log's width makes a bridge easy to walk across with ease of balance. Stumps of former branches jut out three or four inches from the trunk at irregular intervals. Had this tree been harvested, the dense area inside the tree that anchored these branches would have constituted the knots in someone's pine walls or furniture.

Various critters take up residence near the log. One year a green frog lived in the tall grass at one end of it. When I stepped onto the log each morning, the frog leapt into the creek. Two years ago, a snake dwelled in that spot, slithering into the water as I approached the stream. I caught only a brief glimpse of its rust-brown color. My first thought: *copperhead!* I have encountered copperheads downstate in Virginia that same color, also resting on foot bridges where they sunned themselves. They, too, slithered into the water as I approached. A park ranger later told me copperheads seldom venture this high up into the mountains; it was likely a brown water snake, and harmless. Still, each day I scratched through the grass with the tip of a long walking stick before stepping onto the log, just in case.

Amidst Earth's grandeur, there is nothing special or unique about this spot; there are millions of others like it. Any spot is good as long as water flows unhindered, the air is fresh, and imagination can roam at will. You see, it does not matter which stream you sit by, nor if the mountains through which it flows are young and jagged, or worn and venerable, as long as the water flows freely over the rocks, makes a sharp bend here and there, and carves out hollow places under the bank where fish can bask in the cool shadows. Nor does it matter under which tree you seek shade, as long as the leaves overhead whisper quietly when the breeze rustles them; as long as the sun's light filters through the leaves and makes a soft landing on your unshod feet, then warms the earth on which you kneel as you scoop soil into your palm, letting it sift through your fingers. Nor does it matter if you are young or old, because, whoever you are, your feet will be cool and refreshed as you wade into the stream, where you bend low to drink with cupped hands, then rise as the filtered light caresses the back of your neck.

This clearing in the forest is mine, on temporary loan.

I've returned most summers to read and write, sitting in the level clearing along Poplar Creek. The natural beauty, quiet setting, and the venerable age of the Alleghenies lures me year after year. The Alleghenies form part of the longer Appalachian Mountain range, one of the oldest mountain ranges in the world. They once stood as high as the Alps, and as jagged. To give a sense of their age, you need only know that they were once connected to the Lesser Atlas Mountains in Northwest Africa. The continents drifted apart over hundreds of millions of years, stretching the earth into the wide basin that now contains the Atlantic Ocean, just as the Great Basin is now slowly stretching, according to what Fred Buechel told me so long ago. The slow persistent work of water and wind, over hundreds of millions of years, eroded the Alleghenies into the mature, rolling hills they are today, with lush hardwood forests, plentiful rivers and streams, and abundant wildlife. New Germany and the Savage River Forest are located amid these old, mellow mountains, near the Eastern Continental Divide. Poplar Creek flows into the Savage River, then the North Branch of the Potomac, the Potomac itself, the Chesapeake Bay and, finally, the Atlantic Ocean. A few miles west, the streams meander toward the Ohio River valley, into the Mississippi River basin and, finally, to the Gulf of Mexico.

The mountains are familiar with far greater devastation than Hurricane Sandy, whose effect amounted to little more than a brief gust in the history of geological and climactic forces. Four hundred and eighty million years ago, massive collisions of tectonic plates thrust the Appalachians upward. Volcanoes erupted and grew into imposing mountains. Enormous rock formations twisted, warped, and folded. Much later, ice glaciers descended intermittently from the north and placed the land under millennia of deep freeze.

The hardwood and pine forests are mature now, the mountains worn down, and the landscape bucolic. The small farming village of New Germany was founded in the mid-nineteenth century by German immigrants. The original settlers built a dam along Poplar Creek for irrigation and to power a gristmill that drew farmers from the surrounding region. The community had a general store, a one-room school, a post office, and a doctor's office. The area fell into disuse once the gristmill quit operating. During the Great Depression of the 1930s, the Civilian Conservation Corps built a dozen log cabins on the site, re-built the dam, and created hiking trails for visitors. The State of Maryland now manages the forest and park, but I claim one small part of it for my summer office.

I wander around the park to assess the destruction from Hurricane Sandy—trees down everywhere, old ones and young ones, mostly pine, but beech and poplar, too. Brokenness is all around, but the forest will regenerate itself. I follow Katie Creek to its upper reaches, to where the loggers clear-cut the forest many years ago. Trees have begun to grow around the edges of the clearing and a few in the middle. They're getting the better of the brambles. The forest will regenerate, not in my lifetime, but slowly, inexorably.

Uprooted trees have left craters in the ground, some as wide as twelve feet and as deep as three. Dirt and large chunks of slate are ensnared by the exposed lateral root systems. Twisted and broken roots protrude up from the ground; others dangle down. Some are two inches in diameter, while others form a tiny web of filaments, little tendrils reaching for water and dirt to extract minerals from the earth. *How do the root hairs do that, exactly?* They must release chemicals through minute pores, which attract certain minerals and draw them back into the roots. *And how, exactly, does the water flow upwards against gravity to the branches and crowns of the trees, sometimes over one hundred feet high?* I jot down "mineral extraction by root hairs" and "sap v. gravity" on a notepad as a reminder to do some research. It turns out that scientists are still figuring this out. A number of theories have been proposed. The most common is *transpiration*: as water evaporates from the leaves, it creates vapor pressure that draws water upward. But not all tree biologists agree, and consensus remains elusive.

I latch onto the word *transpire*, suggesting breath, spirit. Breathing through, escaping concealment, being revealed.

Tree rings show weather patterns and growth cycles over the years. I like to imagine that even a tree's molecules conceal a record of every vibration—no matter how infinitesimal—of every action that occurred on earth during the tree's life. If true, then the earth's history during the lifetime of a tree is encoded in those molecules; we just don't yet know how to extract it. It would require very sensitive and precise instruments to distinguish, say, the record of a Mennonite farmer urging on his mule from a Civil War soldier shouting *charge;* each would have registered a different vibration of infinitesimal proportions on the cellulose molecules in the trees' xylem. It seems illogical, so I draw on the physicist David Bohm for my implausible theory. Bohm said that a deep, implicate order of undivided wholeness lies beyond, or better undergirds, the visible, tangible world. Space is a kind of plasma stretching as a whole across the cosmos. Electrons light years apart—all of them parts of this stretched plasma—can sense one another in time *faster than the speed of light.* That's wild stuff; it goes against our logical, materialistic conceptions of the cosmos. But it sounds just right to me, so I adopt the theory, tentatively.

Theoretical physics aside, I want to know the age of my log bridge when it fell, and thereby, when it sprouted. I find a recently downed tree that the rangers sawed off near its base. I count the tree rings. They are wide near the center, indicating rapid growth, then tighten and narrow as the tree aged. I mark off ten-year intervals with a pen, rest my eyes, then count another ten. Then another. Eleven tens: the tree was 110 years old, plus or minus a few years, when it fell. It has a 20-inch diameter and a 68-inch circumference. As trees go, not that old or large.

I then measure the circumference of my log bridge just above the spot where it broke away from its roots: 109 inches. I assumed the bark had been ¾ of an inch thick, so factoring that in gives a circumference of 114 inches. I perform a simple algebraic exercise: 68 is to 110 as 114 is to x = 184.4 years. That would have been its age when it fell. I first came across the log twenty-six years earlier. Its bark was already worn off. That would have taken at least a decade, so I add ten more years. I calculate that it sprouted from the ground around 220 years earlier, in 1792. During George Washington's first term as President. I am pleased.

The old log connects me in this way to natural history and geologic events hundreds of millions of years ago; to weather patterns and the dynamics of hurricanes; to the early American Republic, and to the local history of this place. They all blend agreeably into the *gestalt* of time and natural and human history in a way that both satisfies and stimulates the imagination. If my fanciful theory of encoded vibrations is valid, then cannon fire from the War of 1812 is faintly recorded in the tree. Could scientific instruments of great precision in the future extract and translate them into human thought and experience? After all, if root hairs can extract minerals from the earth, and chlorophyll molecules in leaves can turn sunlight to sugar, why couldn't scientists someday extract history (beyond age and weather patterns) from the molecules of a tree? My imagination floats away. I think of the ancient bristlecone pines in Nevada's Great Basin. Some of them are over 4,800 years old. Do they contain a record of Abraham's long journey; of Moses leading the Israelites across the Red Sea; of Christ's anguish on the cross? That is farfetched, I know, but the thought pleases the imagination and makes sense if you adopt Bohm's theory of the cosmos as a stretched plasma.

Death and decay float gingerly over this landscape, whispering in muffled voices. There is newness and promise in this dying and long decay, too. I think about death now and then as I approach the final season of life—not often, nor with dread, but a mist of unknowing does hover above the forward horizon. I have talked to Elizabeth and to the children about my burial or, better, non-burial. "Don't coop me up in a cemetery," I said years ago.

Pour my ashes into Poplar Creek.

Pilgrim River

Go in Spring, if you can, when the stream flows strong and the leaves on the hardwoods turn rich green. Go to the forest where the old log crosses the stream, where we held hands and kissed before tumbling into the water. Pour half the ashes from atop the log into Poplar Creek, or, if you are then frail, let the children do it. Pour the rest below where Katie Creek empties into the stream. Say a prayer and say goodbye. Then, all of you, roll up your pant legs, take off your shoes, and wade into the stream. Feel the grace of the water's gentle but steady press against your shins as the stream flows ever on. Because here's the thing:

If you live as this stream lives: meandering here, surging strongly there, resting now in deep pools; if you descend gratefully to the valley floor where you flow contemplatively in the meadowlands until you merge peaceably with the Great Pilgrim River—then you live your days well. But if you are stubborn like the old tree trunk that, years ago, fell across the stream, blocking its course and gathering debris; then the water will, regardless, find its way around and through you.

Even if you resist, pushing back in protest, the stream will smoothen your rough edges. Day by day it carries away more of the coarse bark, then seeps through the small cracks, softening even the heartwood—that tough inner core—until your molecules, one by one, float away, mingling with the current. Then, old log, you will join the stream and freely glide home to Ocean.

CPSIA information can be obtained
at www.ICGtesting.com
Printed in the USA
LVOW03s2342230318
571041LV00002B/15/P